E X P R E S S
E N G L I S H

Transitions

Intermediate Student Book

LINDA A. FERREIRA

NEWBURY HOUSE PUBLISHERS, INC.

Library of Congress Cataloging in Publication Data

Ferreira, Linda A.
    Express English/Transitions.

    (Express English series)
    1. English language—Text-books for foreign speakers.
I. Title.   II. Series: Ferreira, Linda A.   Express
English series.
PE1128.F28   1984   428.2′4   83-13514
ISBN 0-88377-335-X

Project editor/James W. Brown
Design and production/Designworks, Inc.
Illustrator/Margie Frem
Photo research/Janet Dracksdorf

NEWBURY HOUSE PUBLISHERS, INC.

Language Science
Language Teaching
Language Learning

ROWLEY, MASSACHUSETTS 01969
ROWLEY ● LONDON ● TOKYO

First printing: January 1984
Printed in the U.S.A.   10 9 8 7 6 5

Contents

Credits

The author is grateful to the Center for Moral Education, Harvard University, for permission to use adapted materials on pages 43, 55, 103, 115 and 127.

The author also wishes to thank the following people and organizations for the photographs appearing throughout the book:

© 1983, Cloudshooters/Laurel Spingola: viii, ix; Bruce AF Polsky: 4, 25, 28, 30, 47, 48, 60, 64, 73, 78, 84, 85, 88, 118, 120, 130, 136, 145; Janet Dracksdorf: 13, 47; Sack Theaters: 13; American Airlines: 19, 82; Gerard Fritz: 25; General Electric: 30; The Conference Board, *Across the Board,* "Old is not a four-letter word: 31; Ralph Turcotte: 37; Boston Symphony Orchestra: 37; Carol L. Newsom: 37; The Sheraton Corporation: 61; That's Entertainment, Inc.: 61; Bill Lane, Newburyport Daily News: 70, 107; Philadelphia Museum of Art — Given by Jules Mastbaum: 76; U.S. Geological Survey: 79; Needham, Harper & Steers Advertising Agency, Inc., New York: 91; Virginia Slims ad reprinted with permission of Philip Morris Inc.: 91; U.S. Department of the Interior/ National Parks Service: 94; Ford Division/Public Relations: 100; Greek National Tourist Organization: 109; Cape Cod Chamber of Commerce: 109; Swiss National Tourist Office: 109; National General Pictures: 118; Union Pacific Railroad Museum: 119, 125; Columbia Presbyterian Hospital: 120; The Hispanic Society of America: 124; Brazilian Tourism Authority/Embratur: 126.

UPTOWN — the continuing story of the struggle between powerful New York businessman, Preston Wade, and the tenants of Tudor Village, a small West Side apartment building. These are the people of **UPTOWN** . . .

Susan Wade, 20, the daughter of Preston Wade, returns from London to live with her father. Does she help him or her boyfriend Jeff Ryan in the fight for Tudor Village?

Preston Wade, rich and powerful, wants to build Wade Plaza on Manhattan's West Side. Can the tenants of Tudor Village stop him?

Kemp, Wade's assistant, follows Wade's orders to get the tenants out of Tudor Village. How far will he go?

Butch and **Spike,** mean and ugly, do Kemp's dirty work. Can the police catch them before they destroy Tudor Village?

Mary Ryan, tenant of Tudor Village for over 50 years, has a terrible accident in the dark basement. Will she live to see her children again?

Jeff Ryan, 28 and a Viet Nam vet, fights with Susan about her father's plan to build Wade Plaza. Can Jeff win back Susan's love and save Tudor Village?

Molly Ryan, a top newspaper reporter for the *City Herald,* loves her career. Is she ready to start a new life in Brazil with Paulo Santos?

Paulo Santos, an architect from Brazil, moves to Tudor Village and falls in love with Molly. Will he convince Molly to marry him?

This is Flight 487. The captain is speaking to the passengers.

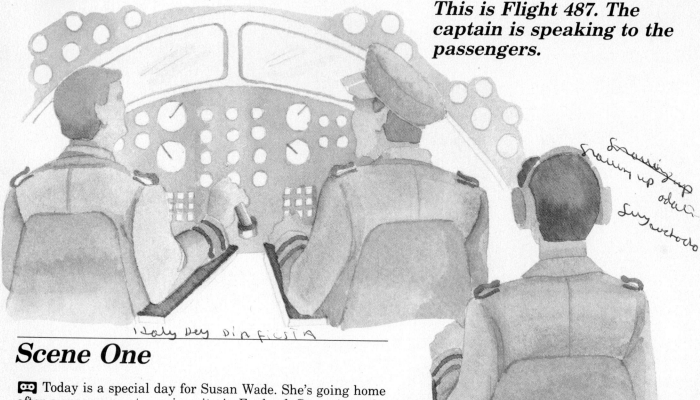

Italy Dey Dinficsta

Scene One

Today is a special day for Susan Wade. She's going home after a year away at a university in England. Susan is smiling and thinking about her father. She misses him very much.

Susan is twenty but she doesn't have many friends. A year is a long time away from her father. She wants to tell him all about London and about her courses at the university. She's studying economics because she wants to help her father in business. But she isn't very interested in economics. She wants only to be with her father.

Susan opens her purse and takes out a photograph. The old woman in the seat next to Susan is watching her. Susan is looking at the photograph now. The smile is returning to her pretty face.

MARY   Look at that big smile! You must be in love. Is that your boyfriend?

SUSAN   Oh, no! It's my father. Here, take a look. His name is Preston Wade. I'm Susan Wade.

MARY   Glad to meet you, Susan. I'm Mary Ryan. My, he is handsome, isn't he? You look like him, you know. You have the same blue eyes.

SUSAN   Do you think so? I miss my father a lot. I don't see him very often. He's an important businessman in New York, and I'm always away at school.

MARY   You are? What're you studying?

SUSAN   Economics. I plan to work for my father's company when I finish my degree. Then I can live in New York with him.

MARY   Well, we're almost there. Are you excited?

SUSAN   Oh, yes. I can't wait to see my father at the airport.

cont wait TO - yo Puedo esperar
depur - grado
handsome - opuesdo
miss - feller Perder
Perch - Cartera
Carl - rojo

Questions

1 Is Susan traveling to London?
   Answer No, she isn't.
   Is she traveling to New York?
   Answer Yes, she is.

2 Does Susan have a photograph of her school? Her father?
   Answer No, she doesn't.
   Does she have a photograph of her father?
   Answer Yes, she does.

3 Is Susan sitting next to a man? A woman?

4 Does Susan look like her mother? Her father?

5 Is Susan studying English at the university? Economics?

6 Does Susan expect to see her father soon? Her mother?

Who's that guy? The one in the back.

Questions

1 Does Mary have children?
   Answer Yes, she does.
   How many children does she have?
   Answer Two.
2 Is Mary's sister living in New York?
   Answer No, she isn't.
   Where is she living now?
   Answer In London.
3 Does Jeff look like his father? Why?
4 Is Molly working? Where?
5 Does Mary have grandchildren?
   Why not?
6 Is Tudor Village an old building? Where?

Scene Two

Mary Ryan is on her way home too. She's telling Susan about her holiday in England. Mary's sister, Barbara, lives in London. When Mary is in London, she and Barbara like to go out a lot. Mary enjoys the theater and so does her sister. Barbara doesn't have any children, but Mary does.

Mary doesn't like to be away from her family. Her husband is dead, so her children are very important to her. They are grown up, but the children still live with her in an apartment in Manhattan. Mary is telling Susan about her son and daughter.

SUSAN Do you have any photographs of your children with you?
MARY Of course! Let me see. Here's one. We're standing in front of our apartment house. That's my daughter Molly on the right. She's a reporter for the *City Herald*.
SUSAN Who's that guy? The one in the back.
MARY That's Jeff, my son. Jeff reminds me so much of his father. He has the same curly brown hair.
SUSAN What does he do?
MARY Jeff? Oh, he's not working right now.
SUSAN Is he married?
MARY No, both my children are single. I'm not a grandmother yet.
SUSAN What a pretty building! It looks like an old English house.
MARY Yes, it does. It's a famous building on the West Side, called Tudor Village. I love that old place.
SUSAN I know what you mean. New York is a special place for me too.

Present Simple vs. Present Continuous

Susan likes Some people don't like	*Vogue.*	Does she Do they	like *Vogue*?	Yes, she does. No, they don't.
Some passengers are Mary isn't	reading.	Are they Is she	reading?	Yes, they are No, she isn't.

We use the **present simple** tense (*V-s third person singular*) to tell about an action or state which occurs or is true *at* this time. We use the **present continuous** tense (**to be** + *verb-ing*) to show that an action or state is temporary and is occurring *about* this time.

A Tell about the story. Susan and Mary are flying from London to New York. They are on board Flight 487.

● Ask about the flight schedule:

1 When do the passengers usually (leave London)?
→ They usually leave London at 8:20 P.M.

2 It's (8:20 at night). What's Mary doing now?
→ She's flying out of Heathrow Airport.

● Ask about *your* schedule:

3 When do you usually (eat dinner)?
4 It's (8:00 in the morning). What are you doing now?

Schedule of Flight 487

8:20 P.M.	leave London	(Heathrow)
9:00 P.M.	have drinks	(juice)
10:00 P.M.	eat dinner	(chicken)
11:00 P.M.	see movie	(*Ragtime*)
8:00 A.M.	have breakfast	(tea and toast)
10:00 A.M.	prepare for landing	(seatbelt)
10:25 A.M.	arrive New York	(Kennedy)

B Susan and Mary are getting to know each other. Susan is reading a magazine, but Mary isn't.

MARY   What magazine are you reading?
SUSAN   *Vogue.* I *always* read fashion magazines. What about you?
MARY   I don't *usually* read *Vogue.* I like *Good Housekeeping.* I'm *always* interested in magazines about food.

● Ask each other about your likes and dislikes.

cues *magazines–read; TV programs–watch; movies–see; snacks–eat; clothes–wear.*

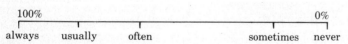
100% ─────────────────────── 0%
always   usually   often   sometimes   never

I ——— I'm	always usually often sometimes never	read look at buy interested in	———. What about you?

C Join these pairs of sentences with *and . . . too, and so . . .* , or *but*.

1 Susan is going home. Mary is going home.
→ Susan is going home *and* Mary is *too.*
→ Susan is going home *and so* is Mary.

2 Mary reads novels. Susan reads novels.
→ Mary reads novels *and* Susan does *too.*
→ Mary reads novels *and so* does Susan.

3 Susan is young. Mary isn't young.
→ Susan is young *but* Mary isn't.

4 Susan likes *Vogue.* Mary doesn't like *Vogue.*
→ Susan likes *Vogue but* Mary doesn't.

5 Susan is coming from London. Mary is coming from London.
6 Mary enjoys the theater. Her sister enjoys the theater.
7 Molly has a job. Jeff doesn't have a job.
8 Susan is excited. Mary is excited.
9 Preston Wade has a daughter. Mary Ryan has a daughter.
10 Susan has a lot of money. Mary doesn't have a lot of money.
11 Jeff is single. Susan is single.
12 Susan is reading *Vogue.* Mary isn't reading *Vogue.*

● Interview a classmate and compare your likes and dislikes.

cues *music, food, sports, movies, TV programs, books.*

→ I like jazz and John does too.
→ John hates pizza and so do I.
→ I enjoy football but John doesn't.

Direct and Indirect Object Pronouns

Direct Object	**Indirect Object**
Susan has *a photograph*.	She's showing the photograph *to Mary*.
	to her.
	She's showing *Mary* the photograph.
	her

These verbs are regularly followed by a *to/for phrase* after the **direct object**: buy, lend, promise, read, send, show, teach, tell. We can replace the *to/for phrase* with an **indirect object** noun or pronoun. The **indirect object** immediately follows the verb.

 Tell about the story. Make sentences with *him, her, it* and *them*.

1 Susan's father is in New York. (write every week)
→ She writes him every week.

2 Susan has a photograph. (keep in her purse)
3 Mary's sister is in London. (visit every year)
4 Susan's watch is from her father. (wear every day)

5 Mary lives with her children. (miss a lot)
6 Susan has a copy of *Vogue*. (read every month)
7 Mary's friends live in Tudor Village. (see all the time)
8 Susan can't wait to see her father. (love very much)

B Mary is showing Susan some photographs of Jeff, Molly and her husband, Michael.

SUSAN It's amazing! They must be in the same family. They look so much alike.
MARY Yes, they do. Both of them have curly brown hair and blue eyes. Jeff reminds me so much of Michael.
SUSAN Molly certainly takes after you. Both of you have red hair and the same smile.

● **Tell about *you* and *your* family.**

My	brother	reminds me of my ____.	He	resembles	him.
	sister		She		her.

→ I look like my mother. Both of us have the same brown eyes.
→ My brother takes after my father. Both of them are tall.

● **Show photographs of your family to your classmates and ask each other:**

Who's in the photograph?
Which one is _____?
Where is he/she now?
What is he/she doing now?

C Agree or disagree with these statements about the story. Practice *indirect object* position.

1 The flight attendant is bringing a fashion magazine *to Susan*.
→ That's right! He's bringing *her* a copy of *Vogue*.

2 Mary is buying dinner *for Susan*.
→ That's wrong! She's buying *her* a drink.

3 The Captain is giving information about the flight *to the passengers*.
4 Mary is showing a photograph of her sister *to Susan*.
5 The flight attendants are bringing books *to the people on board*.

Note the use of *to* + **indirect object pronoun** after these special verbs:

explain something *to* someone
introduce someone *to* someone
return something *to/for* someone

---

6 The Captain is explaining the flight plan *to the passengers*.
7 Mary wants to introduce her son *to Susan*.
8 Mary is returning the fashion magazine *to the flight attendant*.

● **Make conversations like this one:**

S1 I'm getting some juice from the flight attendant.
S2 Can you bring me some tea?

1 get juice/ bring
2 take trip/ send
3 go library/ return
4 get newspaper/ buy
5 do homework/ explain
6 go bank/ lend

ONE Giving and getting information

Kemp, Preston Wade's assistant, is calling the airline. He wants to get information about Susan's flight for his boss.

Listen to the tape. Then complete the conversation as you listen to the tape a second time.

OPERATOR Trans American information and reservations. May I help you?

KEMP I'm calling about _TA 487_.

OPERATOR From _London_ to _New York_?

KEMP Yes, _That's right_. What's _arrival_ time?

OPERATOR _10.25_ A.M.

KEMP Is _it_ on schedule?

OPERATOR Yes, _it is_. Gate _3_.

KEMP Thanks.

OPERATOR Thank you for calling Trans American. Have a nice day.

What information does Susan give her father in the telegram?

> **W E S T E R N   U N I O N**
>
> PRESTON WADE
> WADE PLAZA BUILDING
> NEW YORK NY   USA
> DADDY—ON TA FLIGHT 487 JUNE 26 -STOP-
> ARRIVE KENNEDY 10:25 AM -STOP- CANT
> WAIT SEE YOU -STOP- MISS YOU -STOP-
> LOVE SUSAN

Role Play: Take the roles of Kemp and the operator. Ask and give information about the flights from the other cities to New York.

Airline	Flight	From	Arrival	Gate
Pan American	PA 310	Amsterdam	9:30 A.M.	8
Trans American	TA 487	London	10:25 A.M.	3
British Airways	BA 276	Cairo	12:15 P.M.	12
Swiss Air	SA 315	Lagos	2:45 P.M.	5
United Airlines	UA 452	Tokyo	3:30 P.M.	10

TWO Telling about people

The passengers expect to land at Kennedy Airport at 10:25 A.M. It's quarter past nine in the morning now.

SUSAN What do you think Molly and Jeff *are doing* right now?

MARY They're probably cleaning the house. I'm sure it's a mess. Jeff isn't very neat, and Molly doesn't usually like to do housework.

New York 9 a.m.

Tokyo 10 p.m.

Cairo 3 p.m.

Tell about people *you* know.

S1 What do you think your (father) *is doing* right now?

S2 He's probably _____ right now.

He's *usually*	at home in the office	at ___ o'clock.
He *always*	gets up goes to work has lunch	at ___ o'clock.
He's a	hard worker. busy man.	

London 1 p.m.

At Gino's

Gino's is an Italian restaurant on the corner of 72nd Street and Columbus Avenue. It's a popular place because it serves excellent food at very reasonable prices. *Gino's* is always crowded, especially on weekends.

Parents like to take their children to *Gino's* for lunch on Saturday. There's a family of four at the table next to the window. The mother and father are young. They're about thirty and they're very good-looking. They have two children, a little boy about six years old and a little girl about four. The children are wearing bluejeans and red sweaters. The little boy is wearing a baseball cap and so is the little girl. The little boy is looking at the toy airplane in his hand. The father is telling him all about airplanes. The little boy is smiling. The little girl is still eating her pizza. There's tomato sauce all over her face. The mother has a paper napkin in her hand and she's trying to clean the mess. They are both laughing. They seem like a happy family.

Thinkabout

	True	False
1 *Gino's* serves Italian food.	X	
2 The parents are young, but not very attractive.		X
3 The children are wearing their Sunday clothes.		X
4 The little girl is having a good time and so is her brother.	X	

Talkabout

This is another family at *Gino's* restaurant. What's happening in this scene? How do the parents feel? How do the children feel?

Give your opinion:
- Do parents usually punish their children . . .
- when they break something by accident?
- when they break something on purpose?
- Is it right to punish a child in public?

Tell about customs in your country:
- When do parents punish their children?
- Who usually punishes the children—the mother or the father?
- How do parents punish a small child? a teenager?

Writeabout Description: Creating an impression

Observe a family in action, perhaps in a restaurant, in a park, or on a bus. Is there a good or bad feeling about the scene? Is there joy? anger? humor? sadness? love?

Write a short composition to describe a family scene. Choose your details carefully. Each detail adds to the main impression of your story.

> There's a family of four next to me in a restaurant.
>
> They seem like a very happy family.

←Start with:
Tell about the scene. Who? Where?

←Give details:
Describe the people. Age? Sex? Characteristics? Clothing? Describe what the people are doing. Smiling? Laughing? Talking?

←End with:
Give your main impression of the scene.

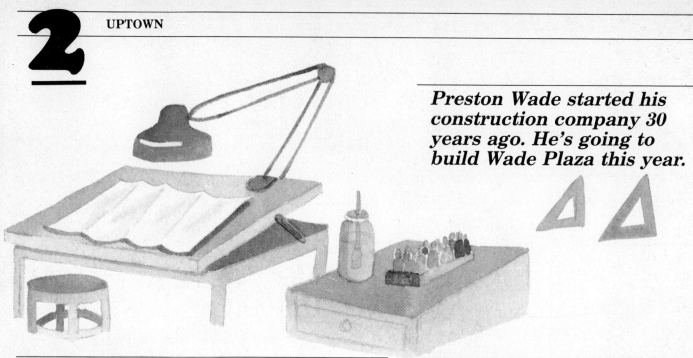

Preston Wade started his construction company 30 years ago. He's going to build Wade Plaza this year.

Scene One

Thirty-five years ago, Preston Wade came to New York and got a job as a builder. He didn't have much money then, but he had a lot of ambition. He soon learned all about the construction business. With his savings, Wade bought some equipment and hired a few men. He had his own company only a year when he made his first million dollars.

Wade used the profits from his construction company to buy property in Manhattan. Ten years ago he built the Wade Building on Park Avenue as his business headquarters. By that time, Wade was a wealthy and powerful man.

Last year Wade began to buy property on Manhattan's West Side. He hired a famous architect to design the plans for Wade Plaza, a new group of luxury apartments, boutiques, shops, and restaurants. At 66, Wade was a man with a dream. He wanted the people of New York to look at Wade Plaza, its beauty and its power. Wade wanted them to remember him long after his death.

As usual, Preston Wade was in his office in the Wade Building by 8:00 A.M.. Kemp, his assistant, wanted Wade to look at a section of the plans for Wade Plaza. Kemp was an impatient man. He wanted Wade to make a decision.

KEMP Well, what do you think?
WADE These plans look complete. Are we ready to build?
KEMP Not yet. There's one problem. Wade Enterprises owns all the land except this corner property here, the section next to the park.
WADE Let me see those plans again. What's there now?
KEMP Tudor Village, an old apartment house. It's a cooperative. All the tenants own the building and they don't want to leave.
WADE Buy them out, Kemp. That's your job.
KEMP Yeah, sure. I can get them out of there.
WADE You do that, Kemp. It's your problem now.
KEMP Right. You can count on me.

Questions

Ask and answer:
1 if Preston Wade got his first job in business or in construction. When?
   Question Did Preston Wade get his first job in business or in construction?
   Answer He got his first job in construction.
   Question When did Wade get his first job?
   Answer Thirty-five years ago, when he came to New York.
2 if Wade was lucky or clever in those early years. How?
   Question Was Wade lucky or clever in those early years?
   Answer He was clever in those early years.
   Question How was Wade clever?
   Answer He worked hard and saved his money.
3 if Wade built the Wade Building or Wade Plaza ten years ago. Where?
4 if Wade is going to build an office building or a plaza complex this year. Where? Why?
5 if Wade needs to buy the park or the Tudor Village property. Why?
6 if Tudor Village is Wade's or Kemp's problem. Why?

Scene Two

🔊 Preston Wade sent Kemp to phone the airline about Susan's flight. Wade put away Susan's telegram; then he picked up a photograph from his desk. It was Kathryn, Susan's mother. Wade began to think about the past.

Wade was 45 years old when he fell in love with Kathryn and got married. Susan was born a year later. As usual, Wade was in his office that night when the doctor phoned from the hospital. Kathryn didn't expect to have the baby so soon. It all happened quickly. The baby was well but Kathryn was dead.

For the rest of that night, Wade sat there and looked at the photograph of Kathryn on his desk. He didn't want to think about the baby. What did he, Preston Wade, know about children anyway? All he understood was his business.

Wade placed the photograph back on his desk. Twenty years was a long time, but the pain was still there. The door opened and Kemp stepped into the office.

WADE Well, what time is the plane going to get into Kennedy?

KEMP At 10:25. It's on time.

WADE You know, Kemp, Kathryn was only 20 years old when I took this photograph.

KEMP She was about Susan's age then, wasn't she?

WADE Oh, yes, Susan. And now my daughter is coming home. You know, Kemp, I'm 66 years old. I'm just too old. I can't learn how to be a father now.

KEMP You don't have to be. Susan can get married. She's old enough. A husband is all she needs.

WADE I'm not sure about that. Susan takes after her mother. She needs a strong man to look after her.

KEMP You have to get to the airport. Let me put away those plans for Wade Plaza.

WADE No, not yet. I want to look them over again.

KEMP But the plane is arriving in half an hour.

WADE Call for the car, Kemp. I want you to go to the airport for me. I'm going to do some more work here.

Questions

Ask and answer:
1 if Wade was happy or sad when he thought about Kathryn. Why? *Because is dead*
2 if Wade received a call from the doctor or his wife. When?
3 if Kathryn or the baby died. When?
4 if Wade or Kemp thinks Susan needs to get married. Why?
5 if Kemp or Wade is going to meet Susan the airport. How?
6 if Wade is going to stay in the office or go to the airport. Why?

I want you to go to the airport for me. I'm going to do some work here.

Simple Past

Did	the plane the passengers	arrive	on time? late?	Yes, it did. No, they didn't.
Was the plane Were the passengers		late? on time?		No, it wasn't. Yes, they were.
When did the passengers arrive? Who arrived at 10:25?				At 10:25. The passengers did.

We use the **simple past** tense to tell about an action or state that happened or was true at a time in the past. When *who* or *what* is the subject of the sentence, we do not use the *did-pattern* to form a question.

A Tell about the story. Complete these sentences with the *past tense* of regular verbs and *was(n't)* or *were(n't)*.

1 The doctor (telephone) with the news about Kathryn. Wade _____ upset.
2 Kathryn _____ very old. Wade (marry) her when she was 21 years old.
3 Wade (pick) up Kathryn's photograph. He _____ sad.
4 Wade (start) his business with a lot of hard work and a little money. He _____ lazy.
5 Wade _____ clever. He (use) company profits to expand his business.

6 Kemp (wait) for Wade to look over the plans. Kemp _____ impatient.
7 Kemp and Wade (discover) the Tudor Village problem. They _____ happy.
8 Kemp and Wade _____ angry. They (want) to build Wade Plaza soon.

B Make *wh-questions* with the *past tense* to ask each other about the story.

1 Someone called Wade. Who? When?
S1 Who called Wade?
S2 The doctor did.
S3 When did he call?
S4 At midnight.

2 Someone telephoned the airlines. Who? Why?
3 Something happened to Kathryn. What? When?
4 Someone wanted to own Tudor Village? Who? Why?
5 Something landed at 10:25 this morning. What? Where?

• Make questions to ask each other with *who, what, where,* and *when* and the past tense of these irregular verbs.

eat/ate	have/had	take/took
buy/bought	go/went	read/read
come/came	make/made	see/saw

1 dinner last night
→ Who had chicken for dinner last night?
→ What did you make for dinner last night?
→ Where did you eat dinner last night?
→ When did you have dinner last night?

2 department store last week
3 school today
4 vacation last year
5 work yesterday
6 television last night
7 breakfast this morning
8 trip last month

C Read about Kathryn and Preston Wade's wedding and complete the story with the correct form of these verbs.

- attend
- carry
- follow
- graduate
- leave

- marry
- perform
- receive
- serve
- wear

Kathryn Davis, New York Heiress, Weds

Kathryn Gayle Davis _____ Preston Wade, New York industrialist and president of Wade Enterprises, in Manhattan yesterday. The Reverend Charles Jenkins _____ the ceremony at St. William's Church on Park Avenue. The reception for 300 guests _____ at the Plaza Hotel.

Miss Davis, daughter of John Davis, founder of Davis Department Stores, _____ from Miss Porter's School and _____ Vassar College. The bride, a fashion editor at *Vogue*, _____ a white silk gown with Belgian lace. She _____ a bouquet of roses and orchids.

Mr. Wade _____ on the City Planning Board and _____ the *Good Citizen Award* from the NY City Council last year.

After the reception, Mr. and Mrs. Wade _____ for a two-week trip to Hawaii.

Going to *Future*

Who's Wade isn't	going to meet	Susan?	Kemp is.
Is Wade Are her friends	meeting		No, he isn't. No, they aren't.

We regularly use the **be going** *to-infinitive* form of the verb to express future plans. When we know the future time of an action or event, we regularly replace the **going to future** with the **continuous present** form.

A Tell about the story. Complete the statements with the correct tense of the verb.

1 Preston Wade (be) a very powerful and wealthy man. He (own) a very large construction company. Wade (build) the Wade Building 10 years ago. Now he (have) a new project. Wade (start) the construction of Wade Plaza sometime this year. The people of New York (remember) him because of this building.

2 Kemp (be) Wade's assistant. A few minutes ago, he (call) the airlines office. Susan's plane (arrive) at Kennedy soon. Kemp (meet) Susan at the airport. She (be) disappointed because she expects to see her father.

B This is the architect's model of the Wade Plaza complex. Use the cues to ask each other about Wade's plans.

S1 Where is Wade going to build (the department store)?
S2 He's going to build it *over* the boutiques.

S1 Is Wade going to build (a café)?
S2 Yes, there's going to be a café *next to* the fountain.

cues *the office building; the boutiques; the parking garage; the restaurants; the athletic club; the luxury apartments; the park; the supermarket; the fountain.*

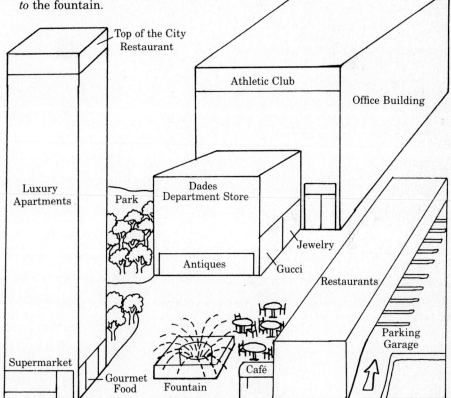

Top of the City Restaurant
Athletic Club
Office Building
Luxury Apartments
Park
Dades Department Store
Jewelry
Antiques
Gucci
Restaurants
Parking Garage
Café
Supermarket
Gourmet Food
Fountain

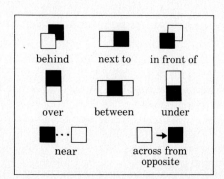

behind   next to   in front of

over   between   under

near   across from opposite

• Tell about a building project in this city or in your country.

The city is going to build a new library on _____ Avenue, next to _____.

There's going to be a new highway from _____ to _____.

11

ONE Giving directions

Kemp is getting into Wade's limousine. He's going to meet Susan at the airport. Kemp is giving the driver directions to Kennedy.

Listen to the tape and look at the map. Then complete the conversation as you listen to the tape a second time.

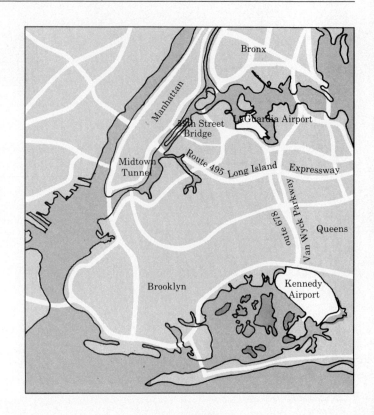

KEMP   Take me to Kennedy International Airport.
DRIVER Do you ___TAKE___ the 59th Street Bridge or the Midtown Tunnel?
KEMP   Go south. Take the Tunnel. Get on Route LONS ISLAND That's the __495__ Expressway.
DRIVER Does the Expressway go _____?
KEMP   No, you have to _____ the Van Wyck Parkway. That's Route _____.
DRIVER Is that _____ to Kennedy?
KEMP   Yes, it goes directly _____.

Role Play: Take the roles of Kemp and the driver. Kemp wants to go to La Guardia Airport. Ask and give directions from the Wade Building to La Guardia Airport. Use the map as your guide and change the model conversation as necessary.

TWO Telling about yourself

Mary told Susan all about herself:

When she was 19 years old, Mary left Ireland. She was in New York only a year when she met her husband, Michael. They got married three years later. Tudor Village was their first home. Mary worked hard all her life, even after the children were born. The Ryans were always poor, but they were a happy and loving family.

Interview each other. Ask each other these questions or make questions of your own. Then write a short paragraph about *your classmate.*

1 When were you born? Where? I WAS born i5T
2 Did you always live there? no
3 Where did you go to school? What did you study?
4 Did you prepare for a particular career?
5 Did you get a job after graduation?
6 Why did you decide to study English?
7 What are you going to do when you finish this class?

Making plans for the evening

You meet your friend on the street. You don't have any plans for the evening, but you feel like going out.

Listen to the sample conversations on the tape.

• Act out a similar conversation between you and your friend. Follow the conversation guide below. Some vocabulary cues are given, but you may choose words of your own.

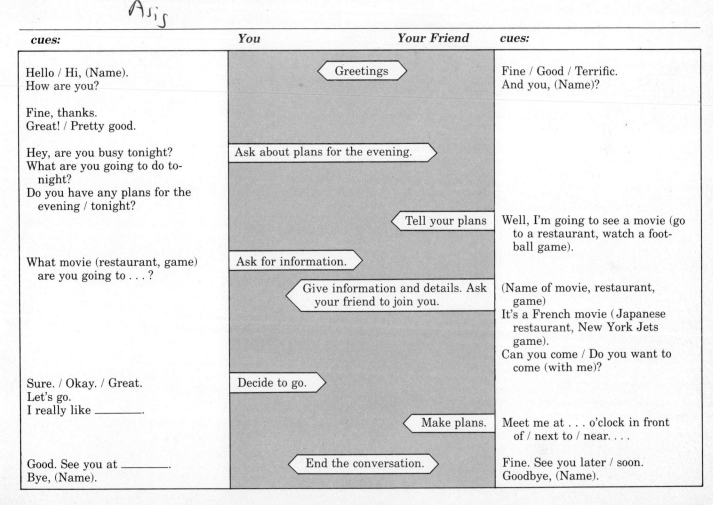

cues:	You	Your Friend	cues:
Hello / Hi, (Name). How are you?	Greetings		Fine / Good / Terrific. And you, (Name)?
Fine, thanks. Great! / Pretty good.			
Hey, are you busy tonight? What are you going to do to- night? Do you have any plans for the evening / tonight?	Ask about plans for the evening.		
		Tell your plans	Well, I'm going to see a movie (go to a restaurant, watch a foot- ball game).
What movie (restaurant, game) are you going to . . . ?	Ask for information.		
		Give information and details. Ask your friend to join you.	(Name of movie, restaurant, game) It's a French movie (Japanese restaurant, New York Jets game). Can you come / Do you want to come (with me)?
Sure. / Okay. / Great. Let's go. I really like _____.	Decide to go.		
		Make plans.	Meet me at . . . o'clock in front of / next to / near. . . .
Good. See you at _____. Bye, (Name).	End the conversation.		Fine. See you later / soon. Goodbye, (Name).

While Susan was waiting for her luggage, she looked for her father.

Scene One

🔊 Twenty minutes ago, Flight 487 landed at Kennedy International Airport. The passengers walked to the luggage area to pick up their suitcases. While Susan was waiting for her luggage, she looked for her father behind the customs booths. Family and friends of the passengers were standing there. Susan couldn't see her father. There were too many people. But Susan wasn't worried. He was probably waiting in his car at the terminal entrance.

A few minutes later, Susan had all of her luggage, but Mary Ryan didn't. Mary couldn't find her large green suitcase. She was getting nervous. Finally Mary saw the suitcase as it was coming down the conveyor belt. Mary and Susan tried to lift it, but they couldn't. It was too heavy for them to lift. They weren't strong enough. A tall, well-dressed man was standing next to Mary. He reached over and easily pulled the suitcase off the conveyor belt.

MARY   Why, thank you, young man. It was kind of you to help us.

PAULO   *De nada.* Oh, excuse me. I must remember to speak English. It was nothing, madame.

MARY   Oh, call me Mary.

SUSAN   Hi, I'm Susan Wade. Glad to meet you . . .?

PAULO   Paulo Santos. I am pleased to meet you, too. Are you both from New York?

SUSAN   Well, I live in London. I go to school there, but I'm really from New York and so is Mary.

PAULO   I'm from Brazil.

SUSAN   Are you going to stay in New York long?

PAULO   Only for a year. I'm an architect. I'm going to teach building design at Columbia University. Last year I was teaching at the University of São Paulo.

MARY   Is your family with you?

PAULO   No, I'm single. In fact, I have to find a place to stay in New York. Perhaps you can give me some advice about a hotel?

MARY   Oh, you don't want to live in a hotel. Hotels are expensive. Besides you need to meet some nice young people. Say, there's an empty apartment in my building! My daughter Molly can help you decorate it. She's a terrific housekeeper.

PAULO   Well, I don't know about your daughter. But I do need an apartment.

SUSAN   . . . and a ride to the City. My father's coming for me in his car. He can take us all into the City.

Questions

1 Did Susan look for her father? Ask where.
2 Were the women able to lift the suitcase? Ask why not.
3 Did Paulo help the women? Ask how. ﻚﺴ
4 Is Mary happy because Paulo isn't married? Ask why. ﻚﺴ
5 Is Mary going to help Paulo? Ask how.
6 Did Susan offer to give them a ride? Ask when.

Scene Two

📼 Kemp got into Wade's Cadillac and told the driver to take him to Kennedy. As he was sitting there, Kemp thought about Preston Wade and about his own father. Kemp's father never owned a car like this. And that was Preston Wade's fault.

Thirty years ago, Wade and Kemp's father started the construction company together. But Wade was too clever for Kemp's father. He cheated Kemp's father and stole a large part of the business from him. When he died, Kemp's father was almost broke. Kemp received his father's small part of the business, and now he was working for Wade.

It was Kemp's turn to get even. He wanted to get control of Wade Enterprises and Susan was the first step. Kemp thought about Susan and all that Wade money. Susan didn't know it, he thought, but her future husband was on his way to meet her.

As the car was turning into the TA terminal entrance, Kemp saw Susan. She was standing with a tall man and an old woman. When Kemp got out of the car, Susan ran towards him. She stopped suddenly when she saw the empty back seat.

SUSAN Kemp, where's my father? He didn't come to meet me, did he?

KEMP Your father had . . . uh . . . an important meeting. You know how it is, Susan.

SUSAN I don't believe you. There was no meeting.

KEMP Oh course there was. He couldn't leave the office this morning.

MARY Are you all right, Susan? You look <u>upset</u>. MOLESTA

SUSAN Oh, Mary. I guess I'm just <u>disappointed</u>. I wanted you to meet my father. DESCORAZONADA

KEMP Say good-bye to your friends, Susan. We have to go now.

SUSAN Can't we give them a ride? We're going to the City and so are Mary and Paulo.

KEMP I'm sorry, Susan. Your father told me to take you home, and I really have to get back to the office.

PAULO Don't worry, Susan. We can take a taxi.

MARY Sure, honey. You have my telephone number. Call me soon. I want you to come over for dinner and meet Molly and Jeff.

KEMP Let's go, Susan. We have a lot to talk about on the way home.

Questions

1 Were Wade and Kemp's father in business together? Ask when.
2 Does Kemp hate Preston Wade? Ask why.
3 Does Kemp plan to get control of Wade Enterprises? Ask how.
4 Did Susan feel disappointed when she looked into the car? Ask why.
5 Did Kemp tell Susan the truth about her father? Ask what.
6 Does Mary expect to see Susan again? Ask when.

Simple Past vs. Past Continuous

Mary	spotted the suitcase	as while	it *was coming* down she *was looking* at	the conveyor belt.
	tried to lift it	when	it *passed* her on	

We use *as* and *while* with the **past continuous (was/were** + *V-ing*) to tell about a past action *in progress* at some time in the past. Use *when* with the **past simple** to show an action *happened* at the same time another action happened.

A Answer the questions and then tell about the story. Make sentences with *while* or *as,* and *when.*

1 a Wade was sitting at his desk. What did he pick up? (while)
 b Wade thought about Kathryn. Was he sad? (when)
→ While Wade was sitting at his desk, he picked up a photograph of his wife.
→ When Wade thought about Kathryn, he was sad.

2 a Susan was waiting for her luggage. Did she look for her father? (while)
 b Susan didn't see her father. Was she worried? (when)

3 a The suitcase was coming down the conveyor belt. Who spotted it? (as)
 b The suitcase passed by. Who lifted it? (when)

4 a Kemp was sitting in the car. Who did he think about? (while)
 b The car turned into the TA terminal entrance. Who did Kemp see? (when)

● Join these sentences with *while* or *when.*

5 a The driver was taking Kemp to the airport. The weather changed.
 b It started to rain. The driver turned on the windshield wipers.

6 a Molly was walking to work yesterday. She saw an automobile accident.
 b The police arrived. Molly told them about the crash.

7 a Jeff was watching television. The telephone rang.
 b The woman asked to speak to Mary. Jeff took a message.

B Mary wants to find a husband for her daughter Molly. That's the reason she told Paulo that Molly was a "terrific" housekeeper. Actually, Molly hates cooking and housework.

Yesterday, Molly burned the steak and dropped the frying pan *while* she was cooking dinner.

This morning, she broke the lamp *when* she knocked over the table in the living room.

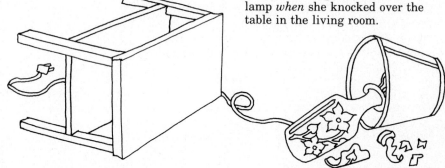

● Tell about something that *happened* to you. Tell what *was happening* at the same time.

cues *have a flat tire; have a car accident; break an arm (leg); meet your wife (boyfriend); find or lose a valuable object.*

→ While I was driving home last week, I had a flat tire. When I discovered the flat tire, I drove to the side of the road and changed the tire.

C Tell about the story. Join these groups of sentences to make one new sentence with *when* or *while.*

1 Kemp was in school.
 It was business school.
 Kemp's father died then.
→ Kemp was in business school when his father died.

2 Kemp was looking through papers.
 The papers were his father's.
 Kemp learned about Preston Wade.

3 Kemp's father and Wade were partners.
 They were in business.
 They started the company together.

4 Kemp's father took care of the equipment.
 It was for construction.
 Wade was managing the office.

5 Wade took control of a part of the business.
 It was a large part.
 Kemp's father was dying of heart disease.

6 Kemp inherited a small part of the business.
 It was his father's part.
 Kemp started to work for Wade.

Too *and* Enough

Mary couldn't			She	was too weak wasn't strong enough		to lift it.
lift the suitcase.		He	was strong enough wasn't too weak	
Paulo could		

| The suitcase was heavy. | Mary was too weak to lift it.
It was too heavy for Mary to lift. |

We use **too** *before* the adjective and **enough** *after* the adjective to show that we need or don't need a particular quality for a certain purpose.

A Tell about the story. Write sentences with *too* or *enough*.

1 Jeff is smart. Can he get a good job?
→ Jeff is smart *enough* to get a good job.

2 Mary is tired. Can she carry the suitcase to the taxi?
→ Mary is *too* tired to carry the suitcase to the taxi.

3 Wade is rich. Can he buy Susan anything she wants?

4 Jeff is lazy. Can he help Molly clean the house?

5 Kemp is clever. Can he take control of Wade Enterprises?

6 Susan is stubborn. Can she convince her father to give her a job?

7 Molly is independent. Can she give up her career to get married?

8 Wade is busy. Can he spend a lot of time with Susan?

9 Molly is talented. Can she win a prize for her stories?

10 Susan is inexperienced. Can she help her father run the business?

● Give your opinion.

Susan is twenty years old. Is she too young to get married? In *your* country, is a twenty-year-old girl old enough to get married? Is a twenty-year-old boy old enough?

cues *to have a job? to live alone? to travel abroad? to own a car?*

B Mary did a lot of shopping when she was in London. She went to these stores and bought presents for her children.

Stores	Presents	Description
Harrod's	a cotton shirt	thin, summer weight
Marks & Spencer	a wool sweater	bulky Irish knit
Asprey's	a china tea service	teapot, 6 cups and saucers
Liberty of London	a silk scarf	36 inches square
Harvey Nichols	a leather wallet	4 inches by 5 inches
John Paine	an ivory chess set	32 pieces, each 3 inches high

● Give your opinion. Which presents did Mary buy for Jeff? for Molly?

S1 What did Mary buy for (Jeff) when she was in London?

S2 She bought him a cotton shirt while she was shopping at *Harrod's*.

● Tell about things *you* bought for someone.

| When I was in ____, | I bought | a(n) ____ for (name). |
| While I was shopping at ____, | | (name) a(n) ____. |

● Mary wants to put the presents in separate boxes. These are the boxes she can get from the stores:

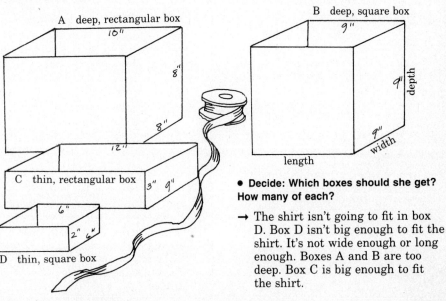

A deep, rectangular box

B deep, square box

C thin, rectangular box

D thin, square box

● Decide: Which boxes should she get? How many of each?

→ The shirt isn't going to fit in box D. Box D isn't big enough to fit the shirt. It's not wide enough or long enough. Boxes A and B are too deep. Box C is big enough to fit the shirt.

ONE   Making excuses

Molly is trying to clean the house before her mother comes home. It's a mess. Jeff doesn't want to help. He hates housework.
Listen to Jeff's excuses on the tape. Then complete the conversation as you listen to the tape a second time.

MOLLY This room is a mess!

JEFF What's _____ it? It _____ to me.

MOLLY Are you kidding? Jeff, _____ pick up those magazines?

JEFF Oh, Sis. I can't. I'm too busy.

MOLLY What _____ "you can't"?

JEFF I'm _____ to get up. Leave me alone.

MOLLY Well, I'm tired of _____. You're _____ to take some responsibility for this house. Get up _____ me.

JEFF When Mom was here, I _____ do the housework.

MOLLY I'm not your mother. Now pick up those magazines.

Role Play: Take the roles of Jeff and Molly. Molly wants Jeff to pick up his clothes and do the wash, but Jeff doesn't want to. Follow the model conversation.

TWO   Describing a trip

While Mary was sightseeing in London, she visited Westminster Abbey and Big Ben. When she went to the British Museum, it was closed. She didn't get to see it while she was visiting her sister.

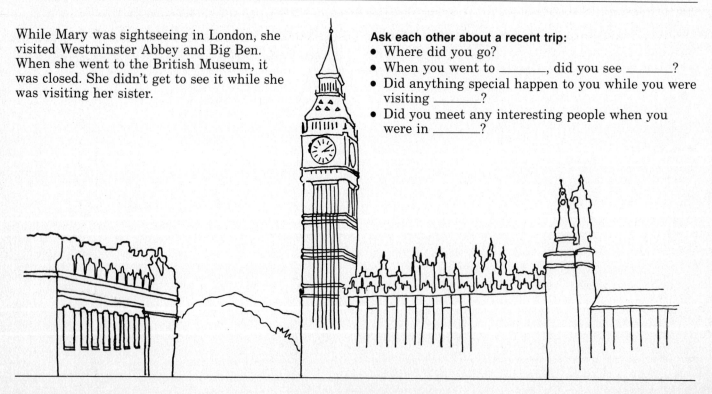

Ask each other about a recent trip:
- Where did you go?
- When you went to _____, did you see _____?
- Did anything special happen to you while you were visiting _____?
- Did you meet any interesting people when you were in _____?

Fear of Flying

Flight 191 from Chicago ended in tragedy today. The plane, with its 258 passengers and 13 crew members, was taking off from O'Hare Airport when the left engine suddenly fell off. Seconds later, the airplane turned, pointed its left wing down and fell toward the earth. When the huge jet crashed, all 272 on board died instantly.

Near the scene of the crash, Michael Delany was walking his dog when he saw the falling plane: "The fuel was coming out of the left side. When the engines stopped, the plane started to drop." Rich Dusek was working outside his store when he heard a big explosion: "When I heard the crash, I turned and saw the flames. The plane was burning. There wasn't much left, just pieces of metal everywhere."

Police and rescue workers were at the scene in minutes. As they walked through the burning pieces of the plane, they looked for signs of life. There weren't any. This was the worst airplane crash in U.S. aviation history.

One of the passengers on Flight 191 was Mrs. Sandra Blake, 47. With tears in her eyes, her daughter Carol told reporters about her mother's fear of airplanes: "While mother was boarding the plane, she turned to me and waved. Her hands were shaking and she looked nervous. You see, Mother was afraid of flying. I laughed when she told me about it. It seemed so silly then."

Thinkabout

1 The engine fell off when the plane was
  a arriving.
  b taking off.
  c landing.

2 When Michael Delany saw the falling plane, he was
  a walking his dog.
  b working in his store.
  c looking for pieces of metal.

3 The rescue workers arrived at the scene
  a when the plane took off.
  b before the plane crashed.
  c after the plane exploded.

4 When Sandra Blake got on the plane, she was
  a smiling.
  b shaking.
  c crying.

Talkabout

These are some of the other passengers on Flight 191. What were they thinking about when they saw the engine fall off?

Marcia Gray, 23. Her boyfriend lives in California. She was traveling to Los Angeles to get married.
Captain Lux, 57. He was a pilot in the Korean War. He was planning to retire next month.
Ron Stern, 28. He finished medical school a week before the crash. He was beginning his career at a famous Los Angeles hospital.

Writeabout   Narrative: Developing a theme

Write a short composition to tell about an accident, perhaps about a friend or relative.

Organize the events of your story chronologically.

> Mrs. Sandra Blake waved to her daughter Carol and boarded Flight 191 from Chicago to Los Angeles.
>
> When the huge jet crashed, Mrs. Blake died instantly.

←**Start with:**
Tell about the person and the situation.

←**Order the events:**
What happened first? second? next? after that?

←**End with:**
Tell about the outcome of the accident.

Scene One

Mary hasn't seen her children for two weeks.

While they were riding in the taxi from the airport, Mary showed Paulo some of the sights. This was his first visit to the United States. She pointed out the United Nations, the Empire State Building, and the World Trade Center. Mary also told Paulo about Molly and Jeff. For the last five years, Molly has worked for the *City Herald*. Newspaper work is difficult, but Molly has become a top reporter. While her friends were getting married, Molly wrote stories for the paper. Mary didn't understand this. She wanted her daughter to have children, not a career.

Paulo asked about Jeff. He saw the sadness in Mary's eyes when she spoke about her only son.

MARY   Well, Jeff's 28 now. He's had a . . . difficult time lately.

PAULO   What's wrong?

MARY   Jeff was in Vietnam. He was in law school when the army drafted him. Jeff didn't want to go, but he had to.

PAULO   How long was he there?

MARY   A year. After that, he didn't want to come home. He lived in Asia and South America. He got jobs there.

PAULO   What's Jeff doing now? Is he working?

MARY   No, he's been home for three months, but he hasn't found a job yet.

PAULO   Has Jeff thought about school since he came home?

MARY   Molly and I have talked to him about it, but he's just not interested. When Jeff was in school he used to be so friendly. He used to love to have fun.

PAULO   How has he changed?

MARY   Jeff's not the same person now. He's so quiet all the time. Jeff is different from Molly. Molly takes after me, I'm afraid. Paulo, have I bored you with all this family talk?

PAULO   Of course you haven't, Mary. Besides, I need to practice my English. Right?

MARY   Don't worry about that. You're going to get plenty of practice around the Ryan family.

Questions

1 Has Paulo ever visited New York City before?
2 Did Mary show Paulo some of the sights? Ask what.
3 Has Molly been a reporter for a long time? Ask where.
4 Was Jeff in Vietnam? Ask how long.
5 Did Jeff use to be friendly? Ask when.
6 Is Molly a quiet person? Ask who.

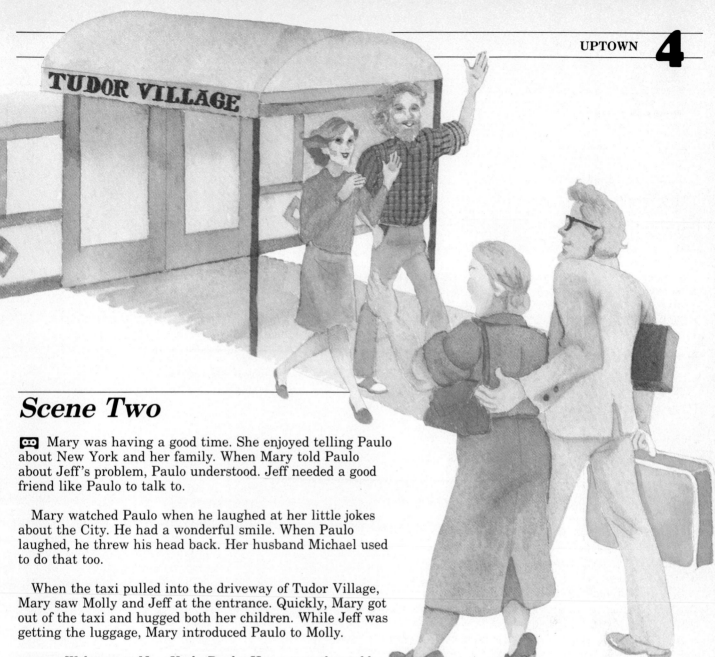

Scene Two

📼 Mary was having a good time. She enjoyed telling Paulo about New York and her family. When Mary told Paulo about Jeff's problem, Paulo understood. Jeff needed a good friend like Paulo to talk to.

Mary watched Paulo when he laughed at her little jokes about the City. He had a wonderful smile. When Paulo laughed, he threw his head back. Her husband Michael used to do that too.

When the taxi pulled into the driveway of Tudor Village, Mary saw Molly and Jeff at the entrance. Quickly, Mary got out of the taxi and hugged both her children. While Jeff was getting the luggage, Mary introduced Paulo to Molly.

MOLLY Welcome to New York, Paulo. Has my mother told you a lot about us?

PAULO Well, she told me about your work on the newspaper. You know, Molly, you *are* too pretty to be a reporter.

MOLLY Paulo, you sound like my mother. She's been saying that for years.

MARY Jeff, those two brown bags are Paulo's. Can you bring them upstairs? Paulo might rent that empty apartment on the ninth floor. You know, the Bradleys' old apartment.

JEFF Let Carlos do it. He's the super, not me. I'm going to find Carlos.

PAULO What's a "super"?

MOLLY He's the building manager. He takes care of the apartments.

MARY We've known Carlos and his wife Maria for years. They're like family.

PAULO Molly, I've looked forward to meeting you and your brother.

MARY C'mon, you two. Carlos can take care of the luggage. I haven't been home for two weeks. This tired old body needs a soft chair and a nice cup of tea.

Questions

1 Did Mary enjoy her conversation with Paulo? Ask why.
2 When did Mary see Molly and Jeff? Ask where.
3 Did Mary tell Paulo about Molly? Ask what.
4 Is Jeff going to bring Paulo's luggage upstairs? Ask who.
5 Has Mary known Carlos and his wife for a long time? Ask how long.
6 Does Mary want a cup of tea? Ask why.

Present Perfect

Has Paulo met Jeff yet?		He	has already met Molly. hasn't met Carlos yet.

Carlos and Maria have	lived been	in New York	for over 30 years. since 1940.

We use the **present perfect** (**have** + *V-ed, en*) to express the time from some moment in the past to the present moment of speaking. The **present perfect** tells that the past action affects the present situation.

A Tell about the story. Paulo has never been to New York. In fact, this is his first visit to the United States. What has happened to Paulo *since he arrived in New York*?

1 Has Paulo made any friends yet?
→ Yes, he has. He's already made friends with Mary and Susan.

2 Has Paulo visited Columbia University yet?
→ No, he hasn't. He hasn't visited Columbia University yet.

3 Has Paulo met Jeff and Molly yet?
4 Has Paulo met Carlos and Maria yet?
5 Has Paulo seen the United Nations yet?
6 Has Paulo seen the Statue of Liberty yet?
7 Has Paulo talked to Molly yet?
8 Has Paulo talked to Jeff yet?
9 Has Paulo taken a taxi yet?
10 Has Paulo taken a bus yet?

Find out what your classmates *have done* or *haven't done* so far today (this week, this month).

today: shave, eat lunch, read the newspaper, open your mail, make your bed.

S1 Have you shaved yet today?
S1 I already have. I shaved this morning.
or I haven't yet. I'm going to shave tonight.

this week: do your laundry, clean the house, write a letter, see a movie

this month: have a haircut, pay your bills, take a trip, go to the bank

B Mary left for London two weeks ago. That was September 14. Now she's home with her family.

Mary hasn't talked to her children *since* September 14.
Mary hasn't seen her apartment *for* two weeks.

Note the use of **for** and **since** with the time expressions:

for	two minutes/hours three days/weeks five months/years	= *length* of time
since	11 o'clock/noon Tuesday/yesterday March 12/1980	= a *definite point* in the past

● Use the cues to make sentences with the *present perfect* tense and *for/since*.

1 Jeff – get a haircut/ six months
Jeff hasn't gotten a haircut *for* six months.

2 Molly – see her mother/ September 14
Molly hasn't seen her mother *since* September 14.

3 Susan – see her father/ a year
4 Mary – open her mail/ 2 weeks
5 Wade – see his daughter/ 198___
6 Paulo – speak Portuguese/ 3 hours
7 Molly – write a story/ Wednesday
8 Jeff – have a job/ 6 months
9 Mary – have a cup of tea/ 9 o'clock
10 Paulo – call his parents/ Sunday

C When Jeff lived abroad, he traveled to a lot of countries. Ask each other about the places Jeff has visited in Europe, Asia, Africa and South America:

S1 Has Jeff ever been to Europe?
S2 Yes, he has. He's been to

_____,

but he's never been to

_____.

Ask each other: Have you ever been to _____?
When were you in _____?

Used to *Past*

Susan used to live in London, but she lives in New York now.
Molly didn't use to live in Brazil, but Paulo did.

Who used to Did Susan use to	live in London?	Susan did. Yes, she did.

We use **used to** with past actions or states which are no longer true.

A Tell about the story. Make questions with *used to* and ask each other. Give correct information about the story.

1 Susan/ live in Paris

S1 Did Susan use to live in Paris?
S2 No, she didn't. She used to live in London.

2 Paulo/ teach in São Paulo

S1 Did Paulo use to teach in São Paulo?
S2 Yes, he did. He used to teach in São Paulo.

3 Jeff/ study medicine
4 Paulo/ live in Brazil
5 Susan/ go to school in New York
6 Mary/ live with her parents
7 Molly/ attend law school
8 Wade and Kemp's father/ be business partners
9 Jeff/ work in Brazil.
10 Molly and Jeff/ live in Ireland

● Ask each other about things you used to do when you were children.

When I was _____ years old, I
    used to _____.
What about you? Did you use to
    _____?

cues *childhood games; activities with your parents; household chores; favorite foods.*

B Molly thinks about her father a lot. She thinks about how it used to be when he was alive. Change the past verbs to the *used to* form to emphasize actions which are no longer true.

Molly's mother and father *owned* a variety store down the street from Tudor Village. Her parents *spent* all of their time together at the family business. Sometimes Molly *helped* out at the cash register, but Jeff *didn't like* to work at the store. The best times *were* at night, when the family *sat* around the big table at the back of the store. Her father *told* them stories about the customers at the store. How he *made* them laugh! Those *were* happy times for the Ryans.

C Molly is working on a story for the *City Herald* about the high cost of living today. She's comparing today's prices with 1950 prices.

Ask how much things used to cost. Compare with today's prices.

How much did a (gallon of gasoline) use to cost in 1950?
What does a (gallon of gasoline) cost today?
How much has the price increased since 1950?

Tell about the change in prices of food and other essentials in your country:

A _____ used to | _____years ago.
    cost _____ | in 19___.

Today, a _____costs _____.

The price of _____ has increased _____(percent) since 19___.

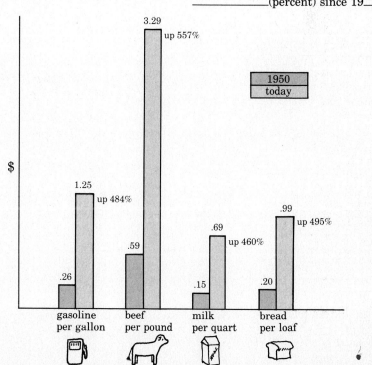

ONE Finding out about jobs

Molly is always trying to help Jeff get a job. She hasn't
been very successful lately. She's trying again now.
Listen to the tape and look at the Want Ads in the *City
Herald.* Then complete the conversation as you listen to
the tape a second time.

MOLLY Did you see today's paper?

JEFF No, I _____ it yet.

MOLLY Look on page _____, under "sales". The Sanderson Hospital Supply Company _____ a
New York area representative.

JEFF What _____ to do?

MOLLY The sales rep _____ hospital and
show _____products.

JEFF What's _____?

MOLLY The starting salary is _____, but you get
_____ percent commission on _____. There are
_____ benefits, too, like free medical insurance
and tuition.

JEFF I'm not sure _____ the qualifications. I
_____ sales work.

MOLLY They _____ any experience. They want
someone with a _____ degree and a _____
personality.

JEFF No, thanks. I'm not interested. I'm not very
good at meeting new people.

Role Play: Take the roles of Molly and Jeff. Use
the information from the other job advertisements and make similar conversations between
Molly and Jeff.

TWO Remembering the past

When Mary came to America, she used to get a
letter from her mother in Ireland every week:

Tell about life in your country 50 years ago.
- How did people use to travel from place to place?
- How did people use to prepare their food?
- How did people use to dress?
- How did people use to earn a living?

**Have times changed or are people doing things
the *same* way now?**

---

32   **City Herald, TUES**

SALES HELP WANTED
MEDICAL SALES
NY AREA REPRESENTATIVE
Start $10,000 + 10% com

Visit hospitals/clinics and show
company products. Excellent
opportunity for college grad with
friendly personality. No experience required. Exc. benefits:
med ins, tuition. Sanderson
Hospital Supply Co. Call 741-
1400. Mr. Brown.

Publishing
BOOK SALES

12,000 base salary plus yearly
bonus. Sales rep for New York/
New Jersey area. Show texts to
school librarians/teachers. Must
have high school diploma.
Company wants ambitious person. Benefits include dental/life/
medical insurance. Submit re-
sume to Vice President, Whit-
ney Publishing Co, 135 W 60th
St., NY, NY 10020.

April 29, 1928

Dear Daughter,
Your father and I have been so busy
this week. Yesterday Father took the
horse and wagon into town and picked
up the seed for the spring planting.
He has already prepared the fields,
so we can put the seed in the ground
tomorrow. Oh, how my back is
going to ache from all that bending!
Father brought back some ice for the
icebox. There's extra ice, so I'm going
to make some ice cream this
afternoon.
Have you gotten my package yet?
I sent you a nice long skirt to keep
your legs warm next winter. I hope
you haven't cut your hair. So many
of the young girls here have. They
say it's the fashion but I think it
looks terrible.
We miss you,
Love,
Mother

P.S. Don't forget to say your prayers every night.

Running into an old friend

You are walking down the street and suddenly you see an old friend. Perhaps this is a person from your childhood, from your old job, or from your school. You haven't seen this person for years! You are happy and surprised to see this person now.

Listen to the sample conversations on the tape.

• Act out a similar conversation between you and your friend. Follow the conversation guide below. Some vocabulary cues are given, but you may choose words of your own.

cues:	You	Your Friend	cues:
Why, it's (Name), isn't it? (Name)! Is that you?	Greetings		(Name)? Is that really you? What a surprise!
How long has it been? When did I see you last? It's been over . . . years, hasn't it?	Ask how long since you saw each other.		
		Give length of time.	We haven't seen each other since . . . / for . . . Since we were . . . / For ages!
What have you done since then? Are you still living in . . . / working at . . .?	Ask what has happened since you saw each other.		Why I haven't seen you . . .
		Give information. Ask about your friend.	Yes, I'm still _____. No, I haven't _____ for years / since _____. What about you? / And you?
I'm . . . now. I've stayed at . . . / moved to . . . How's your family? What happened to (name)? Where's (name) now?	Give information. Ask about other friends and family members.		

		Give information.
		Make plans to meet at another time.
			The (family)'s fine.
			(Name)? Oh, he / she is still . . .
			(Name) is living in . . . / working
			  at . . . now.
			How about lunch / dinner soon?
			Here's my phone number. / Let's
			  get together soon.

How about tomorrow / Wednesday? Let's meet at (restaurant), at noon/ . . . o'clock.	Agree. Make definite plans.		
See you at (restaurant). (Tomorrow / Wednesday), then. at _____. Bye, (Name).	End the conversation		That sounds terrific / fine. / Wonderful. / Great idea. See you then. Good bye, (name).

Jeff and Carlos have been working on the bathroom all morning, but they haven't finished yet.

Scene One

Carlos and Jeff have just brought the suitcases up to the Ryans' apartment. Carlos has been telling Paulo about the vacant apartment. It belongs to the Bradleys, an elderly couple. Mr. and Mrs. Bradley are living in Miami this year. They want to rent their New York apartment while they are in Florida.

All this week, Jeff has been helping Carlos work on the Bradley place. It's a one-bedroom apartment on the ninth floor. It's small, but the stove and the refrigerator are new. The rent is $400 a month. This includes heat, but gas and electricity are extra.

Jeff and Carlos are bringing Paulo to the Bradley apartment. Carlos has been telling Paulo some jokes. The two of them have been laughing since they left the Ryan apartment. Mary and Molly like Paulo too, but Jeff isn't sure. He doesn't trust people easily.

PAULO   What a nice apartment! There's lots of sun. That's good because I like plants.

CARLOS   There are quite a few windows so this apartment gets good light all day. The apartment is in good condition, but the furniture is old.

PAULO   There are a lot of good antiques here. The tables need a little polish, that's all.

JEFF   Carlos and I have been working on the bathroom, but we haven't finished yet.

CARLOS   The tub needs repairing. We want to replace the pipes this afternoon, but we need another person to help us lift the tub.

PAULO   I can help you. I used to do a lot of repairs in my house in São Paulo.

JEFF   You know, I was in Brazil a few years ago.

PAULO   Really? Where?

JEFF   Up north. I had a job on that big road project.

CARLOS   Let's get to work. You two can talk while we're moving that tub.

JEFF   Carlos likes to mix business with pleasure.

CARLOS   Pleasure first. I left some beer in the fridge.

JEFF   So you did. Here, Paulo, try some of our American beer.

PAULO   Thanks. Carlos, do you have the lease to this apartment? I want to sign it before I'm too drunk to read it!

Questions

1 Who used to live in the vacant apartment? Ask where they are now.
2 Who has been fixing the apartment? Ask about the tub.
3 Does the Bradley apartment have a separate bedroom? Ask about the stove and the refrigerator.
4 Is there any furniture in the apartment? Ask how old.
5 Has Jeff ever worked in Brazil? Ask where.
6 When does Paulo want to sign the lease? Ask why.

Have you made any plans, Susan?

Scene Two

Susan and Kemp have been driving into the City. Susan hasn't said a word since they left the airport. She's been very upset. Her father was too busy to see her. All her life she has been hearing this excuse. Preston Wade has always been too busy to spend time with his daughter.

Kemp is angry. He's been trying to talk to Susan, but she's just been sitting there and looking out the window. Kemp's plan to marry the boss's daughter isn't working. Susan doesn't even want to look at him. As the car moves out of the Midtown Tunnel, Kemp tries one last time to talk to Susan.

KEMP   Have you made any plans, Susan?

SUSAN Plans? What plans?

KEMP   You know, about your future.

SUSAN My future is with my father. That's why I've been studying economics.

KEMP   Susan, you have to understand. Your father is a very important man.

SUSAN Is he too important to spend some time with his only daughter?

KEMP   Look, there's no need to get upset.

SUSAN I'm not upset.

KEMP   I think you are. C'mon. Let's relax. Let me show you the City. We can get to know each other.

SUSAN Kemp, I haven't traveled 3,000 miles to New York to go sightseeing with you! I came here to be with my father.

KEMP   That's going to be difficult, Susan. You know your father has been spending all of his time at the office.

SUSAN Then I'm going to be there with him. I've learned enough economics to understand the business.

KEMP   Your father isn't going to like that.

SUSAN Well, let's find out right now! Driver, we've changed our minds. We're not going to the house. Take us to the Wade Building.

Questions

1 What has Susan been doing since she got into the car?
2 What excuse has Susan been hearing all her life?
3 Is Kemp angry? Ask why.
4 Is Susan upset? Ask why.
5 Does Susan want to work for Wade Enterprises? Ask why.
6 Is the driver going to take Susan to the house? Ask where.

27

Present Perfect Continuous

Jeff and Carlos started to paint the bedroom at 10 o'clock.

| They have been painting | since 10 o'clock / for six hours | and haven't finished yet. |

| Have Jeff and Carlos been painting all day? | Yes, they have. |

We use the **present perfect continuous** (**have**+**been**+*V*+*ing*) when the action suggests a *continuous* action from the *past* to *now*. We expect that action to continue into the *future*.

A Tell about the story. Practice the *present perfect continuous* and the *present perfect* tenses.

1 Who has Susan been thinking about since she arrived in New York?
2 Has Susan seen her father yet?
3 What has Preston Wade been planning to build for the last two years?
4 Has Wade started to build Wade Plaza yet?

5 What has Jeff been doing since he returned to the U.S.?
6 Has Jeff found a job yet?
7 What has Paulo been teaching for the past five years?
8 Has Paulo started to teach at Columbia University yet?

B Since Jeff returned, he has been helping Carlos fix some of the apartments. This is the list of repairs. Carlos and Jeff have already made some of the repairs, but they haven't finished all of them yet.

BRADLEY 9D
PAINT LIVING ROOM ✓
FIX TUB AND PIPES
REPLACE KITCHEN SINK ✓
RYAN 12C
FIX TOILET
PAINT HALL ✓
REPLACE BATHROOM WINDOW
LEONARD 5A
PAINT BEDROOM
FIX SHOWER
PUT IN KITCHEN FLOOR ✓
CARLSON 2F
REPLACE LIGHT BULBS
REPAIR DOORBELL ✓
MILLER 8G
CONNECT NEW STOVE ✓
PUT UP BOOKSHELVES
INSTALL CARPET ✓

• Ask about the list of repairs:

S1 Have Jeff and Carlos been working on the *Bradley* apartment?
S2 Yes, they have. They've already painted the living room and replaced the kitchen sink.
S1 Have they finished all of the repairs?
S2 No, not yet. They still need to fix the tub and the pipes.

• Tell about repairs you've been making. What have you finished? haven't finished yet?

C Jeff likes to read mysteries. Since he came home, he has read a lot of books by Agatha Christie. Last month he read *Partners in Crime*. This month he's been reading *Death on the Nile*.

• Ask each other about books you've been reading lately.

S1 Have you read any good books lately?
S2 Last month I read _____. This month I've been reading _____.
S1 Really? I (don't) like _____ books.

mystery

romance

science fiction

adventure

• Tell about your other habits:

1 medicine/take
→ Mary's been taking heart pills for over ten years.

2 breakfast/ eat
3 sport/ play
4 jewelry/ wear
5 newspaper/read

Quantifiers with Count and Noncount Nouns

| How | much | sunlight heat | does the apartment have? | Quite a lot. Not much. Only a little. |
| | many | windows radiators | | Quite a few. Not many. Only a few. |

We use *how much* and *a little* with **mass** amounts that we cannot count. We use *how many* and *a few* with **unit** amounts that we can count. We use *a lot of* with both count and noncount nouns.

A Tell about the story. Make questions with *how much* and *how many*.

1 Carlos and Jeff didn't use a lot of paint. (quart)

S1 How much paint did they use?
S2 Not much. Only a little paint.
S3 How many *quarts* did they use?
S4 Not many. Only a few quarts.

2 Mary didn't drink a lot of tea. (cup)
3 Molly didn't put a lot of lemon in her tea. (drop)
4 Paulo didn't bring a lot of luggage. (suitcase)
5 The Bradleys didn't leave a lot of silverware. (knife and fork)
6 Carlos didn't have a lot of beer in his fridge. (bottle)

● Ask each other about your apartment or house.

1 furniture/have in your room

S1 How much furniture do you have in your room?
S2 Not much. I have a bed, a desk, and a chair.

2 appliances/have in your kitchen
3 sunlight/get in your living room
4 plants/have in your living room
5 heat/get in the winter
6 radiators/have in your apartment
7 hot water/get in the morning
8 showers/take every day

B Mary is nearly 70 years old. She hasn't been feeling well lately. Choose the correct expression to complete this conversation between Mary and her doctor.

DOCTOR Mary, you've gained quite a (few/little) pounds lately. You're going to have to lose a (few/little) weight.
MARY You're right. I have been eating a (lot/little) of sweets these past weeks. How (much/many) pounds do I have to lose?
DOCTOR Not too (much/many). About 20.
MARY That's quite a (few/little) pounds!

DOCTOR Tell me. How (much/many) sugar do you use every day?
MARY Well, I don't eat (much/many) candy or cake, but I usually put a (few/little) spoons of sugar in my tea.
DOCTOR That's too (many/much) sugar! Try a (few/little) lemon instead. I want to see you again in a (few/little) weeks. I hope you're going to lose a (few/little) pounds by then.

● Look at the table below. Find your desirable weight. Are you overweight or underweight?

| Desirable Weights for Women 25 and Over | | | | | Desirable Weights for Men 25 and Over | | | | |
| Height | | Slender Frame | Medium Frame | Large Frame | Height | | Slender Frame | Medium Frame | Large Frame |
Feet	Inches	lbs	lbs	lbs	Feet	Inches	lbs	lbs	lbs
4	10	96–104	101–113	109–125	5	0	112–120	118–129	126–141
5	0	102–110	107–119	115–131	5	2	115–123	121–133	129–144
5	2	108–116	113–126	121–138	5	4	121–129	127–139	135–152
5	4	114–123	120–135	129–146	5	6	128–137	134–147	142–161
5	6	122–131	128–143	137–154	5	8	136–145	142–156	151–170
5	8	130–140	136–151	145–163	5	10	144–154	150–165	159–179
5	10	134–144	140–155	149–168	6	0	152–162	158–175	168–189
6	0	138–148	144–159	153–173	6	2	160–171	167–185	178–199

How many pounds are you overweight (underweight)?
How much weight do you have to lose (gain)?

How are you going to lose (gain) the weight?

ONE *Explaining a process*

Molly has been taking Paulo to some of the New York department stores. Paulo wants to get a coffee maker and a toaster for his new apartment. They are in the house-wares section of *Macy's* department store right now.

🔊 Listen to the tape and look at the kitchen appliances. Then complete the conversation as you listen to the tape a second time.

PAULO What about this coffee maker? It's called *Mrs. Coffee*.

MOLLY I _____ that brand. How _____ does it make?

PAULO From 4 to 12 cups. You can make as _____ as you want.

MOLLY How _____?

PAULO Well, first you set _____, then you add the coffee.

MOLLY Where _____ the water?

PAULO The opening is _____.

MOLLY How _____? I bet it's _____.

PAULO $_____, but _____ special feature. You can select the kind of coffee, from very weak to very strong.

Role Play: Practice a similar conversation between Molly and Paulo. Explain how to use the toaster.

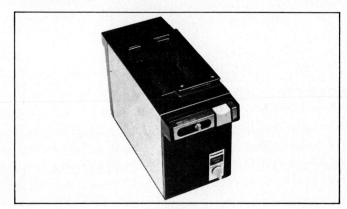

TWO *Talking about future plans*

Have you been planning to . . .
   decorate your house or apartment?
   fix something?
   buy new furniture or appliances?

Ask each other:
S1 I've been planning to _____.
S2 How (When? Why?) are you going to _____?

Sixty Plus

Point of View:
Mildred Kramer

I'm 72 years old and I have a disease. It's called old age.

I've been doing a lot of thinking about my life lately. I've thought about all the good times I've shared with my family and friends. I've had three children and I haven't stopped being a mother. My children have given me grandchildren and a grandmother has a lot of responsibilities. I've held my grandchildren in my arms. I've seen their smiles and heard their laughter. But there are so many wonderful stories I haven't told them yet.

All of my close friends have already left me. At first I was frightened; then I was lonely. I've missed their company. My old friends are dead, but to me they've just stepped into another room and closed the door. There are a lot of empty spaces in my life now, but I've found a way to fill them up.

I've joined a group called the *Sixty Plus* Club at my church. Every Wednesday, we meet to plan social events and community activities. So far this month, we've had a party for our grandchildren and we've seen a play in New York. Some of our younger members have volunteered their help in city hospitals. I've been knitting sweaters and mending clothes at home for poor children. Next week we're going to the mayor's office to talk about a new hospital for the elderly. I have a new group of friends now, and a lot of important work to do.

Thinkabout

1 Mildred Kramer is now suffering from
  a loneliness.
  b heart disease.
  c old age.

2 All of Mildred's old friends
  a have died.
  b have moved away.
  c are in the next room.

3 Mildred helps other people when she
  a volunteers her help in hospitals.
  b knits sweaters and mends clothes at home.
  c sees plays in New York.

4 Mildred is happy because she
  a doesn't have responsibilities.
  b lives in a new hospital.
  c is doing important work.

Talkabout

Clara Wilson is 81 and she lives alone in a small apartment. Her doctor doesn't want Clara to live by herself. Clara doesn't want to go to a nursing home; she wants to live with her son Ronald. Ronald has a big house, but Ronald's wife doesn't want to take care of her mother-in-law. Ronald loves his mother, but he has a responsibility to his wife too.

Should young members of a family take responsibility for old relatives? Does that responsibility mean paying for their care or giving them a home and love? What *should* Ronald do?

Writeabout Narrative: Using experiences to tell a story

Interview an elderly person or tell about one you know. Use the questions below and ask about his or her life. Record the responses. Write a short composition to tell a story about the person's life.

Mrs. Mildred Kramer is 72 years old and lives alone in a one-bedroom apartment in my building.

Mildred is over seventy, but she has the spirit and energy of a young girl.

←Start with:
Tell about the person and the situation.

←Experiences:
What have been the happy times? What have been difficult times? How have you been spending your time lately?

←End with:
Tell about your impression of this person.

Preston Wade should spend some time with his daughter. He could show her around the City.

Scene One

At Susan's request, the driver turned the Cadillac onto 34th Street toward the Wade Building. Kemp was quiet, but angry. Under the black moustache, he was frowning. His dark eyes were filled with hate; they never left Susan's face. Susan was frightened by him. She didn't want to make him angrier. Perhaps she shouldn't go to the office? After all, she could see her father at home that evening. But Susan didn't want to go to the big empty house. She needed to see her father immediately.

The car slowed down and stopped at the entrance of the Wade Building. Quickly Susan jumped out and ran into the lobby. As she got on the elevator, Kemp was right behind her.

The elevator stopped on the fifteenth floor. When Kemp opened the door to Preston Wade's private office, Susan saw her father at his desk. Wade looked up from his papers.

SUSAN Hi, Dad. I'm home.

WADE Susan, what are you doing here? You're supposed to be at the house.

KEMP I told her that, but . . .

SUSAN It was my idea, Dad. I wanted to surprise you.

WADE Well, now that you're here, let's have a look at you. My, you've certainly grown up. You're a young woman now. Come and give me a hug.

SUSAN Daddy, I've missed you so much. But don't tease me. I'm nearly 21 now. I'm old enough to learn the business. And I've been studying economics at school and I have some ideas . . .

WADE Now wait a minute! I don't want you to work in an office all day.

SUSAN But, I want to be with you. We could work together . . .

WADE Susan, I don't want you to work. I want you to have fun. You should shop in the stores and have lunch with your friends. Your mother used to do that when she was your age.

SUSAN Times have changed, Daddy. I want a career. I can't be happy at home all day.

KEMP Susan, you should go home now. Your father and I have a lot of work to do. Preston, we should talk some more about that Tudor Village problem.

SUSAN Tudor Village? But that's Mary Ryan's . . .

WADE Sure, Kemp. Susan, you must be tired. We can talk later at dinner.

SUSAN But, Daddy . . .

KEMP Listen to your father, Susan. Let's go.

Daddy, I've missed you so much.

Questions

1 Where did the driver take Susan and Kemp? Ask why.
2 Did Kemp show his anger? Ask how.
3 Did Wade expect to see Susan at his office? Ask why not.
4 Did Susan want to work for Wade Enterprises? Ask why.
5 What did Kathryn use to do when she was 21?
6 Did Susan tell her father about Mary Ryan and Tudor Village?

Scene Two

🔊 Kemp walked Susan to the car, then he returned to the office. Wade was standing by the window. The plans for Wade Plaza were on the desk, but Wade was watching Susan as the Cadillac drove away.

Kemp took a long hard look at his boss. With the City behind him, Wade looked impressive. He was tall and thin, but his body was still strong from the years of construction work. Only the gray hair and lines around his eyes showed his age. Wade appeared to be a man without feelings, a cold man, like a piece of stone.

Wade was probably thinking about Susan now, Kemp realized. Like her mother, Susan needed lots of attention. Kemp saw his opportunity. With Wade out of the office, he could easily take control of Wade Enterprises.

KEMP Well, she's on her way home.
WADE Oh . . . What did you say? Sorry, I was thinking about Susan. Do you think I was wrong? You know I don't want her around here. Construction can be a tough business.
KEMP I don't think she really wants to work here.
WADE What do you mean? You heard her. She's got some crazy idea about a career. And she's been studying economics.
KEMP Yeah, but that's all talk. Don't you see? Susan just wants to be with you.
WADE You're right. I should spend some time with her. I haven't been a very good father, have I?
KEMP You could show Susan some of the sights. Maybe take her to the museums and the theaters. In fact, you need a break yourself. You haven't taken a vacation in years.
WADE I don't know. There's so much work to do here. Do you really think you can handle the Wade Plaza project for a while?
KEMP I've already got a plan to get those tenants out of Tudor Village.
WADE What are you going to do?
KEMP Don't worry about the details. Just enjoy yourself with Susan. Leave everything to me.

Questions

1 What was Wade thinking about as he stood by the window?
2 Does Wade look like a 66-year-old man?
3 Should Wade spend some time with Susan? Ask why.
4 Where could Wade take Susan around the city?
5 Who's going to take care of the Tudor Village problem?

Have to, Could, Should, Would–*Present Modals*

| Susan has to make a decision. She could see her father | at the office now. |
| | at the house later. |

| Susan | should | go | to the office | because she wants to see |
| | shouldn't | | to the house | her father now. |

Susan would probably like to see her father right now.

Has/have+*to infinitive* expresses necessity. **Could**+*V-stem* expresses a future choice or opportunity, and **should**+*V-stem* expresses a personal opinion about the best choice to make. **Would**+*V-stem* shows how we expect another person to behave.

A Give your opinion about the story. Make questions and answers with *should*.

1 Paulo *could* live in a hotel or in an apartment.
S1 What *should* Paulo do?
S2 He *shouldn't* live in a hotel. It's expensive.
or He *should* get an apartment. He can entertain his friends in an apartment.

2 Susan could work for her father or stay at home.
3 Jeff could go back to law school or get a job.
4 Wade could handle the Tudor Village problem himself or trust Kemp to take care of it.
5 Molly could get her own apartment or continue to live with her family.

● Respond to these situations. Tell what you *could* do and what you *should* do.

1 What are you going to wear to school/work tomorrow?
→ Molly could wear her gray suit or her denim skirt. She should wear her gray suit because she's going to interview the mayor.

2 What are you going to do tonight?
3 Where are you going to go on your next vacation?
4 What are you going to eat for dinner?
5 When are you going to do your laundry?
6 How are you going to get home tonight?
7 Where are you going to eat lunch tomorrow?
8 What are you going to watch on TV tonight?

B Preston Wade is thinking about all the interesting things to do and see in New York City.

Where *could* Preston Wade take Susan?
  Which plays could they see?
  Which museums could they go to?

Which tourist attractions could they visit?
Which restaurants could they go to for lunch?

Susan is twenty years old. What advice can you give to her father about her likes and dislikes?

Susan probably	would	like to	see	———.
	wouldn't		visit	
			go to	

They	should		see	——— first.
	shouldn't		visit	
			go to	

● What suggestions and advice can you give visitors to *this* city?

1 What tourist attractions–
  could they see? (popular)
  should they see? (very popular)
2 What hotels–
  could they stay in? (recommended)
  should they stay in? (highly recommended)

3 What museums–
  could they visit? (interesting)
  should they visit? (very interesting)
4 What restaurants–
  could they go to for some local food? (very good)
  should they go to for some special local food? (especially good)

● What warnings can you give visitors to this city?

They shouldn't	stay in	———.	They wouldn't like to (see) ———.
	visit		
	go to		

Adjectives vs. Adverbs

Molly is a	careful fast good	writer.	She writes	careful*ly.* *fast.* *well.*

English is	an easy language. easy.	Paulo speaks English	eas*ily.* fluent*ly.*

Paulo is a fluent English speaker.

To form **regular adverbs**, add "ly" or change "y" to "i" before you add "ly." Some adverbs, such as *fast* and *hard,* have the same form as the **adjective.** *Well* is the **irregular adverb** form of *good.*

A Tell about the story. Complete the sentences with the correct form of the adjective or adverb.

Adjective	Adverb
bad	badly
fast	fast
friendly	–
good	well
graceful	gracefully
happy	happily
lazy	lazily
old	–
slow	slowly
young	–

1 Carlos doesn't speak Portuguese _____ but he's a _____ Spanish speaker. (fluent)

2 Molly isn't a _____ cook, but her mother cooks _____. (good)

3 Jeff wears _____ clothes like bluejeans and sweatshirts. He always dresses _____. (casual)

4 Molly has worked _____ to become a top reporter. She's a very _____ worker. (hard)

5 The car moved _____ along 34th Street because traffic is always _____ around lunch time. (slow)

6 Paulo waited _____ for the salesclerk to wrap the coffee maker. He's a very _____ man. (patient)

7 Wade has _____ trust in Kemp. He trusts Kemp _____. (complete)

8 Carlos connected the stove in the *Larsen* apartment _____. In fact, it was an _____ job. (easy)

B Paulo and Jeff are looking at the automobile advertisements in the *City Herald.* Which car do you think they are talking about? Use the information from the ads to complete the conversation.

JEFF   I've found a good one.
PAULO What's the make?
JEFF   It's a(n) _____. I think it's made in _____.
PAULO Well, _____ isn't my favorite color, but it does have _____.

JEFF   The mileage is _____ and that's rather (low/high).
PAULO What do you think of the price? It seems (cheap/expensive) at $_____.
JEFF   It looks like a pretty (good/poor) choice to me.

ALFA ROMEO '78
White, light blue interior, AM/FM cassette, new tires and shocks. Many extras. Perfect. 45,000 miles. $5900 firm. 203-529-9744

'81 TOYOTA CORONA
12 months, 12,000 miles Dark green, like new, one owner. AM/FM radio, air conditioning. $4,500 or best offer. (212) 735-3834

BMW BAVARIA '74
Only $4,000 — 60,000 mi YELLOW, sun roof, many new parts. Very attractive. Must see. ORIGINAL OWNER Call 212-730-1003 days before 5

VW '80 RABBIT DIESEL
Red, 4-door, only 2900 miles, radial tires, roof rack. Excellent condition. Asking $5,000. WILLS MOTORS (516) 431-8726

● **Tell about your favorite car.**

1 Is it economical?
Does it use gas economically?

2 Is it automatic?
Does it change gears automatically?

3 Is it fast?
Does it accelerate quickly?

4 Is it comfortable?
Does it seat six people comfortably?

5 Is it reliable?
Does it need service regularly?

ONE Arranging a dinner date

Paulo and Molly have just returned to Tudor Village.
They've been shopping all afternoon. Today is Saturday,
and Paulo wants very much to ask Molly for a date.
Listen to the tape and look at the advertisements for restaurants. Then complete the conversation as you listen to
the tape a second time.

PAULO Are there any good restaurants around here?
MOLLY Actually, there _____ ones.
PAULO Which _____ is your favorite?
MOLLY *Gino's*. It's _____ restaurant. They
serve _____ lasagne and spaghetti and _____
is reasonably priced.
PAULO Is it close by?
MOLLY Not _____. It's _____
93rd and Broadway.
PAULO How about joining me _____? We
_____ to *Gino's* tonight.
MOLLY Well, I'm writing a story and I really
_____ it tonight.
PAULO C'mon. You've _____
lately. Take a break.
MOLLY Oh, all right. But _____ and make a
reservation. They're _____ crowded on week-
ends.
PAULO Let's make it for _____.
MOLLY That sounds fine. Come by for me at _____.

Role Play: Use the information in the advertisements to make similar conversations between
Molly and Paulo.

P I E R R E ' S C A F É

Cuisine française
à la carte choices:
Beef Bourguignon   Coq au Vin
Dinners from $4.95
95th/Amsterdam 581-1293
Call for reservations.

Best prices on the West Side
Hunan Palace
The finest Chinese Food
Sweet & Sour Pork
Orange Chicken
Reservations recommended.
Columbus Ave/83rd Street   Phone 362-8127

GINO'S
93rd/Broadway
Italian specialties
Spaghetti   Lasagne
Reasonable prices.
Reservations suggested.
787-4097

TWO Making observations and judgments

Observations	Judgments
Preston Wade is sixty-five, but he has the body of a young man.	Preston Wade looks powerful.
Age: 65 Hair: gray Eyes: blue Height: 6 feet Body: thin, broad shoulders Features: sharp nose, high cheekbones, thin lips	He looks young. He seems to be in good health. He looks strong. He seems to be in good condition. He looks impressive. He appears to be a man without feelings, a cold man.

- What *observations* can you make about the characters in the story:
  Who is: short? tall? fat? thin? elderly? young?
  Who has: gray hair? curly hair? long hair? a mustache? light eyes? dark eyes?

- What *judgments* can you make about the characters in the story?
  Who looks: neat? messy? serious? attractive? happy? mean?
  Who seems to be: hard-working? ambitious? responsible? lazy? shy? friendly?
  Who appears to be: clever? impatient? talented? kind? selfish?

Declining an invitation

You telephone your friend. You ask your friend to join you for coffee, a concert, or a sports event. Your friend declines your invitation. However, you make plans to see each other at another time.

🔊 **Listen to the sample conversations on the tape.**

• Act out the telephone conversation between you and your friend. Follow the conversation guide below. Some vocabulary cues are given, but you may choose words of your own.

cues:	*You*	*Your Friend*	*cues:*
May I speak to (Name)? This is (Name). Is (Name) there?	Ask to speak to your friend. Identify yourself.		
		Show surprise. Greetings.	Is that you, (Name)? This is (Name). (Name)! What a surprise! How have you been? / Where are you?
I'm fine. / Okay. / Pretty good. I've been working / traveling . . . I'm at . . . Say, how about coffee / a concert / a game of. . .? Do you want to. . . .? / Would you like to. . .? Let's go. / How about (tonight / Tuesday)?	Give information. Tell why you called.		What have you been doing?
		Decline. Explain why you can't make it.	(Tonight? / Tuesday?) Oh, I'm sorry but . . . No, I can't (tonight) because . . . I shouldn't go. I have to . . . But thanks, anyway.
Really? / Oh! That's too bad / a shame. Could we get together (on Wednesday / next week)? How about. . .?	Express disappointment. Suggest another time.		
		Agree. Arrange to call another time.	That sounds terrific / wonderful / fine. I can make it (on Wednesday / then). Call me at the office / at home on _____ .
All right. / Okay. / Good. See you on _____ . Good bye, (Name).	End the conversation.		Good. / Fine. Talk to you later / then. Bye, (Name).

Jeff will meet Susan when she comes for dinner on Sunday night.

Scene One

📼 It's been several days since Mary returned from London. The apartment is quiet. Jeff is sitting in the kitchen, reading the afternoon paper and sipping a cold beer. Molly has just walked into the room. She's carrying a heavy briefcase and looks exhausted. All day she's been working hard, but she still will have to finish her story for Sunday's paper.

When they were teenagers, Molly and Jeff used to be very close. However, since Jeff came back to New York a few months ago, he has been spending most of his time alone. Molly won't be happy as long as Jeff sits around the house all day. She wants him to get a job or go back to law school.

Molly works hard, but her salary barely pays for the household expenses. Right now she's very tired and she's looking at Jeff. He's drinking a beer and reading the sports pages.

MOLLY How long will you continue to sit around the house all day? Won't you even try to get a job?

JEFF But I have tried. I look through the papers every day.

MOLLY The papers! You read only the sports section! You can find a job, but you won't. You refuse to earn any money.

JEFF C'mon. That's not fair. I earn some extra money when I work for Carlos.

MOLLY Are you kidding? That's peanuts! Jeff, Jeff . . . Listen to me. You're just wasting your life. You could go back to school. You used to want to be a lawyer. What happened?

MARY What are you two arguing about now?

JEFF Oh, nothing. My big sister is just giving her little brother some advice.

MOLLY Nothing? Mother, talk to your son. He won't listen to me. Tell him to get out of this house and do something with his life.

MARY Now, honey. He's only been back home a few months. Give him some time.

MOLLY Time? He hasn't got any plans for the future. He hasn't got any friends . . .

MARY Molly's right, Jeff. You should meet people your own age. That reminds me. Remember that sweet girl on the plane, Susan Wade? You know, I told you all about her.

JEFF Ma, I can find my own girlfriends.

MARY Be quiet. I'll call her now. Maybe Susan can come over for dinner on Sunday. She's such a nice girl, Jeff. You'll like her.

Questions

1 What has Molly been doing all day? Ask about Jeff.
2 Did Jeff and Molly have a close relationship? Ask when.
3 Won't Jeff try to get a job? Ask why.
4 What does Molly think Jeff should do? Ask why.
5 Is Jeff dating anyone right now?
6 Who'll telephone Susan? Ask why.

Scene Two

📼 For the past week, Preston Wade has been spending all of his time with Susan. They've been seeing a lot of the sights and going to theaters and restaurants. Yesterday, Wade took his daughter to the big department stores and bought her a lot of new clothes.

Susan was having a good time because she had her father with her every day. She's been too busy to call Mary Ryan and never did tell her father about Mary Ryan and Tudor Village.

This evening Preston Wade and Susan will have dinner at home. Like all the other rooms in the Wade house, the dining room is large. There are high ceilings and on the walls are several modern paintings. Silver candlesticks and good china are on the dining room table.

Just as Susan and her father are sitting down to dinner, the telephone rings.

MARY Susan, is that you? How are you doing, honey? It's me, Mary Ryan.
SUSAN Mary! Oh, it's so good to hear your voice. I've been meaning to call you, but I've been so busy . . .
MARY Never mind about that. You sound so happy, Susan.
SUSAN Oh, yes. Dad has been wonderful. He's been taking me all around the City. But how are you, Mary?
MARY I'm just fine, honey. Susan, will you be free on Sunday? Would you like to come for dinner?
SUSAN I'd love to come.
MARY Good! Is 7:00 okay? My address is 785 Riverside Drive. You can't miss Tudor Village. We're in apartment 12B.
SUSAN Seven is fine. It really will be nice to see you again, Mary.
MARY And you'll meet Molly and Jeff too. I know my Jeff will like you.
SUSAN Oh, Mary. You're teasing me. But, thank you. I'll see you on Sunday.
MARY Bye, Susan.
SUSAN Good-bye, Mary.
WADE Who was that?
SUSAN That was Mary Ryan, a woman I met on the plane. She's so wonderful. I'm going to her apartment on Sunday. She lives on the West Side, in a place called Tudor Village.
WADE Tudor Village? Susan, I want you to tell me all about this Mary Ryan.

Questions

1 What has Preston Wade been doing recently?
2 Do the Wades have a modern dining room? Ask about the Ryans' kitchen.
3 Who received a phone call from Mary Ryan? Ask when.
4 Will Susan see Mary on Sunday? Ask where.
5 What's Mary's address?
6 Did Preston Wade want to know about Mary Ryan? Ask why.

One-Word and Phrase Modifiers

Would you / I'd	like	to see / to try on	the Italian shoes the ones the red silk blouse	in the advertisement. with the black trim.	(?)
Could you show me			the one	from Italy.	

Single-word modifiers regularly come *before* the noun. **Phrase modifiers** regularly come *after* the noun.

 A Make predictions about the story. Give reasons for your opinions.

1 Wade is going to spend a lot of time with his daughter. Will Kemp take control of Wade Enterprises?
2 Susan is going to tell her father about Mary Ryan. Will Preston Wade be pleased when he hears about Tudor Village?
3 Molly is going to have dinner with Paulo. Will Molly go out with Paulo again?
4 Susan is going to see Jeff on Sunday. Will she like Jeff when she meets him?

● Ask each other about possible future plans. Use the cues to tell what you will or won't do.

1 Your parents are going to visit.

cues *cook dinner, go to a restaurant.*

→ Paulo won't cook dinner for his parents. He'll take them to *Gino's* because they like Italian food.

2 Your friends are going to have a party.

cues *bring food or wine, go alone or take a date.*

3 Your apartment rent is going to increase by 15%.

cues *move to a new apartment or stay in present one.*

4 Your boss isn't going to give you a raise in salary.

cues *quit your job, look for another job, or stay in present one.*

B All week Molly has been asking Jeff to help around the house. Jeff *refuses* to do some of the household chores. He says he *won't* do "woman's work." Here is a list of the weekly household chores:

● **Make predictions about which chores Jeff will do, and which Molly will do.**

Which chores *won't* Jeff do? (refusal)
Which chores *will* Molly *have to* do? (must for necessity)

● **What chores won't *you* do this week?** Since you won't do them, who will have to? (your sister? brother? mother? father? wife? husband?)

Are you going to:
make your bed?
cook your dinner?
wash your clothes?
do the dishes?
clean the bathroom?
put out the garbage?

make the beds –Mary
sweep the floors
vacuum the rugs
do the laundry
dust the furniture –Mary
clean the bathroom
wash the dishes
dry the dishes
put out the garbage
shop for groceries
cook dinner –Mary

C Jeff has to make a decision. A friend has asked Jeff to lend him his motorcycle. Jeff is explaining his point of view to Molly.

MOLLY Aren't you willing to help a friend?
JEFF I'll lend my motorcycle to a reliable friend, but I won't lend it to a careless friend. I might lend my motorcycle, but only for an emergency.

willingness	I will (you offer to . . .)
	I might (there's a chance that you will . . .)
refusal	I won't (you refuse to . . .)

● **How willing are *you* to lend *your* car to a friend?**

Your friend is:
a a reliable person, a very careful driver
b a careless person, a bad driver
c late for work
d a doctor on an emergency

Your car is:
a brand new, an expensive Mercedes
b old, not worth much money
c fully insured
d not insured

40

Will *and* Won't *Future*

| Susan is going to have dinner with the Ryans. | *Will* | she like Jeff? her father be pleased? | Yes, she *will.* No, he *won't.* |

We use the **simple future** (**will** + V-stem) to tell about an action or state we expect to happen *after* the moment of speaking. We regularly use the contracted form *won't* in place of *will not.*

A Preston Wade has taken Susan to *Dades*, New York's fashionable department store. Susan is asking the salesclerk to show her some things in the *Dades* ad.

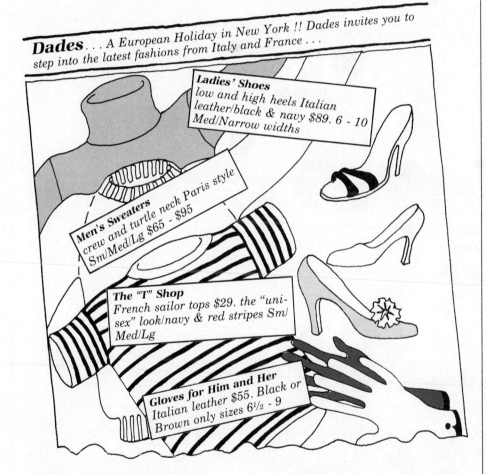

Dades...A European Holiday in New York !! Dades invites you to step into the latest fashions from Italy and France...

Ladies' Shoes
low and high heels Italian leather/black & navy $89. 6 - 10 Med/Narrow widths

Men's Sweaters
crew and turtle neck Paris style Sm/Med/Lg $65 - $95

The "T" Shop
French sailor tops $29. the "unisex" look/navy & red stripes Sm/Med/Lg

Gloves for Him and Her
Italian leather $55. Black or Brown only sizes 6½ - 9

SUSAN Could you show me the Italian shoes in the ad?
SALESCLERK Would you like to see the ones with the high heels?
SUSAN Yes, I would. I'd like to try them on, please. Black, in size 7½ narrow.

• Use information from the ad to make similar conversations between Susan or Preston Wade and the salesclerk.

B Complete the sentences with adjectives in correct order.

1 *leather, wool, green, light* Wade wanted to buy Susan the _____ suit with the _____ buttons.

2 *brown, gold, Italian, dark* The salesclerk showed Susan a(n) _____ handbag with a _____ clasp.

3 *wool, blue, light, Irish* Wade bought himself a(n) _____ sweater in a _____ color.

4 *silk, black, New York, evening* Susan chose a(n) _____ gown from a _____ designer's collection.

5 *brown, large, small, riding* The store didn't carry the _____ boots in _____ sizes.

6 *blue, leather, low, dark* Susan wanted to try on the _____ shoes with the _____ heels.

• Tell about a recent purchase.

S1 I bought my boyfriend a blue denim cowboy shirt with red trim and silver buttons.
S2 Where did you get it?
S1 At *Charivari*, on the corner of Broadway and 85th Street.

	Number	Quality	Color	Origin	Noun	Quality	Noun
the/his	two	dark	green	French		cotton	shirts

ONE   *Making a purchase*

Mary has also invited Paulo and Carlos and Maria Rivera
for Sunday night. Paulo's going to bring a bottle of wine
and a bouquet of flowers to the dinner. He's at the liquor
store now.
Listen to the tape. Then complete the conversation as
you listen to the tape a second time.

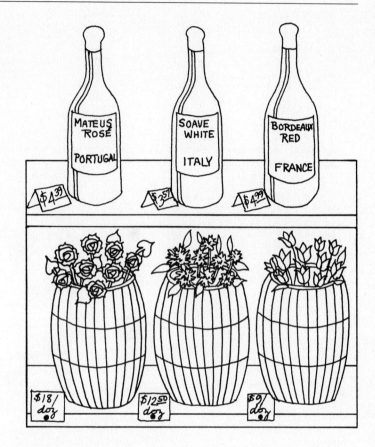

CLERK   May I help you?
PAULO   Yes, I _____ a bottle of wine.
CLERK   What kind _____? We have an excel-
      lent selection of _____.
PAULO   Actually, I think _____ a rosé wine. Do
      you have any wines _____?
CLERK   How about a bottle of Mateus? It's
      _____ popular wines.
PAULO   Fine. I _____.
CLERK   That'll be _____ plus tax.
PAULO   Here's a twenty.
CLERK   Your _____, sir. And your wine.
PAULO   _____.
CLERK   Thank you. Have a pleasant evening and
      come again.

    Role Play: Paulo is at the florist's now. Practice
    a similar conversation between Paulo and the clerk
    in the flower shop.

TWO   *Identifying a lost object*

Molly can't find her gloves:

MOLLY   Has anyone seen my gloves?
MARY   What do they look like?
MOLLY   They're brown leather with black trim.
JEFF   Here they are. You left them on the table.

Ask about Molly's scarf and sunglasses.
Ask each other about something you have with you.
Start with:
Has anyone seen my _____?

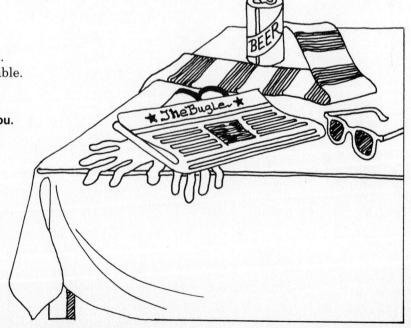

The Car Stealing Plan

James Wilkins is 18 years old and very poor. He wants to go to City College in September so he needs to get a job to pay for the tuition.

Mr. Bolan owns an expensive restaurant. He hires James to park the cars of his customers, but he warns James: "This is a bad neighborhood. There's a lot of trouble around here; but all my customers trust me. They eat in my restaurant because I look after their cars. I'll hire you to park the cars because you look like a good boy. I trust you."

James likes his work and he respects Mr. Bolan, but he isn't making much money to pay for college.

Robert and Alvin, two friends of James's from high school, have a plan to steal some of the expensive cars. Robert and Alvin want James to give them the car keys so that they can make copies of them. Then they follow some of the owners home and use the copies of the keys to steal the cars in the night. Robert and Alvin will give James $500 for each key he gives them.

James is thinking about the plan. He needs the money to go to college, but it's against the law to steal. There's a chance that the police will find out about the plan, then James will go to jail.

Just then, a new Cadillac pulls into the restaurant parking lot. The owner of the car is getting out. He hands James the key: "Here you are, James. Take good care of my car."

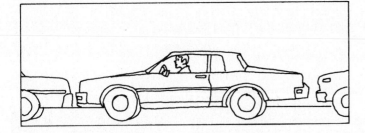

Thinkabout

1 James needs money
  a to buy a car.
  b to go to college.
  c to own a restaurant.

2 Mr. Bolan gives James the job because James
  a is poor.
  b looks like a good boy.
  c has a college education.

3 Robert and Alvin want James to
  a steal the cars.
  b give them the keys.
  c go to the owners' houses at night.

4 James is afraid of
  a the police.
  b the owner of the Cadillac.
  c Alvin and Robert.

Talkabout

Discuss these issues:
a Does James have a duty to Mr. Bolan?
b James has been poor all his life. Should he take this opportunity to make some quick money?
c Do Robert and Alvin respect the property of other people? Does Mr. Bolan? Does James?
d Is there *ever* a good reason to break the law?

What decision *should* James make? Give reasons for your opinion.

Writeabout Expository: Giving reasons to support an opinion

Write a short composition about James's decision to join the car stealing plan. Choose three *strong* reasons to support your position. Give an example or detail to explain each reason.

    James *should / shouldn't* join the car stealing plan to make money for college.

First, . . .

Second, . . .

Third, . . .

In my opinion, it's *foolish to / smart to* . . .

←Start with:
Make your decision.

←Order your reasons:
Reason 1: example / detail

Reason 2: example / detail

Reason 3: example / detail

←End with:
Give your opinion.

Susan isn't permitted to see Jeff again. Her father forbids it.

Scene One

Mary Ryan's dinner party for Susan was a success. Mary invited Paulo, Carlos—the super—and his wife Maria to join them for the evening. Paulo brought a bottle of Portuguese wine and a bouquet of flowers. Everyone is laughing. Mary can't remember the last time she had such a good time.

Jeff was nervous when Susan arrived. But after a while, they were telling each other about their lives abroad. Jeff seemed to like Susan. For the first time in months, Mary's son looked happy.

But Mary had another surprise that evening. Paulo seemed to take a special interest in Molly. During dinner they talked a lot about politics. It was a lively conversation since they both had strong opinions. Later Paulo and Molly took their coffee out on the balcony.

Jeff and Susan went into the kitchen to do the dishes.

SUSAN I'm really glad I came.
JEFF So am I.
SUSAN You have such a nice family.
JEFF Yes, they are pretty terrific.
SUSAN I like your sister a lot. She's so smart.
JEFF Sometimes I think she's too smart. She works all the time.
SUSAN Well, Paulo made her forget about her job tonight.
JEFF Yeah, he's great. Molly needs some fun in her life.
SUSAN What about you? Do you go out much?
JEFF Not lately. But I used to like to go to some of the jazz clubs.
SUSAN I've never been to one.
JEFF Really? Would you like to go sometime?
SUSAN Sure. How about tomorrow night?
JEFF You're free? Okay. Great!
SUSAN It sounds like fun.
JEFF C'mon. Let's finish these dishes. I'll take you home.
SUSAN Do you have a car?
JEFF Nope, a motorcycle.
SUSAN But, I've never been on one!
JEFF Good. Then you'll have to hang on real tight.

Questions

1 Who were the guests at Mary's dinner party?
2 Did Jeff have a good time? Ask why.
3 Did Molly and Paulo have a lot in common? Ask what.
4 Where did Molly and Paulo go after dinner? Ask about Jeff and Susan.
5 Did Jeff and Susan make any plans? Ask what plans.
6 How will Susan get home?

Scene Two

🔊 It was after midnight and Preston Wade was worried. He wasn't very happy when Susan told him about Mary Ryan. He didn't want Susan to know about his plans for Tudor Village. Wade thought about the last few days. Susan was making him happy. She was much like Kathryn, young and lively. He didn't want anything to change. Wade needed Susan's love and he wasn't ready to share her with anyone.

But Wade was getting angry now. It was late and Susan was still out. Then he heard a noise from the street. When he looked out the window, he saw Susan and a young man with long hair and bluejeans. Wade couldn't believe his eyes. They were getting off a motorcycle!

WADE Where have you been? It's almost 1:00!

SUSAN Daddy, you know I went to the Ryans' for dinner.

WADE And who was that out there?

SUSAN Oh. That was Jeff, Mary's son. He brought me home.

WADE Susan, I won't permit you to ride around on motorcycles with hippies. I forbid it.

SUSAN Hippies? Oh, Daddy, he's a nice guy.

WADE Nice guys don't ride motorcycles!

SUSAN That's not fair. You haven't even met Jeff.

WADE And I don't intend to. It's late.

SUSAN Daddy, let's talk about it.

WADE There's nothing more to say. Good night, Susan.

Questions

1 Did Wade tell Susan about his plans for Tudor Village? Ask why not.
2 Did Susan seem like her mother? Ask how.
3 Was Wade surprised when he looked out the window? Ask why.
4 Is Jeff a hippie?
5 Does Susan have her father's permission to see Jeff?
6 Should Susan go out with Jeff again?

Unit Nouns with Of

| How much sugar
How many tablespoons of sugar | do we need? | Only a five-pound bag.
Just one tablespoon. |

We can subdivide *mass* or *noncount* nouns by the use of **unit nouns** (*piece, set, pound,* etc.) with **of.** Some **unit nouns** regularly go with particular mass nouns (a *stick* of gum, a *sheet* of paper, etc.).

A Tell about the story. What do you remember about the Ryan kitchen?

1 Is there a pot of coffee on the stove?
2 Is there a set of pots and pans below the sink?
3 Is there a bar of soap in the sink?
4 Is there a box of soap powder on the counter?
5 Is there a roll of paper towels on the shelf?
6 Is there a book of matches on the counter?

• **Choose from the cues to complete the sentences.**

1 *piece, cup, glass* Molly usually has a _____ of orange juice, a _____ of coffee, and a _____ of toast for breakfast.
2 *bottle, bowl, slice* For lunch, Carlos likes a _____ of chili, a _____ of bread, and a _____ of beer.
3 *bag, stick, bar* Jeff snacks on a _____ of candy or a _____ of potato chips, but Molly prefers a _____ of celery.
4 *dish, mug, box* Mary likes to have a _____ of pretzels, a _____ of ice cream, or a _____ of hot chocolate when she watches TV.

• **Ask each other: What do you usually have for a snack? for breakfast? for lunch? for dinner?**

B Early that morning, Mary and Molly made a shopping list of the groceries they needed to buy for Sunday's dinner. Mary planned to make roast beef with baked potatoes, salad and homemade bread. The chocolate cake for dessert was Molly's idea.

• **Ask about the shopping list.**

Start with:
How much *roast beef* do they need?
Five pounds of roast beef.

• **Ask about Grandmother Ryan's recipe for Irish white bread.**

Start with:
How much *yeast. . . . ?*
or How many *packages of yeast. . . . ?*
Note: Use *how many* with the count noun *egg.*

• **Tell about your favorite recipes. Give the ingredients and explain how to make the dish.**

5 lbs roast beef
1 bottle olive oil
1 jar oregano
2 heads lettuce
1 bunch celery
1 large bag flour
2 cans sweet milk
1 package yeast
4 bars chocolate
1 box baking soda

Grandmother Ryan's recipe for Irish White Bread
Dissolve: 1 package yeast and 1 tablespoon sugar
*   in: ½ cup water*
Let stand in warm place 10 minutes.
Beat in : 1 egg
*   ½ cup shortening*
*   2 cups water*
*   1½ teaspoons salt*
*   ½ cup sugar*
Sift: 8 cups flour
Mix, beat, knead, and shape dough. Place in mixing bowl and let dough rise. Place dough in pan and let rise again. Put pan in 400° oven. After 15 minutes, reduce heat to 375° and bake 25 minutes longer. Remove loaves from pan immediately.

C Paulo is asking Carlos for some help with shopping. Practice similar conversations to ask about shops in this neighborhood.

PAULO Where can I get a bottle of wine?
CARLOS Have you tried *The West End Liquor Mart?* It's on 106th Street, across from the *Shoprite Supermarket.*

cues *a bottle of wine; a pack of cigarettes; a slice of pizza; a cup of coffee; a bottle of aspirin; a six-pack of beer.*

It's Forbidden, Permitted, Allowed

Is Susan	allowed permitted	to ride on a motorcycle?

No, she mustn't. It's forbidden.

We use **is permitted/allowed/ forbidden**+to to show that one person does or does not let another person do something. Use *mustn't* to show that a person doesn't have permission to do something.

A Give your opinion about the story. Remember that Molly is 32 years old and Susan is 20.

1 ride on a motorcycle
→ Is Susan allowed to ride on a motorcycle?
→ Is Molly permitted to ride on a motorcycle?

2 smoke
3 go to a discotheque
4 wear heavy make-up
5 stay out late

B Paulo is asking Jeff about American traffic laws and fire regulations. Explain these signs to Paulo.

 1
 2
 3
 4
5 NO SMOKING

You're not	allowed permitted	to _____.
You mustn't _____.		

C Susan's father is very strict. When Susan was in school, she had to follow a lot of rules too.

London School for Girls
Rules & Regulations

No food in room
No lights in room after midnight
No absences from class
Only school uniforms in dining hall
Visitors only on Sundays and holidays

New students were always asking Susan about the rules:

NEW STUDENT Can I wear bluejeans to breakfast?
SUSAN   No, it's not allowed. You always have to wear your uniform in the dining area.
or   You're not permitted to. You mustn't wear bluejeans in the dining hall. It's forbidden.

● What did Susan tell these students when they asked . . .

1 Can I keep cookies and fruit in my room?
2 Is it all right to cut class once in a while?
3 When can my parents come to see me?
4 Can my boyfriend see my room?
5 Is it okay to stay up all night and type my papers?

● Make a list of the rules in your school. Tell what you're permitted to do and what you're not allowed to do. Include rules about: the library, the cafeteria, the snack bar, parking, the classroom, homework, and test-taking.

8 EXPRESSION

ONE   Offering compliments

It's Sunday night. Mary, her family and her guests are sitting at the dinner table. Mary is serving roast beef tonight.
Listen to the tape and look at the illustration. Then complete the conversation as you listen to the tape a second time.

MARY   Paulo, would you like another piece of roast beef?

PAULO   Yes, _____. This salad is delicious, Mary. _____ your dressing?

MARY   With fresh lemon and _____. I added _____ and other spices.

PAULO   This bread _____. It's so _____. Is it homemade?

MARY   Yes, Molly and I _____. It's my grandmother's recipe for Irish white bread.

PAULO   Molly, _____ pass me _____? I think _____ another _____.

MOLLY   Here it is. _____ more potatoes, Paulo?

PAULO   No, _____. I've had enough. After all, I have to leave room for dessert.

MARY   That's right. Molly made us _____.

PAULO   This is an excellent dinner, Mary. My compliments to the chef and her lovely assistant.

Role Play: Write a similar conversation between Susan and Mary. Talk about the food in the dishes with covers. You might want to tell about special foods from your country.

TWO   Giving warnings

Jeff is taking Susan home on his motorcycle.

Susan is looking at the traffic signs. She's worried because Jeff isn't paying attention to the signs.

SUSAN   Jeff, slow down! There's a speed limit sign ahead. You're not allowed to go over 20 miles per hour.

JEFF   Don't worry. I saw it. I know I have to slow down.

Practice similar conversations about the other signs.

48

Showing surprise

You and your friend are walking down the street. Suddenly you see a very strange sight: a ten-year-old boy on a motorcyle, a woman with a pet snake, or an old woman on rollerskates.

🔊 **Listen to the sample conversations on the tape.**

• Act out a similar conversation between you and your friend. Tell about one of the strange sights above, or one from your experience. Follow the conversation guide below. Some vocabulary cues are given, but you may choose words of your own.

cues:	You	Your Friend	cues:
Do you see / Look at that kid (woman, old lady)(!) Over there. The one with / on the . . . There. Next to / across from . . .	Call attention to something.		
		Show disbelief / surprise.	Where? What kid (woman, old lady)? I can't believe my eyes! Are you kidding? / How strange! That's really weird / strange.
Isn't that something? It's incredible / amazing! (He's / She's) actually . . .	Agree.		
		Try to find an explanation.	Do you think (he's / she's) . . . ? It's my guess that . . . I bet (he's / she's) a . . .
You're probably right. (He / She) must be. I'm certain (he's / she's) a . . . I'm sure (he's / she's) a . . .	Agree.		
		Ask about the "rule."	Isn't it dangerous to / against the law to . . . ? Is (he / she) allowed to . . . permitted to . . . ?
No, I don't think so. But I could be wrong. It doesn't seem possible. . . , but . . . I'm sure / certain . . . it's (not) allowed / permitted.	Give information.		
		Approve or disapprove.	It looks like fun / dangerous. It's ridiculous / wild! (He / She) must be (crazy, nuts, interesting).
I'll never do that! I'll (never) try it / get a. . . .	End the conversation.		Maybe times have changed? You won't see me do that. Maybe I should try it / get a . . .

Kemp hired two men who are going to cause problems for the tenants.

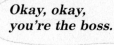

Okay, okay, you're the boss.

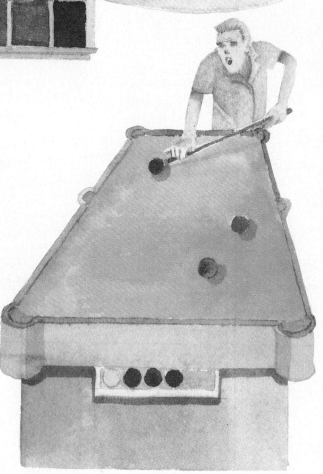

Scene One

With Wade out of the office, Kemp didn't waste any time. Each night he looked through the files and account books of the business. Wade owned a lot of valuable property, the construction company, and the *City Herald*, the city's major newspaper. In all, Wade Enterprises was worth over 400 million dollars.

During the last few years, Kemp has been stealing from Wade Enterprises. Because he stole only a few thousand dollars at a time, Wade never found out about it. Kemp used the money to gamble. But he wasn't very lucky and he had a lot of gambling debts. He was in trouble and he needed to get his hands on some big money fast.

While Wade was on vacation, Kemp was able to take another $50,000. But he was worried. A lot of money was missing from the accounts. There wasn't enough money to pay the tenants full price for their apartments. Kemp had to get the tenants to leave Tudor Village in a hurry and to sell their apartments cheaply. Kemp needed some help. He picked up the phone and dialed.

KEMP   Butch, I've got a job for you and Spike.
BUTCH   Yeah, Kemp. What's up? I hear you owe a little money to our friends.
KEMP   Shut up. I want you two to go over to Tudor Village, that old apartment building on Riverside Drive.
BUTCH   Yeah, I know the place. It's got those fancy roofs and windows.
KEMP   Yeah, that's it. Walk around the place. Watch the super. Find out about all the entrances and the fire escapes. Got it?
BUTCH   Yeah, I got it. What else?
KEMP   That's all for now.
BUTCH   Hey, Kemp, are you planning on moving into the place?
KEMP   Just do what I say.
BUTCH   Okay, okay. You're the boss.

Questions

1 Is Kemp allowed to take money from the accounts?
2 Does Kemp owe a lot of money? Ask why.
3 What is Kemp worried about?
4 What are the names of the men who are going to help Kemp?
5 What did Kemp tell them to do?
6 Who thought of the plan?

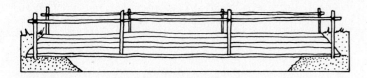

Who's Going to Blow up the Bridge?

Captain McKay is in charge of eight soldiers. A large company of enemy soldiers is chasing them. Of all the men, Captain McKay is the only one who knows the way through the jungle. It's his responsibility to get his men back to the camp safely.

Captain McKay led his men across a wooden bridge which spans a wide river. He knew that the enemy wasn't very far behind them. There was only one way to escape. Someone had to stay behind and blow up the bridge, and the soldier who stayed behind would probably be killed by the force of the explosion.

The Captain's first thought was to blow up the bridge himself. However, no one else could lead the men back to camp. The Captain told his men about the plan. He asked for a volunteer, but no one offered to go. The Captain had to order one of the men to stay behind and blow up the bridge.

The Captain took a long, hard look at the eight soldiers. One was 52 years old. Another was a troublemaker who was always stealing things and fighting with the other men. One man wasn't married; the others had wives and children back home. The Captain also thought about the soldier who was experienced with dynamite and other explosives.

By this time, they could hear the enemy soldiers who were getting closer and closer to the bridge. The Captain had to make a quick decision. Who should stay behind and blow up the bridge so that the others could escape?

Thinkabout

		True	False
1	The Captain was leading his men to the enemy.	____	____
2	The only one who could lead the men through the jungle was the captain.	____	____
3	The soldier who wasn't married offered to blow up the bridge.	____	____
4	No one knew how to use dynamite.	____	____

Talkabout

Discuss these issues:
a Should the Captain order a man to stay behind and blow up the bridge or should he do it himself? Why?
b Is it *right* for the Captain to send one man to almost certain death in order to save the lives of the others?
c Is there a way to decide whose life is *the least important*? Should the Captain choose:
   a man who is old?
   a man who is a troublemaker?
   a man who isn't married?
   a man who is experienced in using dynamite?
Is it fair to make a life and death decision from personal qualities or other considerations?

What decision *should* the Captain make? Give reasons for your opinion.

Writeabout Narrative: Ordering events to show conflict

Good writers can tell a story and create conflict at the same time. These writers organize the events of a story like the steps of a ladder—each step adds more suspense to the story.

Write about a difficult decision which *you* had to make (for example, to leave home, to get married, to change jobs or schools). Tell about the events which caused the situation. *Order the events* so that the reader experiences your conflict. The last sentence should state your decision.

When I (was) . . . , I had to . . .

Event 1:

Event 2:

Event 3:

Event 4:

Event 5:

Finally, I decided to . . .

←Start with:
Describe the situation. When? Where?

←Order the events:
What happened first?

   second?

   third?

   next?

   then? after that?

←End with:
State your decision.

10

Kemp had Butch and Spike meet him in the park next to Tudor Village.

Scene One

As Susan walked up the long staircase to her bedroom, she didn't turn around to look at her father. Jeff or her father, was that her choice? She hardly knew Jeff. Sometimes she thought she also didn't know her father.

The next morning, Susan made her decision. She decided to see Jeff that night. He took her to a little jazz club in Soho, which is in lower Manhattan. Susan loved the music, especially the slow, dreamy sounds of the saxophone. They had a wonderful time. When Jeff brought her home, she promised to meet him the next day at Tudor Village.

When Susan arrived, Jeff was waiting for her near the entrance. The sun was shining. There wasn't a cloud in the sky. As they were walking in the park next to Tudor Village, Susan asked Jeff about Vietnam.

SUSAN   Why did you go?

JEFF   Susan, I had to. I was in my first year of law school. I'll never forget the day when I got the letter from the army. It was the last day of classes. Two weeks later, I was in the army training camp in Georgia. It happened so fast.

SUSAN   Do you still think about Vietnam now?

JEFF   Sometimes. It seems so long ago now. So much has happened since then.

SUSAN   What made you go to Brazil?

JEFF   I didn't want to come home right away. I looked for a place where I could be alone. I needed some time to think about things.

SUSAN   There's so much that I don't know about you.

JEFF   It's so easy to talk to you, Susan. You can stay for dinner, can't you? We could go and hear some music later.

SUSAN   Really, I can't stay. It's late and I have to get home. My father is probably looking for me right now.

JEFF   When am I going to meet the great Preston Wade? Seriously, Susan, I'd like to get to know your father.

SUSAN   Not yet, Jeff. It's too soon.

JEFF   I don't understand.

SUSAN   I can't explain now. I'll call you tomorrow, okay?

JEFF   All right. Susan, you know that I care about you.

SUSAN   I know that, Jeff.

Questions

1   Did Susan have to make a decision? Ask what it was.
2   Where did Jeff take Susan on their first date?
3   Did Susan agree to see Jeff again? Ask where.
4   Did Jeff finish law school? Ask why not.
5   Why hasn't Jeff met Susan's father?
6   How does Jeff feel about Susan? Ask how she feels.

Hey, isn't that Wade's kid? Who's that guy she's with?

Scene Two

Butch and Spike have been watching Tudor Village. They've written down all the information that Kemp wanted—Carlos's schedule, the location of the fire escapes and the entrances, and the times when the tenants aren't usually at home. As soon as Kemp joins them, they're going to discuss the next step.

Kemp has the taxi driver drop him off near the park where they've planned to meet. From his pocket, Butch takes a piece of paper and hands it to Kemp. Kemp is pleased. He thinks about all the trouble he's going to have Butch and Spike make for the tenants. Kemp wants to frighten the tenants so that they'll be afraid to stay at Tudor Village.

Kemp starts to explain his plan.

BUTCH You mean you want us to cut the telephone wires on all their phones?

KEMP Right. Have those wires cut tonight. Spike can do it. Here are some chemicals. Get Spike to put these chemicals into the building's water supply.

BUTCH Sure, Kemp. I'll have him do it. Hear that, Spike?

SPIKE Yeah, I'm listening. Hey, Kemp what about Butch? How come I'm doing all the dirty work? Make Butch do something.

BUTCH I can break some windows. And after the super puts out the garbage, I can set it on fire.

KEMP Good. That should shake 'em up.

SPIKE Hey, look over there, under that tree. Isn't that Wade's kid? Who's that guy she's with?

BUTCH I've seen him before. He's a friend of the super.

KEMP Keep your voices down. I don't want her to see me here. Well, well. Susan Wade. How interesting.

Questions

1 What have Butch and Spike been doing?
2 Where did Kemp have the taxi driver drop him off?
3 What is Butch going to make Spike do? Ask when.
4 What will Butch do to the garbage?
5 Who's paying Butch and Spike to do the dirty work? Ask why.
6 Who was in the park besides Kemp and his men?

Who, Which, That *as Non-subject of Relative Clauses*

Spike took out a screwdriver	*which* *that*	S V he used to open the door.
Butch is the man	*who(m)* *that*	Molly saw.
Jeff can't forget	the time *when* he was in Vietnam. the place *where* the army sent him.	

The relative pronoun can be omitted when it is the **object** of the **relative clause**. When the relative pronoun *who* is in object position, we use *whom* in formal English. *When* and *where* can replace *in which, at which,* and *on which.*

A Tell about the story. Join these sentences with *which* and *who(m)* in *subject position* (a) and in *non-subject position* (b). We can also use *that* to join the sentences.

1 Susan had to make a decision. (which)
   a It was difficult.
   → Susan had to make a decision which was difficult.
   b She didn't want to make that decision.
   → Susan had to make a decision which she didn't want to make.

2 Butch handed Kemp a piece of paper. (which)
   a It was in his pocket.
   b He took it from his pocket.

3 Ben Greene is the editor. (who(m))
   a He read Molly's story.
   b Molly respected this editor.

4 Preston Wade read the story. (which)
   a The story described the Wade Plaza project.
   b Susan showed him the story.

5 Kemp met the two men. (who(m))
   a They were waiting for Kemp in the park.
   b Kemp hired them to watch Tudor Village.

6 Jeff took Susan to a club. (which)
   a It had a terrific jazz group.
   b Jeff liked the club a lot.

B Molly and Paulo are looking at greeting cards. Paulo is curious about American holidays and customs.

PAULO What's Mother's Day?
MOLLY It's the day *when* Americans honor their mothers. Mother's Day is the time *when* you give flowers or other gifts to your mother. It's always the second Sunday in May.

● Ask about these times when Americans celebrate special events: New Year's Day; Thanksgiving; Father's Day; Valentine's Day.

● Tell about the days when you celebrate special events in *your* country.

C Molly is telling Paulo about the places where he can shop. She's drawing him a map of the shops near Tudor Village.

The West End Liquor Mart is the place *where* you can get wine or liquor. You have to go to the Shoprite Supermarket for beer. It's right across the street, on the corner of Broadway and 106th Street.

● Use these cues to ask each other:

S1 Where can I get _____?
S2 __(Name)__ is the place *where* you can get _____. It's (next to, across from, between) _____.

cues *a bottle of aspirin; a spool of thread; a bottle of scotch; a gallon of paint; a loaf of bread; a cup of espresso.*

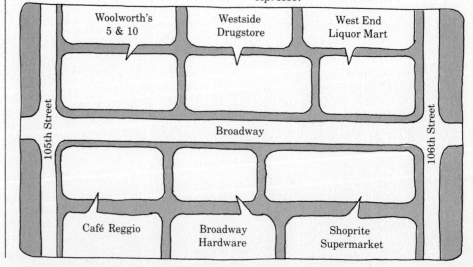

Get Someone To Do Something—*the Active Causative*

| Have
Make
___
Get | Spike | cut
___
to cut | the wires. | Have
Make
___
Get | him | do
___
to do | it. |

We use the **active causative** form (**have/make**+*V-stem* or **get**+*to-V*) when one person *forces* or *persuades* another person to do something.

A Tell about how one person forced or persuaded another person to do something.

1 Ben Greene is Molly's boss.
He ordered her . . .
  a to write the Wade Plaza story.
  b to visit the architect.
  c to interview Kemp.

• What did Ben Greene *make* Molly *do*?

→ He made her write the Wade Plaza story.

2 Mary can't do all the housework herself.
She asked Jeff . . .
  a to vacuum the rugs.
  b to put out the garbage.
  c to dry the dishes.

• What did Mary *have* Jeff *do*?

3 Susan has a lot of influence on Jeff.
She persuaded Jeff . . .
  a to cut his hair.
  b to buy a new suit.
  c to look for a job.

4 She couldn't persuade Jeff . . .
  a to shave his beard.
  b to stop drinking.
  c to go back to law school.

• What | did
didn't | Susan *get* Jeff *to do*?

• Has anyone ever gotten *you* to do something you didn't want to do?

What did he/she | have
make | you do?

B What do you think will happen in the story? How will one person influence another person?

1 Kemp wants to scare the tenants.
He wants them to move out of Tudor Village.
Will Kemp get the tenants to leave?

2 Molly wants Jeff to get a job. Jeff wants his sister to leave him alone.
Will Molly get her brother to take responsibility for the family?

3 Susan wants to go out with Jeff.
Wade doesn't want his daughter to see Jeff again.
Will Wade get Susan to forget about Jeff?

4 Molly wants to have a career.
Mary wants her daughter to get married.
Will Paulo make Molly forget about her career?

C Molly got Jeff to fill out this questionnaire which was in today's paper. Now, they're arguing!

For Men Only		
Do you know how to . . .	YES	NO
1. sew on a button?		✓
2. make coffee?		✓
3. wash clothes?	✓	
4. iron shirts?		✓
5. fry eggs?		✓
6. type a letter?		✓
7. mend socks?		✓
8. polish furniture?	✓	
9. make a stew?		✓
10. wash windows?	✓	
11. fix a toaster?	✓	
12. change a flat tire?	✓	

Jeff won't learn how to sew a button!

He'll | have
get | his mother | –
to | sew it on for him!

• What else won't Jeff do? Why not?

• Can you do these things yourself? If not, tell who *you* can get to do them for you.

ONE Reminiscing

Susan is telling Jeff about her life at school in London. Susan's experiences remind Jeff about his life in the army.

Listen to the tape. Then complete the conversation as you listen to the tape a second time.

SUSAN I'll never forget the time when I was at that school. It was awful. The teachers _____ at 7 o'clock in the morning, even on Saturday and Sunday. We _____ in class by 8:00.

JEFF You think that's bad? When I was in the army, they had us _____ A.M.! Then they _____ line up for inspection. The sergeant walked up and down and checked our uniforms. Sometimes _____ shine our shoes again before we could eat breakfast.

SUSAN They _____ uniforms at school too. We had to wear old-fashioned _____ skirts and _____ blouses. When we were in class, we had to wear our _____ sweaters. They made _____ on even in hot weather.

JEFF At least you were in a classroom all day! I spent all my time in the mud. The sergeant had us march 10 miles a day in the heat. We had to carry _____ of equipment on our backs. It's a part of my life _____.

Role Play: Practice a similar conversation with your classmate.

- Compare your experiences in school or at home.

What did your	teacher / parents	make / have / ___ / get	you	do? / ___ / to do?

- How did you feel about these experiences?

I want to	remember / forget about	the time I was ____.

Start with:
I'll never forget the time I was _____.

TWO Stating preferences

These are some of the records in Jeff's collection:

Jeff wants to play some music. He is asking his family and friends for their preferences.

- Practice short conversations between Jeff and Paulo, Susan, Molly and Carlos. Give your opinion about their choices.

JEFF Is there a special album you'd like to hear, Mom?

MARY How about *Irish Folk Songs?* That's the kind of music I really enjoy.

or Choose the one you like. Only please don't play *Disco Delights.*

I	don't care for / don't like / can't stand	that kind of music.

- Ask each other about *your* preferences.

Making recommendations

You are telling your friend about a new restaurant, a new nightclub, or a new discotheque you've been to recently. You recommend it highly, and you want to tell your friend all about it. You hope your friend will want to go there too.

- Act out a similar conversation between you and your friend. Follow the conversation guide below. Some vocabulary cues are given, but you may choose words of your own.

Listen to the sample conversations on the tape.

cues:	You	Your Friend	cues:
I went to a great / terrific / wonderful restaurant (nightclub / disco) last night. I've just been to . . . I found a great . . .	Introduce the topic.		
		Show interest.	Really? / Oh? Which one? Where is it? What's the name of the place where . . . ?
It's called ___(Name)___. It's on the corner of . . . / next to . . . / on _____ Street.	Give information.		
		Ask for more information.	What's it like? What's so special about it?
It's a place where you can . . . The prices are . . . reasonable / high / inexpensive.	Give details.		
		Show more interest.	Maybe I should try it. I like _____ (food / music), too. It sounds interesting / like fun.
Why don't you have (Name) take you? / Get (Name) to go with you. Maybe you can persuade (Name) to go?	Make a suggestion.		
		Agree.	That's a good idea. / You're right. We could go tonight / next. . . . Yes, (Name) should really like it.
It's a wonderful / special place. I'm sure (Name) will love it. You'll have a great time.	End the conversation.		I know we'll like (Name of place). Thanks for telling me about (Name). Maybe we'll see you at (Name).

Who could be responsible for the accidents at Tudor Village?

Scene One

🔲 Later that night, Butch and Spike returned to Tudor Village. At about midnight, Carlos turned off the lights in the lobby. Butch kept his eyes on the windows of Carlos's apartment. All of the lights in the living room were on. Carlos could still be awake. An hour later, someone turned off the lights. The other apartments were dark too. The tenants must be asleep, Butch and Spike thought.

Butch opened his jacket and pulled out a pair of huge wire cutters. Cautiously, he made his way to the side of the building. He reached up and grabbed the telephone wires. With a few quick motions, he cut the thick cables.

Meanwhile, Spike climbed the fire escape to the roof. In his pocket was the package of chemicals. The water tank was old. It might be rusted, he thought. Spike had to use all of his strength to remove the cap on one of the pipes. Slowly, he poured the white powder into the opening.

Before they left Tudor Village, Butch poured gasoline into one of the garbage cans. Then he lit a match and tossed it into the middle of the garbage. As they ran away, Spike threw a few rocks at the windows. Then they jumped into their car and drove away before anyone could see them.

Molly woke up when she heard the crash of the windows. She looked out of her bedroom window and saw the flames of the burning garbage. Quickly, she ran to wake up Jeff.

MOLLY Jeff, Jeff. Wake up! There's something wrong.
JEFF Mmpf . . . What? Go away.
MOLLY Jeff. Get up! There's a fire outside the building.
JEFF A fire? What are you talking about?
MOLLY Look out the window. Hurry. You call the fire department. I'll wake up Mom.
MARY What's all the noise? You two should be in bed. It's 3 A.M.
MOLLY There's a fire, Mom. We could be in danger. Grab your coat. We've got to wake up the other tenants and get out of the building.
JEFF There's something wrong with the phone. It's dead. I'm going to pull the fire alarm in the hall.
MARY Get Morris. I'm not going anywhere without my cat.
MOLLY Mom, I've got him. C'mon. Put on your coat.
MARY Molly, I feel dizzy. I might be sick. Get me one of my heart pills and a glass of water, honey.
MOLLY Here you are. Hurry, Mom.
MARY Ah, that's better. You go first. I'm right behind you.

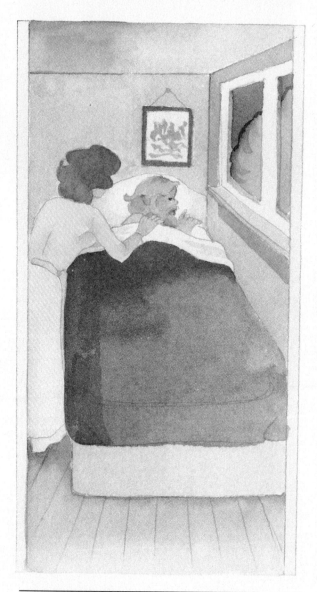

Questions

1 Who turned off the lobby lights? Ask what time.
2 Was everyone at Tudor Village asleep at 1 A.M.?
3 Who put the chemicals into the water? Ask about the telephone wires.
4 Why did Molly look out the window?
5 Did Jeff telephone the fire department? Ask why he couldn't.
6 Who wanted a glass of water? Ask why.

Scene Two

Within ten minutes, three fire engines arrived at Tudor Village. By then, all of the tenants were safely out of the building. Molly and the others watched as the firemen turned their water hoses on the fire. They put out the flames before the fire spread to the main building.

When Carlos saw the cut wires and the broken windows, he called the police. The fire could be an accident, but Carlos knew that someone must be responsible for the other damage. The police didn't find anything. Butch and Spike didn't leave behind any clues.

Mary was one of the tenants who became ill the next morning. Because so many of them were ill, Carlos called the Health Department. When the tenants learned about the chemicals in the water, they were frightened. Some even talked about leaving Tudor Village. Jeff and Molly wanted to find the people who were responsible for the trouble.

MOLLY   Look at this mess. Who would cut the phone wires and throw rocks at the windows?

JEFF   It doesn't make any sense to me.

CARLOS   Could it be some of those teenage boys who live down the street?

JEFF   I don't think so. This is serious business. Those boys wouldn't set fires or cut phone wires.

MOLLY   It has to be someone who knows about chemicals and electrical work. It must be a professional job.

JEFF   Carlos, have you seen any strangers around the building lately?

CARLOS   Well, there are always strangers around here now. They're working on that Wade Plaza project next door.

MOLLY   That's it! Don't you see? Wade wants to get us out of Tudor Village. They need this land for Wade Plaza.

JEFF   That's crazy, Molly. Wade's a rich man. Why would he do anything like this?

MOLLY   He could be giving the orders. He lets other people do the dirty work. Besides, I met Kemp, his assistant. He's probably part of all this. He looks like a crook.

CARLOS   I think Molly might be right. Jeff, let's get Paulo and some of the others. We're going to stay up all night until we catch those guys.

JEFF   Hey, good idea. We'll get them ourselves.

MOLLY   Believe me. There's got to be a connection between Wade Plaza and these troubles.

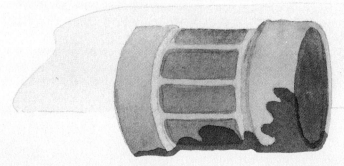

Questions

1 Did the police find the men who were responsible for the damage? Ask about the clues.
2 Was Mary sick the next day? Ask what made her sick.
3 Did Jeff think the boys down the street set the fire? Ask what Molly thought.
4 Why are strangers around Tudor Village?
5 Did Molly think that Wade was responsible for the trouble at Tudor Village? Ask why.
6 Does Carlos have a plan to catch Butch and Spike? Ask what it is.

PRACTICE ONE

Might, Could, Should, Must, Will—*Degrees of Certainty*

Jeff thinks the fire might be an accident. (It's a possibility.)
Carlos thinks it could be teenage boys. (It's a good possibility.)
The police think there should be some clues. (It's expected.)
Molly thinks it must be the strangers Carlos saw. (It's a conclusion.)
Carlos thinks that the two men will be back. (It's a certainty.)

The modal auxiliaries express degrees of certainty. Use **might** and **could** to tell about something that is possible. Use **should** for something that is likely and **must** for something that is almost certain.

A Give your opinion about future events in the story. Practice *might be, could be, should be, must be* and *will.*

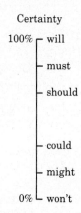

Certainty

```
100% ┌ will
     ├ must
     ├ should

     ├ could
     ├ might
  0% └ won't
```

1 Wade won't permit Susan to see Jeff, but Susan is in love with Jeff. Is Susan going to see Jeff again? What's a certainty?

→ Susan will see Jeff again. I'm certain of it.

2 Paulo is spending a lot of time with Molly. Is Paulo in love with Molly? What's a good possibility?

3 Kemp is unlucky in cards and has lost over $50,000 so far. Is Kemp a heavy gambler? What do you conclude?

4 Molly enjoys Paulo's company, but she spends most of her time at the *City Herald.* Is Molly in love with Paulo? What's a possibility?

5 Preston Wade is rich and powerful. Is Wade a happy man? What do you expect?

6 Mary is old and overweight and she has a bad heart. Is she in poor health? What do you conclude?

B Complete these conversations about the story with the correct *modal* form:

1 *must be, could be*
   JEFF There's a man in uniform in Carlos's apartment.
   MOLLY He _____ a fireman or a policeman. I can't see him clearly.
   PAULO There's a police car out front.
   JEFF Then he _____ a policeman. The fire engines left half an hour ago.

2 *should be, must be*
   CARLOS I checked the water pipes. Someone has removed one of the caps.
   MOLLY Then, it _____ something in the water! There's no other explanation.
   CARLOS I've called the Health Department. An inspector _____ here in a few minutes.

3 *might be, must be, could be*
   JEFF Wade _____ responsible for these accidents, but I doubt it very much.
   MOLLY He doesn't have to know. Some of his men _____ responsible without Wade's knowledge. It's a good possibility.
   CARLOS Well, we're sure of one thing. There _____ a connection between these accidents and the Wade Plaza Project.

4 *must be, could be, might be*
   MARY I don't feel very well. My stomach is upset.
   MOLLY Well, I'm not sure, but it _____ the fried onions you had for dinner. They were greasy.
   MARY I don't think so. They've never bothered me before.
   MOLLY Do you think it _____ the excitement? You had to take a heart pill, didn't you?
   MARY No, I'm certain it _____ something I ate.

C Molly is looking through her desk at the office. She can't find her notebook. She always leaves it in the top drawer. Give suggestions about where to look.

It should be _____.
It might be _____.
It could be _____.

• **Where do you usually keep your special things?**

Tell:
where it should be.
where it might be.
where it could be.

All, None—*Pronoun Substitutes*

Most of the lights were off. Not *all* of the tenants were asleep.	Did *anyone* see Butch and Spike? *No one* saw them get away, but *someone* noticed the fire. There were no clues. They left *nothing* behind.	**No one** means *not anyone* and **nothing** means *not anything*. We can use "body" in place of "one" as in *anybody*. For questions and negatives, we regularly use **anything** and **anyone** in place of *something* and *someone*.

A Tell about the story. Complete the conversations with: *someone, something, anyone, anything, no one* or *nothing*.

1 Butch and Spike didn't leave any clues.

JEFF   No one knows for certain who's responsible for the accidents.

MOLLY They left nothing behind. Not one clue.

2 Mary has a bad stomachache because she drank the water with the chemicals.

MARY   I think it was _____ I ate.

JEFF   Is there _____ I can do?

MARY   No, there's _____.

3 Ben Greene had Molly interview a TV personality.

MOLLY Is he _____ I've met?

BEN   No, but he's _____ you've heard about.

4 Molly is discussing politics with Paulo. Suddenly Paulo gets up and starts to leave.

MOLLY Was it _____ I said?

PAULO No, I just remembered _____ I have to do.

5 Molly has been on the telephone for half an hour.

MARY   Was that _____ I know?

MOLLY No, that was _____ I met at the office.

● **Ask each other.**

S1 Is there anything you've been meaning to do but haven't done yet?

S2 Yes, there is something. I have to _____.

or No, there isn't anything. I have nothing to do.

B Practice pronouns such as *all, most, a few, . . .* Use *I think so* or *I don't think so* instead of repeating the complete statement.

		COUNT					
100% — All — Most —	Many Much	— Some —	Several A Little	A Few	— None —	— 0%	
		MASS					

1 The tenants are out of the building. Will they be safe now?

JEFF   Are the tenants okay?

CARLOS *I think so.* MOST of them are frightened, but NONE of them is seriously injured.

2 The tenants drank the water with the chemicals. Will they be all right?

3 The tenants are frightened. Will they want to leave Tudor Village?

● Discuss the issues in the news. Tell what the people in *your* country think will happen:

All Most Some A few None	of them	agree(s) think(s) believe(s) feel(s) argue(s)	that _____.

● Tell what you think might or might not happen. Agree or disagree with each other's predictions:

Agree	Disagree
I think so. I suppose so.	I don't think so. I suppose not.

cues *Will someone ever start a nuclear war? Will someone ever solve the problem of world hunger? Will someone ever discover a cure for cancer?*

ONE   Showing determination

Molly is watching Jeff. He took the sink apart to clean out the chemicals. He's been working at it for hours.
Listen to the tape. Then complete the conversation as you listen to the tape a second time.

MOLLY Dinner's ready. We're waiting for you, Jeff.

JEFF Start _____. I'm busy.

MOLLY Haven't you _____ yet?

JEFF Not _____. I just need _____ more minutes.

MOLLY It _____ too difficult for you. Why don't you get Carlos _____?

JEFF Because I'm determined to _____ myself. That's why.

MOLLY You always _____ everything yourself. I've never met _____ so stubborn.

JEFF Stop talking, Molly, and _____ that wrench.

MOLLY The one _____?

JEFF Right. That's _____.

MOLLY Here _____.

JEFF Thanks. There, I've got it. The sink _____ okay now.

MOLLY Well, it's about time. You've _____ all afternoon.

JEFF *I* might be stubborn, Molly, but at least *I'm* patient!

Role Play: Practice similar conversations about these situations.

1 You're watching a friend. She's trying to solve a very difficult math problem which she's determined to work out by herself. You've watched her now for two hours.

2 You're watching your brother. He's trying to fix the transmission in his car. He wants to do all the work himself. You can see he's having a hard time.

Start with:
Haven't you _____ yet?

TWO   Discussing personal finances

Molly is always broke. She doesn't know how she spends her money. How do *you* spend your money?

After savings and taxes, this is where the average American consumer's dollar goes:

Draw a chart to show how you spend your money. Tell about your budget. Use expressions, such as:
- Most of my money goes for _____.
- I spend some of it on _____.
- A few (dollars) go for _____.
- I spend several (dollars) on _____.
- I don't spend any of it on _____.
- None of my money goes for _____.

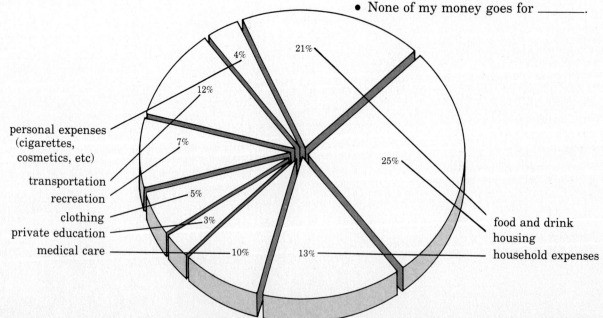

The Technological Revolution

From the invention of the first stone tools to today's complex computers, man has developed the power to change the world around him. Computer technology in particular could be taking over our economic life.

On the farm, modern tractors and threshers have taken the place of field workers. With their help one man can plant and harvest enough wheat and corn to feed thousands of people. In addition, many farmers have been using computers to process information about soil chemistry, insect control and plant genetics. By the year 2000, much of the food we eat could be the result of these new machines.

In business, computers do the job of accountants and secretaries. In minutes, office computers type out hundreds of letters and, by satellite transmission, send out bills to customers around the world. Business managers use computers to collect huge amounts of information and, in seconds, to do calculations beyond the power of the human brain. In the future, the most important decision-maker might be the computer, not the company executive.

In industry, computerized robots have replaced many workers on factory assembly lines. Because technology supplies the muscle power, workers are now free to use their brain power to make new discoveries. In the automobile industry, graphics computers help engineers design the shape of the car and calculate the size of engine parts.

The human brain has not changed in size in the past 100,000 years. However, man was able to invent hand tools, then the steam engine and now the computer. Man has used his brain to create "intelligent machines" to do his work for him.

Thinkabout

	True	False
1 The invention of the tractor and thresher has resulted in more jobs for farm workers.	___	___
2 The computer solves mathematical problems that man can't.	___	___
3 Computer graphics help engineers design parts of cars.	___	___
4 The human brain has increased in size in the past 100,000 years.	___	___

Talkabout

Do machines, such as computers, *give* us freedom or do they *take away* our freedom?

One opinion . . .

"Machines are wonderful. Think of all the hard work they do for us and all the time we save! Because of technology, man now has the freedom to use his imagination to create more interesting things."

And another . . .

"Before we had modern machinery, we made things with our hands. We put the pieces together and we were satisfied when we saw the final product. Workers in a factory see only pieces of things. They never see the whole product—the result of their work. That's why workers today are very unhappy and dissatisfied. They feel like human robots."

Writeabout Expository: Using examples to support an idea

Write a short composition about technology in your *daily* life. Give examples of machines and appliances in your home and explain their functions and use by you and your family.

More and more, technology has been taking over the daily life of people in (*your country*).

By the year 2000, there might be machines which could _____.

←**Start with:**
State the main idea.
←**Development:**
Kitchen:
    Examples 1 & 2   Functions

Living Room:
    Examples 1 & 2   Functions

Bedroom and Bath:
    Examples 1 & 2   Functions

←**End with:**
Give your opinion about the future.

We should wait for the police.

Molly was convinced that Kemp was behind the troubles at Tudor Village.

Scene One

▣ The next night Butch and Spike returned to Tudor Village to continue their work. The building was dark so they couldn't see the tenants who were hiding in the shadows. Quickly, they moved toward the door which led to the basement. The door was locked. Spike took out a screwdriver and broke the lock. Just then, Butch turned around. Molly was watching him from the shadows and saw his face clearly in the small light above the door. There was a long scar on one cheek.

Molly ran upstairs to call the police as Jeff and the others followed Butch and Spike down the basement steps. Inside, it was dark but Carlos knew the building by heart. He led the others to a room where the light switches were. But when they tried to turn on the lights, nothing happened. The wires were cut.

PAULO They cut the wires. We'll have to use flashlights.

JEFF I think I hear them. They must be in the boiler room in the front of the building. Let's go.

CARLOS They might have guns. We should wait for the police.

JEFF No, they could leave before the police get here.

CARLOS Look, they're running away. They heard us!

JEFF C'mon, let's get them.

CARLOS Paulo, go back to the main entrance and bring the police.

JEFF Where did they go? Do you see them?

CARLOS No, and I don't hear them either. I think they got away.

JEFF Check the boiler. Is it damaged?

CARLOS It looks all right. The boiler wasn't touched. At least we stopped them.

JEFF Yeah, for tonight. But they'll be back. I'm sure of it.

Questions

1 Was the basement door locked? Ask how it was opened?

2 Did anyone get a good look at Butch's face? Ask who, how.

3 Was anything wrong with the basement lights? Ask about the wires.

4 What does Paulo suggest? Ask if Jeff agrees.

5 Was anything damaged? Ask about the boiler.

6 Is Jeff certain of anything? Ask what.

Scene Two

📼 By the time the police arrived, Butch and Spike were gone. Carlos gave the police a full report but, as usual, no clues were found. Molly remembered the face with the scar. Because she might be able to identify one of the men, Molly went with the police to the station. There she spent the rest of the night until she picked out Butch's face from the police records.

For the next few days, the police looked for Butch, but without success. As a reporter, Molly was used to getting information fast. She went to all the bars and pool halls where Butch might go and talked to some people who knew him. Molly found out a lot; she even discovered that Butch occasionally did some rough jobs for a man named Kemp. It all started to make sense. Molly was convinced that Kemp was behind the troubles at Tudor Village.

Molly told the police about her suspicions. They wanted to help but Molly didn't have any evidence. They promised to investigate Kemp. Molly wasn't satisfied, so that night she and Jeff called a meeting of the tenants. It was time for them to take some action of their own.

PAULO   You mean that Wade Enterprises is responsible for all our troubles?

MOLLY   I'm sure of it. Kemp is Preston Wade's assistant and he's the one behind all this. It's obvious that Kemp hired the men who are trying to frighten us.

MARY   Will the police arrest Kemp?

MOLLY   No, we can't prove anything. The police advised us to wait.

PAULO   Kemp is very clever. He's trying to get us to leave Tudor Village.

MARY   But what can we do? How can we stop him?

MOLLY   We can fight back! We can organize a protest! Jeff has a plan.

JEFF   A group of us will go down to Wade's office tomorrow. We'll make so much noise that he'll have to talk with us. We'll find out if Wade knows anything about these problems.

MOLLY   Jeff's right. Kemp won't be able to stop us from seeing Wade. There'll be too many of us.

PAULO   Jeff, what about Susan? Are you going to tell her about all this?

JEFF   No, this has nothing to do with Susan. Besides, she wouldn't believe anything bad about her father. I don't want her mixed up in any of this.

CARLOS   Let's get to work. Molly and Paulo can make some signs. Mary, put on a pot of coffee. It's going to be a long night.

Questions

1 Did the police catch Butch and Spike? Ask about the clues.
2 Who identified Butch's photograph? Ask how.
3 What is Molly certain about? Ask why.
4 Was a tenants' meeting called by Jeff and Molly? Ask why.
5 What are the tenants planning to do? Ask when.
6 Why won't Jeff tell Susan about the plan?

Passive Voice in Simple Present and Simple Past

Active	Passive
Someone takes Molly to the station.	→ Molly *is taken* to the station.
Someone asked Molly to look at photos.	→ Molly *was asked* to look at photos.

We use the **passive voice** when the subject of the verb is the *receiver* of the action of the verb. We form the **present passive** with *is* or *are*+V-*ed*, -*en*. The **past passive** is formed with *was* or *were*+V-*ed*, *en*.

A Preston Wade has been out of the office all week. He is meeting with Kemp to check on the progress of the Wade Plaza Project.

WADE Have you *finished the plans* yet?
KEMP No, the plans aren't finished. I haven't taken care of them yet.

This is Kemp's list of things to do.

> *1. finish plans*
> *2. pay architect ✓*
> *3. arrange financing*
> *4. hire construction crew ✓*
> *5. rent equipment*
> *6. solve Tudor Village problem ✓*

● Make similar conversations between Wade and Kemp.
Start with:

Have you _____ yet?

● Tell about a building project in this city or in your country.

What parts of the

project	are / aren't	finished?

B Carlos is telling the police about all of the problems at Tudor Village. One of the policemen is making a list of all the accidents.

Carlos says: "Someone broke the lock on the basement door." The policeman writes: The lock on the basement door *was broken*.

● What does the policeman write in his notebook when Carlos says:

1 Someone broke four windows on the third floor.
2 Someone cut the wires on the light switch.
3 Someone moved the barrels behind the building.
4 Someone burned the garbage in the barrels.
5 Someone damaged the mailboxes in the hall.

● Ask each other about the last break-in.

S1 Was the _____ damaged?
S2 Yes, it was. The _____ was (broken) when they _____.
or No, it wasn't. They didn't get a chance to _____.

cues *boiler; lock; elevators; doorbell; light switches.*

C Has there ever been a terrible fire, storm, or earthquake in your country? Describe what happened.

Was anything destroyed?
Was anything damaged?
Was anything saved?
Was anyone killed?
Was anyone injured?
Was anyone warned?

Reported Commands with Warn *and* Advise

The police told the tenants, "Don't leave the doors unlocked!"

The police	warned advised	*the tenants them*	to lock their doors.
The tenants	were	warned advised	not to leave their doors unlocked.

For **reported commands** with *warn* and *advise,* we put the command in the *to-infinitive* form. Use the indirect object to show who receives the command. In **passive voice,** the indirect object becomes the subject of the sentence.

 A The police gave the tenants a list of instructions:

> **Ask for the names of all visitors.**
> **Don't open the doors to strangers.**
> **Lock your windows at all times.**
> **Leave a light on in your apartment.**
> **Don't stand near your windows.**
> **Don't walk outside alone at night.**

1 What did the police *advise* the tenants *to do*?
→ The police advised them to ask for the names of all visitors.

2 What did the police *warn* the tenants *not to do*?
→ The police warned them not to open their doors to strangers.

3 Practice the **passive voice**:

→ The tenants *were advised* to ask for the names of all visitors.
→ The tenants *were warned* not to open their doors to strangers.

● What advice and warnings do you usually give visitors to your city or country?

I advise them to _____.
I warn them not to _____.

cues *eat/drink certain foods; shop in certain stores; go to certain places.*

B What warnings and advice are given on the labels of products, such as these?

1 The manufacturer advises us to _____.
We are warned not to _____.
We have to _____.

2 The druggist warns the consumer to _____.
Parents are advised to _____.
I would keep this medicine in/on _____ so that a child couldn't reach it.

3 The Surgeon General warns the smoker that _____.
The smoker is (not) advised to _____.
In my opinion, we should(n't) smoke because _____.

4 The manufacturer advises the consumer that _____.
The user is warned (not) to _____.
We have to _____.

● Tell about products you use which carry warning labels.
What does the manufacturer advise? What is the consumer warned (not) to do?

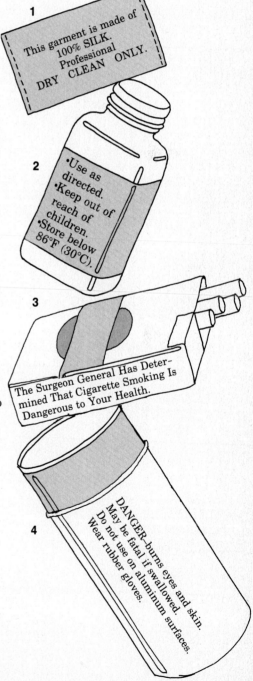

1 This garment is made of 100% SILK. Professional DRY CLEAN ONLY.

2 •Use as directed. •Keep out of reach of children. •Store below 86°F (30°C).

3 The Surgeon General Has Determined That Cigarette Smoking Is Dangerous to Your Health.

4 DANGER—burns eyes and skin. May be fatal if swallowed. Do not use on aluminum surfaces. Wear rubber gloves.

ONE Making a complaint

Paulo and Molly are having dinner at a restaurant Ben Greene recommended. They made reservations for 8 o'clock, but they weren't seated until 8:30. The waiter led them to a table next to the kitchen. Paulo complained, so the waiter found them another table near the window. It has been quite a while since they gave their order to the waiter.
Listen to the tape. Then complete the conversation as you listen to the tape a second time.

MOLLY   Can you believe this place? First they made us wait for a half-hour, then they brought us to that horrible table.

PAULO   Well, we _____ this wonderful table _____. Why don't you just _____ the view?

MOLLY   Relax! How can I relax when _____? Where's our food? Our order _____ hours ago!

PAULO   C'mon, Molly. It _____ that long. Besides, the waiter _____ our food now.

MOLLY   Paulo, I can't eat this roast beef. It's well done. And these potatoes! They _____ in oil. I wanted _____.

PAULO   Waiter. We specifically ordered _____ and _____. We'd like to have the food we ordered.

WAITER   I'm sorry for the mistake, sir. I'll take this back _____ and get your order.

MOLLY   Terrific. Now_____ another half-hour!

PAULO   Molly, _____ more wine. Here, let me _____ your glass.

MOLLY   Oh, all right. But pass me the bread. I'm starved.

Role Play: Practice a similar conversation between you and the waiter. Complain about the food. Talk about a dish which is popular in your country.

The (food) is	undercooked. overcooked.	It's	rare. well done.

The (food) is	fried. broiled. baked.	It's too	oily. dry.

Start with:

YOU   Waiter, we can't eat this _____. It's _____.

WAITER   How do you like your _____ cooked?

TWO Expressing certainty

Carlos is listening to the weather report on the radio:

"Snow warnings were issued for the Metropolitan Area for this evening. Six to eight inches are expected by the early morning hours. Motorists are advised to leave their cars at home tomorrow and to take public transportation to work. All schools are ordered closed by the City's Department of Education. Stay tuned to this station for further snow bulletins."

Give a weather report about a bad storm in your country.
- What is expected to happen?
- What are people advised to do?
- What is certain to happen?

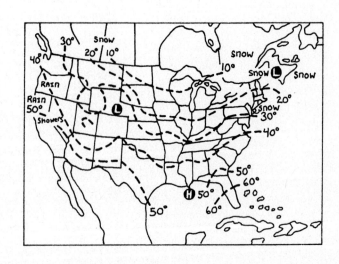

Getting service

Your watch is broken, or your dress / suit is ripped, or your car is damaged. You take it to a shop in your neighborhood.

🔊 **Listen to the sample on the tape.**

- Act out the conversation between you and the other person. Follow the conversation guide below. Some vocabulary cues are given, but you may choose words of your own.

cues:	You	The Other Person	cues:
		Offer assistance.	May I help you? / What can I do for you? Need some help?
There seems to be something wrong with this _____. I have a problem with my _____. It's my _____. It's . . .	State the problem.		
		Ask for information.	Could you show me the place where it's (broken)? Let me see the _____ / take a look at _____. Where's it (broken)?
Here, next to . . . / on the . . . It's (broken) here, next to . . . There, you can see it next to . . . It happened when I was . . .	Point out the problem area.		
		Agree to take care of the problem.	I can fix it for you. We'll take care of it. No problem.
I'm glad to hear that. Good. / Terrific. / Great. Thanks for your help.	Show appreciation.		
		Tell when the customer can pick it up.	You can pick it up on _____. It'll be ready on _____. How about next (Thursday / week)?
Fine. That's good. How much will it cost? What's the charge? What do you charge for . . . ?	Agree. Ask for the charge.		
		Give information.	That will come to $_____. It should be about $_____. We charge $_____ for . . .
Good. / Fine. I'll stop by on _____. I'll come and pick it up on _____.	Agree. Make final arrangements. End the conversation.		Very good. / Okay. / Fine. / Sure. It will be ready then. See you on _____.

**If the tenants don't leave
the Wade Building, Kemp
will call the police.**

Scene One

📼 Early the next morning, the tenants met in the lobby of Tudor Village. Many of them were carrying signs as they took the subway to the Wade Building on Park Avenue. By the time they got there, it was already 10:00.

Jeff led the tenants into the reception area in the lobby. A few of the men started shouting at the receptionist until Jeff told them to calm down. If we don't see Wade soon, Jeff thought, the situation will get out of hand.

Molly was there too. She planned to write a story for the *City Herald*. She watched her brother closely as he talked to the tenants. Molly saw the old Jeff, the confident and capable student leader she knew long ago. She realized what was happening to Jeff. He *cared* about these people. He didn't have time to worry about his own problems now. Just then the elevator came down and Kemp stepped out. At once, the room was quiet.

KEMP I'm Mr. Wade's personal assistant. Can someone tell me what's going on here?

JEFF We want to see Preston Wade.

KEMP You can speak to me. No one sees Mr. Wade without an appointment. If you're quiet and orderly, I'll listen to you.

MOLLY Don't you dare talk to us like that! We're not children.

KEMP Oh, Miss Ryan. So you're here too. Your editor will hear from me.

JEFF We demand to see Preston Wade. We're going up.

KEMP I'm afraid I didn't make myself clear. This is private property. You're trespassing. If you're not out of here in ten minutes, I'm going to call the police.

JEFF You can't threaten us, Kemp. Give Wade this message: Tell him if he isn't down here in ten minutes, we'll come up and get him!

Questions

1 How did the tenants get to the Wade Building? Ask when.
2 Has Jeff changed in the last few days? Ask how.
3 Did someone speak to the tenants? Ask who.
4 Did Molly get angry at something Kemp said? Ask why.
5 What will happen if the tenants don't leave Wade's office?
6 What does Jeff say is going to happen if Wade doesn't come down to see the tenants?

If you're not out of here in ten minutes, I'm going to call the police.

Questions

1 Where did Susan have the taxi drop her off?
2 Did Susan realize that the tenants were angry? Ask how she knew.
3 Could Susan find Molly and Jeff in the crowd? Ask where they were.
4 Did Molly say that Preston Wade was causing the troubles? Ask what Susan thought.
5 Did Jeff agree with Molly or Susan? Ask why.
6 Does Susan believe Jeff? Ask what she thinks.

Scene Two

When Susan stepped out of the taxi in front of the Wade Building, there were several police cars near the entrance. She was surprised when she walked into the reception area and saw the tenants.

With amazement, Susan read the signs that the tenants were carrying, and she saw the angry looks that were on their faces. As soon as Susan spotted Jeff and Molly, she pushed her way to the front of the crowd.

SUSAN Jeff, tell me what's happening! Why are all of you here?
JEFF Susan! This hasn't got anything to do with you. We're here to see your father.
SUSAN My father? But you're all screaming and yelling. Are you crazy?
MOLLY Susan, we think that Wade Enterprises is causing all of the troubles at Tudor Village.
SUSAN What are you talking about, Molly?
MOLLY Someone is trying to frighten us so that we'll leave Tudor Village. There was a fire and the telephone wires were cut. Mother is still ill from something in the water.
SUSAN Oh, no! Mary ill? But it can't be because of Wade Enterprises—because of my father!
JEFF I'm sorry, Susan. But your father . . .
SUSAN Stop it! Stop it! If this is true . . . But, no, I just don't believe it. It's all so crazy.
JEFF Susan, please listen to me. I didn't mean . . .
SUSAN No, no. You're all wrong. I want to talk to my father. You'll see. Maybe he was right about you, Jeff. Goodbye!

Present Real Conditional with If

Condition		Result	
If Kemp has his way, If Jeff isn't careful,	the tenants	will are going to	go to jail.
		won't aren't going to	see Wade.

The **first conditional** with **if** tells about the result of some possible or real event which can happen. When both the *if-condition* and the *result* take place in the future, we use the future tense *will* or *going to* only in the result.

A What do *you* think will *probably* happen or not happen in the story?

1 Molly might write a story for the *City Herald* from the tenants' point of view. Will she get fired?
→ If Molly writes the story, she'll get fired because Wade owns the paper.
or
→ If Molly writes the story, she won't get fired because Ben Greene is her friend.

2 The tenants might damage the furniture and some other property in Wade's office. Will they go to jail?
3 The situation might get out of hand. Will Jeff be able to control the tenants?
4 Jeff might try to call Susan. Will she speak to him?
5 Susan might realize her mistake. Will she apologize to Jeff?

● If Molly loses her job on the paper, there won't be any money to pay the bills. She's asking herself:

What will happen:

if the gas and electric bills aren't paid?
if the telephone is disconnected?
if there's no money for food?
if she can't pay the mortgage on the apartment?

● If you (or a family member) lose your job, what will or won't happen to you and your family?

Who will pay the bills?
How will your life change?
Where will you go for help?

B What are each of these people thinking about? Complete the statements with the results.

1 If the tenants see Wade, he _____. I've got to stop them!

KEMP

If we see Wade, we _____. We've got to talk to Wade!

MOLLY

2 If I explain the situation to Susan, she _____. Susan's just confused right now.

JEFF

If Jeff tries to call me, I _____. I never want to speak to him again.

SUSAN

● Tell what's on *your* mind.

If I get home early tonight, I _____

If I can save some money, I _____

If I have time this weekend, I _____

If I get up early tomorrow, I _____

If I study very hard, I _____.

Reported Speech and Wh-Noun Clauses

Wade	asks,	S V "What's going on out there?" "Who wants to see me?"
	didn't know	S V what was going on out there. who wanted to see him.

When the **wh**-word is the subject of the **noun clause**, use regular (S-V) word order. Follow sequence of tenses rule (page 53) for the verb in the **noun clause**.

A Tell what has happened in the story:

1 Can you remember what is happening in the reception area?
Did Wade know what was happening?

2 Do you know who is responsible for the accidents at Tudor Village?
Did Susan understand who was responsible?

3 Do you know who is lying to Wade?
Did Wade realize...?

4 Can you guess what is troubling Susan?
Did Jeff try to understand...?

5 Do you know who is trying to frighten the tenants?
Did Molly explain to Susan...?

B Use the cues to make excuses.

1 Paulo is standing in front of the *City Herald*. He's been waiting for Molly for over half an hour. He's getting angry. When she comes, Paulo asks:
Could you please tell me what has taken you so long?
Molly says...

cues *important phone call; broken typewriter; finish a story.*

2 Wade is beginning to notice that Susan hasn't been home very often. Wade asks Susan for an explanation:
I'd like to know who has been taking up so much of your time lately.
Susan says...

cues *classmate from London in town; new girlfriend; next-door neighbor.*

C Jeff watches a lot of television. One of his favorite programs is a quiz show called *The Category Game.* Look at today's game board. How many points can you make?

Directions: Form two teams. Five names are given in each column. Each team member takes a turn, selects one of the names (silently), then makes a clue-question in indirect speech. Give information in your question so that your team can guess the correct name. You are not allowed to repeat the name in your question. Each name has a point value. Keep score. The team with the most points wins!

Steps:
1 Choose a name.
2 Ask your team:
Do you know...
who wrote _____?
when _____ is celebrated in the US?
where _____ is/are sold?
what is used to _____?
who is/was married to _____?
3 Your team guesses.
4 Keep score.

● ● ● ● The Category Game ● ● ● ●

	Authors	Holidays	Specialty Stores	Kitchen Things	Famous Spouses
10 points	Shakespeare	January 1	pharmacy	toaster	Adam
20 points	Tolstoy	Last Thursday in November	bakery	iron	Jackie Bouvier
30 points	Gabriel García Marquez	July 4	hardware store	percolator	Yoko Ono
40 points	Dante	First Monday in September	barber shop	wok	Richard Burton
50 points	Karl Marx	October 31	stationery store	blender	Helen of Troy

ONE Making a threat

Kemp wants Ben Greene to fire Molly. After all, Wade owns the *City Herald* so he should have some control over who works there. Kemp is on the telephone now with Ben Greene.
Listen to the tape. Then complete the conversation as you listen to the tape a second time.

GREENE City Desk. Greene speaking.

KEMP Greene, this is Wade Enterprises. I'm _____ Preston Wade.

GREENE I hope Mr. Wade liked _____ on The Plaza. Molly Ryan did _____ on that article.

KEMP That's exactly the person _____. I want you _____. Immediately.

GREENE Now, hold on. Molly's _____ top reporters. Who are you?

KEMP Kemp's the name. Mr. Wade's personal assistant. Let me make myself clear. Miss Ryan and her brother _____ a tenant protest here at Wade Enterprises. Mr. Wade _____ political people. Do you understand?

GREENE Sorry, Kemp. Molly's personal life is her business. My concern is what _____.

KEMP Listen carefully, Greene. If _____ fire her, you'll have to answer to Preston Wade.

GREENE Don't you _____, Kemp! I run this paper, not Wade Enterprises.

KEMP Get rid of her, Greene, or I'll see that _____, too.

GREENE You try that, Kemp, and we'll see who leaves—you or me. Get lost!

Role Play: Preston Wade decides to call Ben Greene himself. Ben Greene tells Wade that Molly is the *City Herald*'s top reporter and a good friend of his. He refuses to fire Molly.

Practice a short conversation between Preston Wade and Ben Greene.

Start with:

WADE Greene, this is Preston Wade. I'm calling about one of your reporters, Molly Ryan.

End with:

GREENE I'm sorry you feel that way, Mr. Wade, but I'm not going to fire Molly. Goodbye.

TWO Agreeing and disagreeing strongly

Give your opinion:

1 A lot of men say that women should have little responsibility in business and politics. What do *you* think?

2 Some government officials are concerned about the birth rate. They say that the world is already over-populated. Do *you* think that the government should force people to have small families?

Practice:
They're wrong! / right!
I don't care who says _____, I believe that _____.
How can they say that! / What a great (terrible) idea!
A lot of people believe that _____, but I know _____.

A Volcano Is Born

On March 27, Mike Nelson and Sandy Moore, with four of their friends, set up camp 30 miles from the peak of Mt. St. Helens. Mike and Sandy were up at sunrise. The morning was unusually quiet. No birds were singing that day. On March 27th, at 6:34 a.m., the top of Mt. St. Helens blew off. A volcano was born.

Mike first felt the earth move beneath his feet. Then he heard the explosion. He and Sandy looked up to see clouds of hot ash and steam bursting from the top of the mountain. Moments later, the hot ash was coming down on them and a sea of melted rock and yellow mud was moving their way.

Mike ran towards the tent. If we don't wake the others, he thought, it will be too late. Trees were falling down all around them. He used his body to protect Sandy from the hot ash and broken trees. In five minutes, they were buried in the ash. After a while, they started to dig themselves out from under the ash and logs.

Later that day, Mike and Sandy found pieces of the tents. Two of their friends were dead. The two others were alive, but they were badly burned.

Mike and Sandy walked 15 miles down the mountain, over a desert of white ash and fallen trees. After a ten-hour journey, they were finally found by a helicopter rescue team. As they guided the pilot to their friends' location, they looked in horror at the lifeless scene below. For miles around Mt. St. Helens, it looked like the surface of the moon.

Thinkabout

True False

1 The campers were awakened by the volcano explosion. ____ ____

2 Two of the campers died in their tent. ____ ____

3 Mike and Sandy decided to wait until they were rescued. ____ ____

4 The land around Mt. St. Helens was completely covered by white ash and broken trees. ____ ____

Talkabout

These are two other people who died on Mt. St. Helens. They were warned about the explosion, but they decided to stay. Do you agree with their decision *not* to leave?

1 *David Johnston,* 30, a geologist, was doing tests on the mountain peak. It was his job to predict the time of the volcano explosion. He knew that the time was very near, but he wanted to complete his work.

2 *Harry Truman,* 84, lived with his 16 cats just north of the peak. He didn't believe the warnings from those "city people." Many reporters visited Harry. He became famous because he stubbornly refused to leave his home. If I leave, Harry perhaps thought, people will think I am afraid.

Writeabout Narrative / Expository: Using a story to give information

Write about a situation that happened in your country, perhaps a natural disaster such as an earthquake or a flood, or an event, such as an election or a strike. *Give information about the event through the experience of one person—you, a relative, or a friend. Use time expressions to link your events in chronological order.*

(Name) , who is _____ , was in / at _____ when _____(Event)_____ .

the next day . . .
that night . . . later . . .
after that . . .
then . . .
the following day . . .

In the end, _____ .

If people like _(Name)_ don't (help others? take action?), then _____(Result)_____

← Start with:
Describe the situation. main character? place? time?

← Order the events:
Tell what happened from the experience of the main character.

← End with:
Describe the final stage or result. Give your opinion.

Wade always gets what he wants. He made the tenants an offer they couldn't refuse.

Scene One

Susan is confused. For the past few weeks, she has been happy. The Ryans have been kind to her and Jeff has been wonderful. Yet, didn't Jeff say those terrible things about her father? Now, she didn't know what to believe.

Susan opened the door to Wade's private office. Kemp was there, talking to some policemen. Reporters and cameramen were asking her father a lot of questions. As Susan heard her father deny the tenants' charges, she knew that he was telling the truth. Jeff must be wrong about the problems at Tudor Village. Someone else was causing the trouble.

WADE Gentlemen, you've heard the tenants' side of the story. They've accused us of causing all the accidents at Tudor Village.

REPORTER Mr. Wade, do you deny those charges?

WADE Absolutely! There has been no wrongdoing on our part. That's a dangerous neighborhood. There's always been a lot of crime there.

REPORTER Isn't it true that Wade Enterprises wants the Tudor Village property for the Wade Plaza project?

WADE That's correct. But we intend to make a generous offer to buy the property from the tenants. My assistant, Mr. Kemp, will explain.

KEMP Wade Enterprises is offering the tenants more than the market value for their apartments. Mr. Wade has also reserved a group of apartments in the new Wade Plaza building for those tenants who want to remain in the neighborhood.

REPORTER Suppose they don't want to move out?

KEMP That's not likely. If more than half of the tenants accept our offer, the others will have to sell. Tudor Village is a cooperative. We feel that the majority of the tenants will vote to sell.

REPORTER Will the police arrest the tenants in the lobby?

WADE Wade Enterprises has no quarrel with them. We expect them to act responsibly. And now, if you excuse me, gentlemen, I have a business to run.

Questions

1 Is Susan confused? Ask why.
2 What was happening in Wade's private office?
3 What did Susan know about her father?
4 Who denied the tenants' charges? Ask about what he said.
5 What will Wade give the tenants if they sell Tudor Village?
6 Will all the tenants have to sell if more than half agree? Ask why.

Scene Two

Kemp knew what he had to do. If the tenants vote to sell, they'll want a high price for Tudor Village, he thought. But Kemp needed that money. He had gambling debts and they had to be paid soon.

Kemp was in trouble. Wade didn't realize how much money was missing from the company accounts. Before Wade got suspicious, Kemp had to get the tenants out of Tudor Village.

Late that night, Kemp drove to the sleazy hotel where Butch was hiding.

BUTCH Hey, Spike, there's someone at the door.
SPIKE Who do you suppose it is? Maybe it's the cops!
KEMP Butch, open up. It's me, Kemp.
BUTCH Okay, okay. C'mon in. I'm surprised to see you here, Kemp.
KEMP There's been some trouble.
SPIKE Yeah, we read about it in the papers. Those tenants gave us a rough time too. We almost got caught the other night.
KEMP Well, you're going to go back there again. You haven't finished the job yet.
BUTCH I don't know. Thanks to that Molly Ryan, the police are after me.
KEMP That's your problem. This time, really frighten those tenants. It's an old building so make it look like an accident.
BUTCH How about if we loosen some of the boards on the stairs, or maybe cut the wires on the elevator?
SPIKE Wait a minute! Suppose someone gets hurt?
KEMP *That's* the idea.

Questions

1 Did Kemp need money? Ask why.
2 What didn't Wade know about the company accounts?
3 Who did Kemp see late that night? Ask where.
4 Why was Butch hiding?
5 What does Butch suggest? Ask if Spike approves.
6 Will Kemp be sorry if one of the tenants gets hurt?

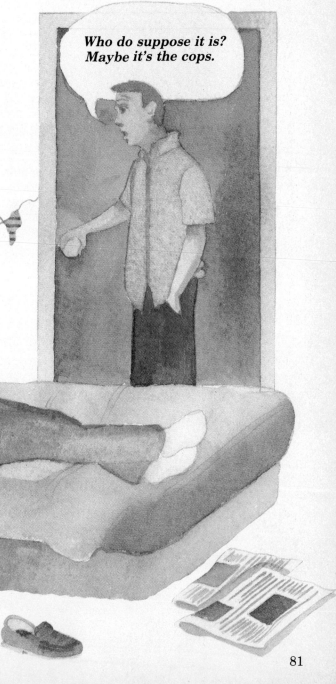

Who do suppose it is? Maybe it's the cops.

81

Reported Speech with Wh-words as Non-Subjects

Susan	asks,	"Why are the tenants in my father's office?" "What do the reporters want to know?" "What question will my father answer?"
	didn't know	why the tenants *were* in her father's office. what the reporters *wanted* to know. what questions her father *would answer*.

When the **wh**-word is *not* the subject of the **noun clause**, use *statement* word order (S-V) *after* the **wh**-word. Follow sequence of tenses rules (page 53) for **noun clauses** in object position.

A Tell what you know about the story:

1 Do you remember where Butch was hiding?
Did Kemp know where Butch was hiding?
2 Do you know what the protest is all about?
Did Susan know what the protest was all about?
3 Do you understand why Susan is angry at Jeff?
Did Jeff realize. . . ?
4 Do you recall what Kemp wants Butch and Spike to do?
Did the tenants learn. . . ?
5 Can you remember why Kemp needs to take cash from the accounts?
Did Wade realize. . . ?

B After the press conference, a reporter asked Kemp these questions:

1 "What complaints do the tenants have?"
2 "When will the construction start?"
3 "Why won't Wade meet with the tenants?"
4 "How much does Wade expect to pay for Tudor Village?"
5 "How many tenants are going to sell?"

Change to reported speech:
→ The reporter asked what complaints the tenants had.

C Molly is on assignment for the *City Herald*. Ben Greene told her to get on the first plane to Los Angeles. Molly is at Kennedy Airport right now. She's asking for information.

Excuse me, do you know where I can buy a ticket?
Could you please tell me when the next plane to Los Angeles is departing?

I'd like to know what time the plane will arrive in L.A.
I wonder if you could tell me how much the ticket costs.

● Ask each other for information about:

places: the ladies' room (the men's room); the main entrance; the snack bar; the library.

S1 Excuse me, do you know where I can find the men's room?
S2 Sure. It's down the hall on your right, just across from the library. You can't miss it.

times: the building opens; the snack bar closes; the bank is open; the library is closed; the next test is scheduled.
costs: next term's fees; bus fare; subway fare; a cup of coffee; a pack of cigarettes; a book for class.

● When friends ask you about your school, what do they want to know? Make a list of their questions:

→ They want to know what class I'm in.
→ They usually ask me how much the fees are.

cues *class or level, fees, location, teacher's name, textbook, classroom tapes, conversation practice, schedule.*

Suppose *and* Supposed to

Molly *supposes* she'll get married someday.
(believes/expects it will happen.)

Mary thinks that all women *are supposed to* get married.
(it is expected/required to happen by custom or law.)

Suppose refers to a state of mind or feeling. It cannot be used with continuous tenses. Other *state* verbs are: *believe, desire, doubt, forget, hate, know, love, prefer, remember, understand* and *want*. We use **is supposed to** when we refer to normal practice.

A Tell what you expect to happen in the story:

1 Kemp made Butch and Spike go back to Tudor Village.

What are they supposed to do?
Do you suppose that someone will get hurt?

2 Kemp stole $50,000 from the company accounts.

Is he supposed to take money without Wade's permission?
Do you suppose Kemp will get caught?

3 Mary wants Molly to get married.

Is Molly supposed to give up her career for marriage?
Do you suppose Molly will get married soon?

B Tell about the laws and customs in your country. What are people *supposed to* do?

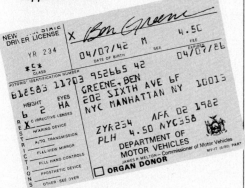

1 get a driver's license?
2 get a passport?
3 vote in an election?
4 get into the university?
5 send a telegram?
6 get married?
7 get a job?

C Kemp knocked on the door of the hotel room where Butch and Spike were staying. They weren't expecting Kemp.

BUTCH Hey, Spike. There's someone at the door.
SPIKE Who *do you suppose* it is? ("I have no idea who it is.")

● Read each situation. Then make a "guess."

1 Molly is reading a book at home. Suddenly the lights go out. What do you suppose has happened?
2 Jeff is riding his motorcycle. Suddenly the engine makes a strange noise. What do you suppose has happened?
3 Carlos sees a shining object in the night sky. It seems to be moving. What do you suppose it is?

Guess:	YES ⌐ I suppose it's . . .
	It could be . . .
	It might be . . .
	NO ⌐ It's definitely not . . .

● Tell about your own experiences. Give reasons for your guesses.

1 You receive a special delivery letter. Who do you suppose it's from?
2 Your best friend gives you a present in a very small box. What do you suppose it is?

3 There's a knock on your door at midnight. Who do you suppose it is?
4 Your teacher wants to see you after class. Why do you suppose he/she wants to see you?

ONE Conjecturing

When the tenants learned about Wade's offer, they called off the protest. Jeff and the others are discussing the situation while they are waiting for the subway to Tudor Village.

Listen to the tape. Then complete the conversation as you listen to the tape a second time.

JEFF   What do you suppose Wade is up to?

CARLOS   What do you mean? You heard _____. He offered us a lot of money _____. And he's going to give us new apartments at Wade Plaza.

JEFF   Molly, _____ Mom will want to sell our apartment?

MOLLY   I _____ so. She cares a lot about Tudor Village. Do you realize how long _____ _____? Almost fifty years. No, I don't think _____.

CARLOS   What about the money? Doesn't Mary care about _____ with the money? She could buy new furniture, or take trips.

MOLLY   Mom really doesn't need the money. She has _____. The money _____ to her.

JEFF   I suppose you're right. I'm sure Mom won't vote to accept Wade's offer.

Role Play: Molly and Jeff are discussing how the Bradleys will vote. They are the elderly couple who own Paulo's apartment. They are living in Florida now, and they don't have much money. Practice a short conversation between Molly and Jeff.

Start with:

JEFF Do you suppose the Bradleys will want to sell their apartment?

TWO Denying

Direct	Indirect
Absolutely (not)!	I'm afraid I don't agree with you.
You're wrong!	Actually, I don't think so.
Of course not!	I'm sure you have made a mistake.

A reporter asks Wade: "Do you deny the tenants' charges?" Wade replies in a very *direct* manner: "Absolutely! There has been no wrongdoing on our part." Another reporter asks Wade: "Isn't it true that Wade Enterprises is forcing the tenants to leave Tudor Village?" Wade replies in an *indirect* manner: "I'm afraid I don't agree with you. We are making a generous offer for the apartments. We expect most of the tenants will want to sell."

What would you say in these situations? How would you deny your guilt or responsibility—in a *direct* or *indirect* manner?

1 sister to brother: Did you use my shampoo?
2 policeman to driver: Did you go through that red light?
3 boss to secretary: Have you misplaced the file on the Perry account?
4 girlfriend to boyfriend: Have you been seeing another girl?
5 teacher to student: Isn't it true that you got someone to write your composition for you?
6 husband to wife: Did you take $100 out of our bank account?
7 manager to clerk: You were late for work this morning, weren't you?
8 student to student: You borrowed my pen again, didn't you?

Settling an argument

You are driving down the street when suddenly another car crashes into your car. The other driver has just gone through a red light, ignored a stop sign, or come down a one-way street the wrong way.

Listen to the sample conversations on the tape.

• Act out the conversation between you and the other driver. Decide whether the other person is a teenager, an elderly woman, or a big man. Follow the conversation guide below. Some cues are given, but you may choose words of your own.

cues:	You	The Other Driver	cues:
Hey, you hit my car! My car! Do you realize that (you hit my car)? Do you know what you've done? You've just (gone through a red light).	State the problem.		
		Tell about your problem.	Your car? Take a look at (my car). Look at the damage / what you've done to my car!
It was your (fault / mistake). You caused the accident. You're responsible for . . . I suppose you didn't see that (red light)?	Accuse the other person of the accident.		What (red light)?
		Deny the charges.	Me? / My fault? / That's not true. You're wrong / crazy. Absolutely not! I'm afraid you're mistaken.
Didn't you see me? / look where you were going? / see (the light)? You didn't see the (red light), did you? You don't know how to drive!	Make a specific charge.		
		Say it's the other person's fault.	Me? You weren't . . . I know how to drive / what I'm doing. You don't. I'm an excellent / good driver. I'm afraid you don't know how to . . .
Let's exchange information. Why don't you give me your driver's license. We should let the police / the insurance companies handle this.	Make a suggestion.		
		Give and ask for information.	Here's my license. My insurance company is _____. I don't know what your name is / insurance company is.
Here's my license. I don't know where to call you / what your telephone number is.	Give information.		
I'll call you at _____. If I don't hear from you, I'll call you on _____ / at _____. Okay. / Good.	Make arrangements to speak again. End the conversation.		It's _____. Call me tomorrow / after _____ / at _____ o'clock. Fine. / Okay.

Some tenants didn't want to sell; others preferred to live in Wade Plaza because it was safer and more comfortable.

Scene One

🔊 Jeff was afraid that most of the tenants were going to vote to sell Tudor Village. The new Wade Plaza apartments would be larger and more comfortable than the ones they had now. With the money Wade was paying them, they could buy more expensive furniture. For some, the money was less important than safety. Because of the accidents at Tudor Village, these tenants wanted to live in a safer place such as Wade Plaza.

Some tenants, like the Ryans and the Riveras, didn't intend to sell their apartments. Tudor Village was important to them, and they weren't going to give up easily. The problem was how to convince the others not to sell.

MARY Who would want to leave this wonderful old place?

JEFF Not everyone feels the same way about Tudor Village, Mom. Look at what Wade is offering the tenants—a lot of money and a new apartment in Wade Plaza.

MARY So what? Are modern apartments better? Tudor Village is just as good as Wade Plaza. It's even better because it has more character.

MOLLY But a lot of people prefer a newer building because of the comforts and conveniences—like air conditioning and dishwashers.

JEFF And after all the trouble we've had here, the tenants probably feel it's much safer at Wade Plaza.

MARY Can't the police help us? If we can prove that Wade Enterprises is responsible for the trouble here, the tenants won't want to leave.

MOLLY There's just no evidence to connect Wade or Kemp with the trouble. The police can't arrest Kemp without some proof.

JEFF I'm going to call Susan. It's our only hope. If she watches Kemp for us, we can get the evidence we need. Susan has to help us.

Questions

1 Do most of the tenants want to sell? Ask about the rest of the tenants.

2 Do some people prefer modern buildings? Ask why.

3 Did Mary understand why other tenants preferred Wade Plaza? Ask what Wade was offering to do.

4 Is Wade Plaza safer than Tudor Village? Ask why.

5 Can the police arrest Kemp? Ask about what they need.

6 What is Jeff going to get Susan to do? Ask how.

Scene Two

📼 It was late afternoon and Susan was reading the newspaper. On the front page, there was a long story about the tenants' protest at her father's office. There was also a photograph of Wade talking to the reporters in his office; a smaller one showed Tudor Village. When Susan looked closer, she saw the fire damage in front of the building. The newspaper told about the other troubles at the building.

Susan didn't know what to think. It was clear that these weren't accidents. Someone had to cut those wires and set that fire. But not Wade Enterprises. Susan pushed the thought out of her mind.

When she read about the tenants and their problems, Susan thought of Jeff. She missed him and the wonderful times they had together. But Susan was her father's daughter. Her father's love was more important than her friendship with Jeff.

The telephone rang.

JEFF   Susan, is that you? Please don't hang up.
SUSAN I don't think I want to talk to you.
JEFF   I want to explain, Susan. Please, listen to me . . .
SUSAN Oh, Jeff. I'm too upset to talk to you. I feel caught between you and my father. Maybe I should just go back to England.
JEFF   Oh, God. Susan, no! My feelings for you haven't changed. I still care about you.
SUSAN And I still care about you too. That's part of the problem.
JEFF   Susan, think of my mother. We've got to stop these accidents or someone else is going to get hurt. We need your help.
SUSAN My help? I can't do anything to help you.
JEFF   Yes, you can. I want you to watch Kemp and your father. See if they know someone named Butch. I'm sure that he's responsible for the accidents.
SUSAN Are you crazy? You want me to spy on my own father? And Kemp? What does he have to do with this?
JEFF   Susan, Kemp is an evil man. Molly thinks he's hired this guy Butch to do his dirty work.
SUSAN That's enough. Just leave me alone, Jeff.
JEFF   But, Susan . . .
SUSAN Goodbye!

Questions

1 What did Susan see in the smaller photograph? Ask about the larger photograph.
2 What was more important than Susan's friendship with Jeff?
3 Did Susan miss Jeff? What else did she miss?
4 Why did Jeff phone Susan?
5 What might happen if Susan doesn't help the tenants?
6 What does Jeff think of Kemp? Why?

Comparatives of Adjectives

Is Molly	as	smart pretty interesting	as	Susan?
		smarter prettier more or less interesting	than	

The **as . . . as** pattern indicates equality. Use **than** before the person or thing that is to be compared. When we compare two things, we add **-er** to one- and two-syllable **adjectives**. Use **more/less** before **adjectives** of more than two syllables.

A Use the cues to ask about the characters in the story.

1 old/ Susan or Molly

S1 Is Susan as old as Molly?
S2 I don't think so. Molly is older than Susan.
or I'm not sure, but I think Susan is younger than Molly.

2 young/ Jeff or Paulo
3 beautiful/ Molly or Susan
4 handsome/ Jeff or Paulo
5 ugly/ Butch or Spike
6 ambitious/ Kemp or Jeff
7 responsible/ Molly or Jeff
8 clever/ Wade or Kemp

B Many of the tenants prefer to move to a newer building, but Mary would rather stay in Tudor Village. Tell about your preferences.

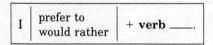

I	prefer to would rather	+ **verb** ____.

1 listen to classical or rock music?
2 drive a large car or a small one?
3 buy antique or modern furniture?
4 go to a museum or to a football game?
5 see a movie or a play?

cues *enjoyable; safe; exciting; relaxing; comfortable; fast; valuable; cheap; beautiful; interesting.*

C Choosing a place to live. You are trying to decide whether to rent an apartment in the city or to buy a house in a suburb.

Considerations	City Apartment	Country House
expense	$350 rent a month	$500 mortgage a month
convenience to job	½ mile away	30 miles away by car
living space	3 rooms	6 rooms
air quality	dirty, unhealthy	clean, healthy
recreation	theaters, movies, museums, etc.	hiking, fishing, gardening, etc.
safety	high crime	low crime

● Discuss the advantages and disadvantages of city life and country life:

I think it's more expensive . . .
It seems to me that it's more convenient to . . .
My guess is that it's more comfortable to . . .
I'm sure it's healthier to . . .
I bet it's more fun to . . .
It might be safer to . . .

● Tell about where *you* live.

How + *Adjectives of Measure*

How	long wide	is			18 feet 6 yards	long.
What's the	length width	of		that room?	It's	12 feet 4 yards	wide.

We use **how** + **an adjective of measure** to ask about the *degree* (large to small, high to low, light to dark) of a specific quality. *Measure phrases* (six feet tall) also express degree.

A Compare the building specifications of Wade Plaza and Tudor Village:

	Wade Plaza	**Tudor Village**
Height (tall)	800 feet	400 feet
Width (wide)	100 feet	200 feet
Length (long)	100 feet	400 feet
Size (big)	200 units	75 units
Value (valuable)	$8 million	$2 million

1 Ask about: *height, width, length.*

S1 What's the *height* of Wade Plaza?
S2 It's 800 feet tall. How high is Tudor Village?
S1 It's 400 feet tall. Wade Plaza is taller than Tudor Village.

2 Ask which is: *bigger; more valuable.*

S1 Which building is bigger?
S2 Wade Plaza is. It has 200 units.
S1 That's more than Tudor Village. It has 75 units.

3 Ask about: *the same* (height); *as* (tall) *as.*

S1 Is Wade Plaza the same *height* as Tudor Village?
S2 No, Tudor Village isn't as tall as Wade Plaza.
S1 Wade Plaza is taller than Tudor Village. They aren't the same height.

cues *width; length; size; value.*

B Can you help some of the tenants with their home improvement projects?

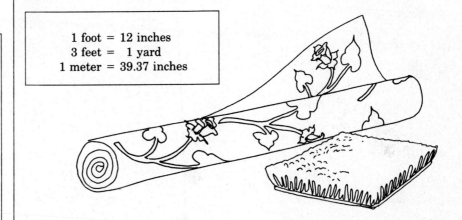

1 foot = 12 inches
3 feet = 1 yard
1 meter = 39.37 inches

1 Carlos has a board which is 7½ feet long. He wants to make three shelves which measure 27 inches each.
The length of the board is _____ feet or _____ inches long.
The length of each shelf is _____ inches long.
Three shelves require _____ inches of board.

● **Is the board long enough to make the shelves?**

2 Paulo wants to put wall-to-wall carpeting in the living room. The room measures 6 meters by 8 meters. He must buy the carpeting in square yards.
The length of the room is _____ inches or _____ feet or _____ yards.
The width of the room is _____ inches or _____ feet or _____ yards.

The area of the room (length × width) is _____ square yards.

● **How many square yards of carpet does Paulo need to buy?**

3 Molly wants to wallpaper her bedroom which is 12 feet long and 10 feet wide. The height of the walls is 9 feet. The room has one door (78″ × 30″) and one window (54″ × 36″). The wallpaper that Molly likes comes in rolls 22 feet long and 18 inches wide.
The area of the walls is _____ square feet *minus* _____ square feet (the area of the window *plus* the area of the door).
Molly needs a total of _____ square feet of wallpaper. The wallpaper comes in rolls of _____ feet long and _____ feet wide.

● **How many rolls of wallpaper does Molly need to buy?**

ONE   Talking about likes and dislikes

Molly and Paulo are trying to forget about the Tudor Village problem, at least for a little while. They are looking at the paper and trying to decide what to do this weekend.

Listen to the tape and look at the newspaper listing. Then complete the conversation as you listen to the tape a second time.

PAULO What about going to the football game at Giants Stadium?

MOLLY Football? Are you kidding? I _____.
How about _____? There's a performance of *Aida* at Lincoln Center.

PAULO No, thanks. You know _____ the opera.

MOLLY All right. Then why _____ to a concert? Ella Fitzgerald is at Carnegie Hall. And Elton John _____ in Central Park.

PAULO Won't the park be crowded and noisy? Well, what _____?

MOLLY Well, I _____ to Carnegie Hall. It's a lot _____ and _____ there.

PAULO Fine. I'd really like to see Ella Fitzgerald. Besides I'm not _____ rock music.

MOLLY Okay. I'll _____ the tickets after work tomorrow. It's my treat.

PAULO Molly, I can't let you _____.

MOLLY Oh, yes you can. You'll pay me back when you help me wallpaper my bedroom.

Role Play: Choose from the weekend activities and make a similar conversation to talk about your likes and dislikes.

Happening This Weekend

Soccer Championship
Cosmos vs T-men
Giants Stadium

Jazz Concert
Ella Fitzgerald
Carnegie Hall

Elton John
Rock Festival
Central Park

Aida
NYC Opera Company
Lincoln Center

Hamlet
Shakespeare
Public Theater

Swan Lake
American Ballet Theater
City Center

I prefer (not) to + V
I'd rather (not) + V
I (don't) really enjoy + N
I'm (not too) crazy about + N

Start with:
"What about going to _____?"

End with:
"I'll pick up the tickets _____."

TWO   Describing a person

Molly is showing a photograph of Paulo to one of her friends at the *City Herald*.

FRIEND He's very handsome. How tall is Paulo?

MOLLY I guess about 6 feet. He's the same height as my brother Jeff.

FRIEND He looks young. You say Paulo's 36?

MOLLY He'll be 37 next month. Paulo's four years older than I am.

Show a photograph of a family member or a friend to your classmate. Practice a similar conversation.

You Are What You Buy

Today's advertisements on television or in magazines promise the consumer a better, happier, and more exciting life. In these ads, we actually see the kind of people who use the product and the style of life which they enjoy. As a lesson in psychology, modern advertising tells us a lot about ourselves.

A popular cigarette ad shows a handsome man dressed in bluejeans, boots, and cowboy hat. With his horse next to him, he is standing in the middle of a quiet place in the American West. Behind him are high mountains and a beautiful sunset. The man is smoking a cigarette. The reader of the ad is invited to come to "Marlboro Country" too. With the purchase of this brand of cigarettes, he can become just as strong and independent as this cowboy who smokes Marlboros, or so the ad promises.

Ads for the new lighter and thinner cigarettes fill the pages of women's magazines. These ads, like the one for Virginia Slims, also carry the message of more independence and freedom for the modern woman. In the Virginia Slims ad, an old-fashioned housewife stands with broom in hand. We also see the same woman today in a silk evening dress with cigarette in hand. The message is clear: "You've come a long way, baby!"

Advertisers give us what we want, and that isn't always information about the product. You and I might not need to buy cigarettes, perfumes, or even a new car, but we do need to feel good about ourselves. Successful ads promise us the dream of a better life, and that's what we buy.

Thinkabout

		True	False
1	Modern advertising uses a lot of techniques from psychology.	____	____
2	Marlboro ads give information about the kind of tobacco in the cigarette.	____	____
3	Women with old-fashioned ideas are attracted to Virginia Slims ads.	____	____
4	Advertisers know that people have dreams about better lives.	____	____

Talkabout

What are the psychological messages of these ads? In your opinion, what kinds of people are attracted to these ads? Why?

Writeabout Expository: Using an example and details to support an opinion.

Write about an advertisement which is popular in your country. Give details from the ad to show why the ad appeals to a man or a woman and what message the ad is giving.

The (TV) advertisement for _____ is very popular in (your country).

←**Start with:**
Identify the ad.

←**Describe the ad:**
What does it say?
What are the actors doing?

←**Give details:**
Why is the product "good?"
What message do people get?

←**End with:**
Give your opinion.

The restaurant was the most expensive one in town, but Susan didn't like it. It was her father's choice, not hers.

Scene One

Preston Wade felt like celebrating. After all, the Tudor Village problem was solved. How could the tenants refuse his offer? Wade didn't care how much it cost. He was going to use his power and money to get what he wanted.

After the press conference, Wade called Kemp into his office. He instructed him to work with the Wade lawyers to buy the apartments from the tenants. Wade was determined to start the building of Wade Plaza by the end of the month. Kemp had to get the tenants to leave Tudor Village or he was out of a job.

It was Wade's idea to invite Kemp to join them for dinner. But Susan was depressed about Jeff and she certainly wasn't in the mood to listen to Kemp and her father talk business all evening. Susan preferred to go to a small quiet place, but the restaurant her father chose was the best and most expensive one in town.

WADE Toast! To Wade Plaza—an old man's dream, now a reality.

KEMP I'll drink to that. Congratulations, Preston. Susan, you're not drinking? This is wonderful champagne.

SUSAN I'm sorry, but I don't feel like celebrating. I keep thinking about all my friends at Tudor Village. What will happen to them if they don't want to leave?

WADE Frankly, Susan, they'd better decide to take my offer. I'm losing my patience with them. Nothing is going to stop Wade Plaza now.

KEMP Forget about those tenants, Susan. They're nothing special.

SUSAN What a horrible thing to say! They're good people, and they're frightened. Didn't you read about all those accidents?

WADE Tudor Village is one of the oldest buildings in the City. The place is falling apart, that's all. It's about time that building was torn down. It's unsafe.

SUSAN I can't help feeling this way. I'm afraid something terrible is going to happen.

KEMP Susan, don't worry about it. Forget about Tudor Village. I'm taking care of it.

SUSAN What do you mean by that?

KEMP Oh, just business. Here, have some champagne. Drink up.

Questions

1 Was Wade in the mood to celebrate? Ask why.
2 Who can lose his job if the tenants don't leave Tudor Village?
3 What kind of restaurant did Wade choose? Ask what Susan preferred.
4 Did Susan get angry at Kemp? Ask what Kemp said.
5 Did Wade have an explanation for the Tudor Village accidents? Ask what it was.
6 Who was worried about the tenants? Ask why.

Scene Two

🔊 Down the street from Tudor Village, there's a bar and grill called the *West End* where all the young people go. You can get sandwiches and beer there. In a booth in the back, Paulo is sitting with Molly. Jeff is with them, but right now he's at the bar getting another pitcher of beer.

Paulo and Molly are concerned about Jeff. Since Jeff last talked with Susan, he hasn't been interested in anything. They're taking him out tonight to cheer him up, but so far all he's talked about is Susan. He's having a hard time understanding her. Jeff can't accept the fact that Susan won't talk to him. His whole world seems to be falling apart. He's been so upset that he's talking about going abroad again.

MOLLY Jeff's been so down these past few days. It's the worst I've ever seen him. I'm getting worried.
PAULO It's natural that he should feel that way.
MOLLY Do you think he'll ever be himself again?
PAULO Oh, of course. Just give him some time. He'll be all right.
MOLLY I hope so.
PAULO You know, Molly, it's time you started thinking of yourself for a change.
MOLLY What do you mean?
PAULO You're always so concerned about other people. What do you want for yourself?
MOLLY Well, I've got my family, and my career. My mother needs me. And Jeff certainly does, especially now.
PAULO Is that all you want out of life? What about me? I want to be part of your life too.
MOLLY Paulo, you are. I care for you deeply. But I've got to think of the family first.
PAULO Never mind about Jeff. You're making a lot of excuses to yourself. Molly, I love you, I want to marry you. We could have a wonderful life in Brazil.
MOLLY Paulo, do you realize what you're asking me to do? I can't give up everything and go away with you. No, it's impossible. It's out of the question.
PAULO The problem with you is that you're afraid of life.
MOLLY That's not true! Don't you see? I don't have a choice. Someone has to take care of this family.

Questions

1 What kind of place is the *West End*? Ask where it is.
2 Is Jeff upset? Ask why.
3 Is Molly worried about Jeff? Ask why Paulo isn't.
4 What's most important to Molly—career, family, or Paulo?
5 What does Paulo want Molly to do? Ask what Molly replied.
6 Did Paulo get Molly to change her mind? Ask about Molly's excuse.

Superlative of Adjectives

| It was a special restaurant. | Of all the restaurants in town, it was | the best.
the finest.
the biggest.
the most expensive.
the least inexpensive. |

When we compare more than two things, we add **-est** to one and two-syllable **adjectives**. Use **most/least** before **adjectives** of more than two syllables.

It was better than the others. It was the best restaurant in town.

A Give your opinion about people in the story.

1 Who has the most interesting career—Paulo, Molly, or Kemp?
2 Who is the friendliest person—Mary, Susan, or Molly?
3 Who has the most pleasant manner—Wade, Paulo, or Carlos?
4 Who is the most emotional person—Jeff, Susan, or Molly?
5 Who has the worst personality—Butch, Spike, or Kemp?
6 Who has the best job—Carlos, Paulo, or Molly?

B The Wades and the Ryans live in New York City, the largest city in the U.S.

● Tell about this city:

What's . . . (the most expensive restaurant)?
cues *expensive restaurant; large department store; tall building; good club; elegant street; bad neighborhood; interesting museum; pretty park; popular tourist attraction.*

C Paulo and Molly are trying to decide which movie to see tonight. They are looking at the reviews in the *City Herald*. Complete the reviews with the correct form of the adjective.

The Critic's Corner

*½ **Crazy Cats** (*Cinema I*)—Probably (bad) film of the summer, with (weak) plot and (terrible) acting I've ever seen on the screen. If you have two hours to waste, this movie is for you!

*** **A Romantic Afternoon** (*Loew's*)—Jacques Monet, one of France's (talented) directors, has once again brought us a winner. Monique Orley is by far (lovely) actress on the screen today. Her performance is (good) than expected, but with a face like that, who cares?

** **Danger Island** (*Center*)—About as (dangerous) as putting your socks on. (exciting) part of the entire film is the opening airplane crash which takes about 30 seconds of the film's three hours. This movie is even (boring) than the popcorn advertisement!

**** **Escape!** (*Star*)—The (interesting) adventure film of the year and not to be missed. John Randolf, as (clever) of all the criminals, gives (good) performance of his career. From start to finish, *Escape!* is (thrilling) than any other film out this year.

● Which of these films would you like or not like to see? Tell why or why not.

cues *the most interesting; the most boring; the best; the worst.*

● Give your opinion:

1 What's the most exciting movie you've ever seen?
2 Who's the most popular actor in films today? the most popular actress?
3 What country makes the best films?
4 What movie has used the most fantastic special effects?
5 What are the five *best* movies of all time? the five *worst* movies?

Possessive Pronouns

Singular Fill up	my your his/her	glass.	Mine Yours His/Hers	is the empty one.
Plural Fill up	our your their	glasses.	Ours Yours Theirs	are the empty ones.

When **possessives** are used independently as **pronouns**, we put stress on them when speaking: *Mine* is empty and so is *yours*.

A After dinner, Kemp is at the check room. He is picking up the coats while Wade is paying the restaurant bill. There is some confusion. Complete this conversation with: *mine, his,* and *hers.*

CLERK This black coat is ___yours___, isn't it?

KEMP No, _____ is brown. It's the one on the right.

CLERK Is this the young lady's fur?

KEMP Yes, that's _____. Now can you find Mr. Wade's coat?

CLERK It must be here. I think this is _____.

KEMP That's right. _____ is the brown tweed one.

● **Describe something you are wearing. Tell about the differences between your shirt (sweater, coat, etc.) and a similar one another classmate is wearing.**

His Hers	is blue too, but	mine yours	has

white buttons and long sleeves.

B Complete the sentences with the missing possessives. Identify the *possessive pronouns.*

1 ___My___ glass is full, but ___yours___ is empty.

2 Mary doesn't want to sell _____ apartment and Carlos doesn't want to sell _____ either.

3 Paulo has _____ career and Molly has _____.

4 We won't sell _____ apartment but the other tenants might sell _____.

5 You might prefer to live in _____ new building, but I'd rather have _____.

6 Molly misses _____ father, but Kemp doesn't seem to miss _____.

7 Kemp finished _____ steak but Susan and her father didn't eat all of _____.

8 Preston Wade has _____ dream and I have _____.

C This is Carlos and Maria's bathroom. Which things are *his? hers? theirs?*

● **Do you have any special things that you don't share with other members of your family?**

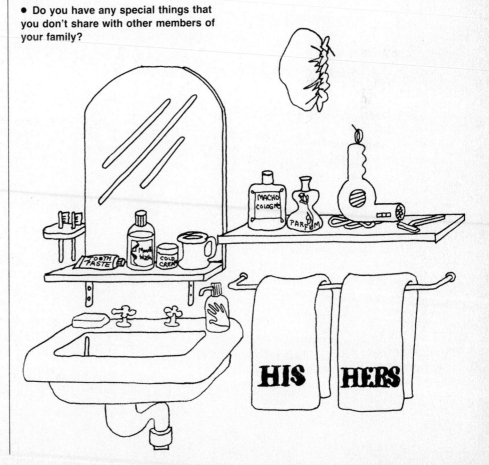

95

ONE   Agreeing and disagreeing with tact

Paulo and Jeff are having a man-to-man talk. It's obvious to Paulo that Jeff is very depressed. Paulo is agreeing with *some* of the things that Jeff is saying but Paulo also is trying to get Jeff to consider *other* points of view.

Listen to the tape. Then complete the conversation as you listen to the tape a second time.

JEFF   Susan is the kindest and most wonderful person I've ever met. She's _____ that's ever happened to me.

PAULO It's certainly true that Susan _____ _____.

JEFF   She's _____ of my life, and now I've lost her.

PAULO I can see that, Jeff, but _____ you've lost her forever. She'll _____ _____.

JEFF   I don't know about that. She's pretty angry _____. Susan's father is _____

_____ than I am. Do you really think she _____ her mind?

PAULO I'm sure of it. I know that Susan is _____ right now, but she _____ very much. Give her some time to think about everything. Don't worry. She'll see what's really _____ .

JEFF   I hope you're right.

Role Play: Practice a similar conversation between Paulo and Carlos. Paulo is telling Carlos about Molly's refusal to marry him. Carlos thinks that Molly will change her mind.

Start with:

PAULO Molly is the smartest and most interesting woman I've ever met.

Agreement	Disagreement with Tact
It's certainly true that . . .	I can see that, but . . .
I'm sure of it.	I don't know about that.
I hope you're right.	I know that _____, but . . .

TWO   Giving strong advice and warnings

Ben Greene is sending Molly to Seattle, Washington to cover a story for the *City Herald*. Mary is helping her daughter pack some clothes for the overnight trip.

MARY You *had better* take my raincoat. It rains pretty hard in Seattle.

MOLLY I probably *should* borrow yours, but mine is lighter. I don't want to wear a heavy coat all day.

MARY You *could* take an umbrella too.

MOLLY I suppose so. But I don't really need it. I'll be gone for only two days.

You are planning a weekend camping trip to the mountains. There are no stores around you and you will have to sleep in tents. Everything you need must be carried on your back.

List the things . . .

you *had better* take with you (absolutely necessary)

you *should* take with you (recommended)

you *could* take with you (not essential)

Decide who can bring these things.

Clothing	Equipment	Miscellaneous
coat	tent	food
jacket	sleeping bag	water
sweater	blanket	matches
rain gear	stove	playing cards
boots	knife	pots & pans
hat	ax	radio
gloves	rope	book
pajamas	compass	beer

Persuading

You are trying to convince your wife (husband, mother, father, etc.) that you need something. It could be a larger apartment, a bigger car, or a better TV set. You get angry during the conversation and the other person agrees to consider your point of view.

Listen to the sample conversations on the tape.

- Act out the conversation between you and the other person. Follow the conversation guide below. Some vocabulary cues are given, but you may choose words of your own.

cues:	You	The Other Person	cues:
Don't you think we need (a larger apartment)? Why don't we get a _____? I thing we should . . .	Make your point.		
		Express surprise.	What do you mean? A (larger apartment)? What's wrong with this _____ / ours? Our (apartment) means a lot to me. But (this apartment) is fine.
It's obvious that (this apartment) is too small / not big enough. I'd rather (live in a larger apartment). Can't you see that . . . ?	Give reasons.		
		Disagree. Tell your preference.	I prefer a smaller _____. I'd rather live / have . . . I'm not crazy about . . . Ours / The one we have is fine.
A (larger apartment) is —more spacious —more comfortable —more luxurious	Argue your point of view.		
		Give reasons for your point of view.	It's more expensive / harder to keep clean / too big for us . . . We can't afford it. We don't have the money to . . . Let me think about it.
That's not true. / You're wrong. That doesn't make sense. Of course we can afford a _____. We have the money to . . .	Get angry.		
		Compromise.	Well, if it means that much to you, we can take a look at . . . Maybe we have the money to . . . Let me think about it.
If you think about it, you'll realize I'm right. You know we really need . . . I still think we should get / buy a new _____.	End the conversation.		We'll see. Let's discuss this later / at another time. You're probably right. / I'm not so sure.

17

17

17

UPTOWN

If Kemp married Susan, he would have Wade's money. Whatever he tries, Kemp can't get Susan to like him.

You're drunk. I think you're disgusting.

Scene One

🔊 It was a long and rather boring evening for Susan. Although the restaurant was lovely and the food was excellent, Susan didn't enjoy herself. There was something about Kemp that Susan didn't like. All through dinner, he kept looking at her. She felt uncomfortable. Each time Kemp filled up his glass, he tried to get Susan to drink some more. She could see that he was getting drunk.

Finally, Wade paid the bill and Kemp went to the parking lot to get the car. When they arrived at the house, Kemp insisted on coming in for another drink. Wade excused himself, and went to his study to make a phone call. Susan sat down on the living room couch; she hoped Kemp wouldn't stay too long. But he walked over to the bar, took out some glasses, and started to pour more drinks.

SUSAN Don't you think you've already had too much to drink?

KEMP It seems to me that you haven't had enough. Here, try some of your father's fifty-year-old brandy.

SUSAN No, thank you. It's rather late and I'm exhausted.

KEMP You know, Susan, I've always thought you were a very beautiful girl. C'mon. Have a drink with me.

SUSAN You're drunk! I think you're disgusting.

KEMP You and I would make a perfect couple. We should get married. Keep Wade Enterprises in the family, so to speak.

SUSAN What? Marry you? I could never love *you*!

KEMP So, you're still thinking about that hippie boyfriend of yours? If I were you, Susan, I would forget about him. Give me a chance. I can give you everything you could ever want.

SUSAN Leave me alone, Kemp, or I'll call my father.

KEMP Your father? What can he do? If I didn't take care of the business, there wouldn't be a Wade Enterprises. Your father needs me, Susan, and you do too.

SUSAN I know what you're like, Kemp. What are you going to do now? Send some of your men after me, like you did to the tenants at Tudor Village?

KEMP You're making a big mistake, Susan.

SUSAN No, you are. Now, get out of here.

KEMP I'm leaving, Susan. But only for now.

Questions

1 Did Susan feel uncomfortable at dinner? Ask why.
2 Where did Wade go after they returned to the house? Ask about Kemp and Susan.
3 Did Kemp pour a drink for Susan? Ask what kind.
4 Why did Susan refuse the drink?
5 Who wanted to marry Susan? Ask why.
6 Is Susan afraid of Kemp?

98

Scene Two

🔊 Spike was reluctant to return to Tudor Village, but Butch persuaded him to go. Butch wanted the money Kemp owed them. If they refused to go back, Kemp wouldn't pay them.

Butch and Spike chose a good night. The area around the building was quiet. No one was in the lobby, not even Carlos, who usually watched the front entrance. It wasn't easy to break the new lock on the basement door, but Butch and Spike managed to do it. Slowly and cautiously, they made their way to the back stairs next to the laundry room. Spike took out a screwdriver. One by one, he loosened the screws which held the stairs together. Butch watched the door at the top of the stairs.

BUTCH Hurry up! I'm getting nervous.

SPIKE I'm working as fast as I can. Some of these screws are pretty rusty. If I had more time, I could get them all out.

BUTCH Make sure you get most of them out. Kemp will be really mad if we don't do this right.

SPIKE Then do it yourself! It's your fault that we came back. If you weren't so greedy, we wouldn't be here now.

BUTCH Keep your voice down. Do you want those tenants to hear us?

SPIKE That's it. I've finished.

BUTCH Good. If I were a tenant, I wouldn't come down these stairs. Whoever steps on them is in for a big surprise.

SPIKE I bet it'll be that super. I wouldn't mind seeing him in the hospital for a while.

BUTCH What was that?

SPIKE I didn't hear anything. Is somebody coming?

BUTCH Shhh. Whew! It's only a cat.

SPIKE C'mon. Let's get out of here. This place gives me the creeps.

Questions

1 Would Kemp pay Butch and Spike if they didn't go back to Tudor Village?
2 How did Butch and Spike get into the building?
3 Where in the basement did they go?
4 Was it easy to remove the screws? Ask why not.
5 What could happen to the first person who used the stairs?
6 What frightened Spike?

Present Unreal Conditional with If

I'm not Susan.	Condition If I were Susan,	Result I would be angry at Kemp. I wouldn't listen to Kemp.
I don't have a rich father.	If I had a lot of money,	I wouldn't want to work. I could quit my job.

The **second conditional** is used when the condition is *not possible* and the result refers to a present or future situation. We regularly use the **past tense** (*were, had, etc.*) in the *condition*-clause and a **present modal** (*would, could, should* + V-stem) in the *result* clause.

A Give your opinion about the story:

1 Wade doesn't know that Kemp is behind the accidents at Tudor Village. If Wade knew, would he say that Tudor Village was unsafe?
2 Kemp isn't an honest man. If Kemp were, would he tell Wade about his gambling debts?
3 Mary doesn't want to move. If Mary did, would she sell her apartment?
4 The police don't have any evidence. If the police did, could they arrest Kemp?
5 Susan doesn't believe Jeff. If Susan did, would she help the tenants?

● **What advice do you have for people in the story?**

1 If you were Susan, would you believe your boyfriend or your father?
2 If you were Jeff, would you try to forget the girl you love and leave town?
3 If you were Molly, would you give up your career to get married?

→ If I were you and I were going to medical school, I would specialize in heart surgery. It's so exciting.

● **Do you have a decision to make?**

cues *choosing a career; moving to another place; buying property.*

B Respond to these situations about people in the story. Then tell about yourself.

1 If Molly doesn't pay the bill, the telephone company will shut off her phone.
If I were Molly, . . .
If I didn't pay my bill, . . .

2 If Paulo takes a vacation, he'll go to Brazil to visit his family.
If I were Paulo, . . .
If I took a vacation, . . .

3 If Jeff goes back to school, he can become a lawyer.
4 If Susan goes shopping, she'll buy a fur coat.
5 If Carlos has time this weekend, he can wallpaper the living room.
6 If Mary cooks tonight, she'll make spaghetti and meatballs.
7 If Jeff buys a new car, he'll get a *Honda*.

C Every week Carlos buys a lottery ticket. He hopes his number will be the winning one. If he were the big winner, he would win a million dollars. If he won, he would buy a luxurious car and take Maria and the kids on a trip to DisneyWorld.

● If you buy this lottery ticket, do you think you'll win $1,000,000?

● If you | were the big winner, | what would you do with the money?
were the big winner, won $1,000,000,

Wh + ever *Clauses and Idioms with* Get

Whoever Whenever someone	stands on the stairs,	— he or she	will get hurt.

Who, when, where, how + ever indicate *any* person, time, place or way *at all*. **Wh + ever** can be part of a noun clause which is the subject or object of the sentence.

A Spike is a rather unpleasant fellow. *Whoever* meets him can't stand him. But Spike can't understand why people don't like him. He is complaining to Butch:

"No matter where I go, people don't talk to me."

→ "*Wherever* I go, people don't talk to me."

● Change these statements to the correct "ever" form:
whenever, wherever, whatever, however.

1 No matter when I say anything, people don't listen.
2 No matter where I sit, people move away.
3 No matter what I do, people complain.
4 No matter how I try, people can't stand me.

Susan is just the opposite. People like Susan because she is such a pleasant person.

● Complete these sentences with the appropriate "-ever" form:

1 Susan makes friends _____ she goes.
2 _____ meets Susan finds her pleasant and friendly.
3 _____ Susan walks into a room, all eyes turn in her direction.
4 Susan looks pretty _____ she's wearing.
5 _____ tired Susan is, she always has a smile on her face.

B Jeff is very angry. He's telling Molly about how he feels about Kemp.

"Whatever I have to do, I'm not going to let Kemp *get away with* this." (escape without consequences)

"However I do it, I'll *get even with* him for all these accidents." (take revenge)

Note these other expressions with **get**:

get across (make easy to understand)
get after (criticize)
get along in years (grow old)
get along with (be friends with)
get by on (manage)
get on with (continue)
get over (recover)
get together (meet)

● Complete these statements with expressions with *get*.

1 Molly thinks that Jeff should make a decision about a career. It's time he *got on with* his life.
2 Spike hasn't got any friends. He doesn't _____ people.
3 Molly doesn't make much money. The family can barely _____ her salary.
4 Maria is always finding fault with Carlos. She _____ him all the time to fix things around the house.
5 Mary doesn't understand why the other tenants want to leave Tudor Village. Molly can't seem to _____ to her that some people prefer to live in a modern building.
6 Jeff can't seem to _____ his break-up with Susan. He hopes they'll be able to _____ soon and talk about it.
7 Mary is nearly seventy. She's _____.
8 So far, Kemp has managed to _____ all his dirty work, but Jeff is determined to _____ Kemp for what he did to the tenants.

● Give your opinion:

1 How much money does a student need in your country to *get by on*?
2 What kind of personality do you have to have to *get along with* other people?
3 What does your wife or husband (mother or father) *get after* you about?
4 What do boys *get away with* that girls don't?

101

ONE Making hypothetical decisions

Preston Wade is a member of the City Emergency Council. He is meeting with the mayor and other leading businessmen. There is a financial crisis. The bottom line of this year's budget ($30 million) must show 25% less spending for next year. The Council must decide which cuts to make and how much to cut.

Listen to the tape and look at the illustration. Then complete the conversation as you listen to the tape a second time.

WADE   I propose that we cut the welfare budget in half. There's a lot of waste there. Those people on welfare could get jobs.

MAYOR   That's _____, Mr. Wade. Most of the people on welfare are _____ or too disabled _____. Besides, there _____.

WADE   The City has to create jobs for people. Why don't we _____ for building projects? New construction means new jobs.

MAYOR   The City can't afford to _____. We have to cut the budget, not _____.

WADE   What about _____? Do we really need _____ for preschoolers and the gifted?

MAYOR   If _____, Mr. Wade, I would _____ the future of this City. We need to train _____ for leadership positions.

WADE   I'm _____. We didn't need those special programs when I went to school. Let's hear what the other Council members have to say.

This Year's Budget

$8,000,000	**Welfare**—aid to the poor, the old, and the disabled
$10,000,000	**Education**—preschool programs, elementary and high school education, special education for the handicapped, the bilingual, and the gifted
$2,500,000	**Fire & Police Departments**—salaries and equipment
$2,000,000	**Transportation**—buses, road repairs
$1,000,000	**Recreation**—public parks maintenance, weekly band concerts, summer program for children, new swimming pool and football field
$700,000	**Libraries**—main building and five neighborhood libraries, three trucks to bring books to the elderly and the disabled
$800,000	**Sanitation**—daily garbage pick up
$3,000,000	**Building Projects**—new city hall and apartments for the elderly
$2,000,000	**Health Care**—medicine and equipment for city hospital, three neighborhood clinics, special program for alcoholics
$30,000,000	**Total**

Role Play: You are all members of the City Emergency Council. Propose a budget for next year with 25% less spending. Tell where and how much *you* would cut the budget.

Be prepared to defend your budget cuts to the class.

TWO Refusing an invitation

Molly wasn't prepared for Paulo's proposal of marriage. In fact, she thinks they have been spending too much time together. When Paulo called that night, he invited her to a movie. Molly didn't say no directly; she gave Paulo this excuse:
"No, really, I can't tonight. I'm exhausted. If I weren't so tired, I'd love to go. Maybe another time."

Extend an invitation to a specific event. Your classmate refuses politely by making an appropriate excuse.

S1 What about going / Would you like to go | to _____ | tonight?

S2 No, really, I can't. I'm | exhausted / busy / going to _____ / doing my _____ | tonight.

If I weren't | so tired, / so busy, / going to _____, / doing my _____, | I'd love to go.

Maybe another time.

Disaster at Sea

A violent storm in the Atlantic Ocean caused a large passenger ship to sink in the freezing water. Twenty of the passengers were able to get into a lifeboat. After a few hours, the passengers realized that the lifeboat was sinking. The lifeboat was very small and there were too many people on board. The boat would certainly sink if some of the passengers didn't get out.

Someone said that two of the heaviest people could jump into the water and hold on to the side of the boat. However, if these people stayed in the freezing water for more than five minutes, they would die. Some of the others suggested a lottery to decide who could stay in the boat and who must go overboard. If everyone drew a lot, they would all have an equal chance to remain on the lifeboat. Another group of passengers believed that it was wrong to make any decision to kill people. If the passengers did nothing, their lives would be in the hands of chance—they could all be saved or they could all die.

After they had discussed each of these options, the passengers were quiet for a very long time. Slowly but surely, the icy water was creeping over the side of the lifeboat. The passengers knew they had to make a life or death decision.

Thinkabout

1 When the large passenger ship sank
  a there was a violent storm.
  b two people were able to get into a lifeboat.
  c the water got very cold.

2 The lifeboat was in danger because
  a there were too many people on board.
  b the passengers couldn't swim.
  c the passenger ship was sinking.

3 If the heaviest passengers were thrown overboard, they could
  a die in the freezing water.
  b hold on to the side of the lifeboat for hours.
  c swim to the shore.

4 The passengers had to make a life and death decision because
  a some of the passengers were dying.
  b it was getting dark.
  c the lifeboat was sinking.

Talkabout

a What options do the passengers have? Can you make any other suggestions?
b Is a lottery a fair way to make a decision? Why or why not?
c Is it right to kill some of the passengers in order to save the others?
d Is there a way to decide whose lives are *the most important*? Suppose you had more information about the twenty passengers, such as:
one of them is the richest man in the world
four are women and six are children
five of them are famous scientists
three of them are over 65 years of age.
Would your opinion change if you knew about the passengers? Why or why not?
e In your opinion, what *should* the passengers decide to do?

Writeabout Expository: Analyzing a situation

Write about what the people in the lifeboat can do. What are their *options*? What might happen if they choose one option or another?

When a passenger ship sank, twenty of the people on board _____. If some of the people didn't _____, then all of the people _____.
These people could _____.
If they _____ then _____.
However, they could also _____. If they _____ then _____.
There is a third option. They could _____. If they _____ then _____.
If I were in the lifeboat, I would _____ because _____.

←Start with:
Describe the situation.
State the problem.

←Possible actions:
Give option #1 / result.

Give option #2 / result.

Give option #3 / result.

←End with:
Choose the best option and give your reason(s).

Jeff was disappointed. Most of the tenants had decided to sell before the meeting started.

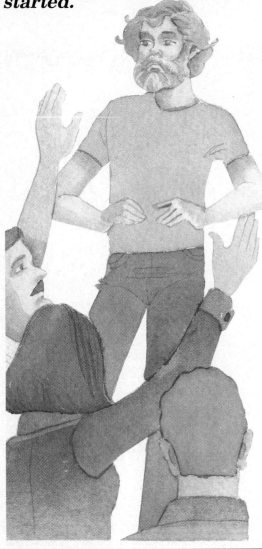

Questions

1 Where were the tenants? Ask why.
2 How did Jeff feel about the other tenants?
3 Were some of the tenants worried? Ask what about.
4 Was Carlos frightened by the accidents at Tudor Village? Ask about the other tenants.
5 Do the tenants think they can stop Wade from building Wade Plaza? Ask what Mary thinks.
6 Did the tenants agree with Mary's suggestion? Ask why.

Scene One

🔊 The tenants were gathered in the Rivera apartment on the tenth floor. Carlos had called the meeting to vote on the sale of Tudor Village to Wade Enterprises. The room was noisy and crowded. Many of the tenants were arguing and shouting at each other. It wasn't going to be easy to make a decision.

Jeff looked around the room. He had known most of these people all his life. If the tenants decided to sell Tudor Village, he wouldn't see many of them again. Jeff felt sad about losing these old friends. He wondered how many of the other tenants felt the same way.

CARLOS Okay. Okay. Let's get the meeting started.
JEFF We're here to vote on whether or not to accept Preston Wade's offer to buy our apartments.
TENANT Do we have a choice? The way I see it, either we get out now, or we live in fear of another accident. I vote we sell and get out of this broken-down building.
CARLOS No, wait a minute! None of us wants to leave. Those weren't accidents we had. Somebody is trying to force us to leave. They're trying to scare us out.
TENANT If I were you, Carlos, I would vote to sell. Aren't you worried about your family? I have a wife and three children to consider. Take my advice! Sell!
JEFF Carlos is right. We've got to find out who's causing all these accidents.
TENANT What's the point of fighting back? We can't stop the building of Wade Plaza. Wade Enterprises is too powerful. We haven't got a chance.
JEFF We shouldn't take a vote now. We need more time to think this over.
TENANT No! Let's vote right now!
MARY I want to say something. Please.
CARLOS Quiet! Quiet! Let Mary speak.
MARY Please. Please. Let's wait until Sunday before we take a final vote. Give Molly and Jeff a chance to find the men who are responsible for these terrible things. If they aren't caught by then, I'll vote for the sale.
TENANT Okay. I guess a few days won't make any difference. We're doing this for you, Mary, because we know how much Tudor Village means to you. But I, for one, won't change my mind, even for you.

Scene Two

📼 The tenants' meeting broke up just before midnight. For the time being, Molly and Jeff had prevented the tenants from voting to sell Tudor Village. But the situation seemed hopeless to them. Most of the tenants were ready to give up. Molly couldn't blame them. What if the next accident in the building hurt one of the children?

It was late when the Ryans returned to their apartment. Mary remembered that she had left some clothes in the washing machine in the laundry room. She didn't want to leave them there all night, so she asked Molly to go with her to the basement. They got off the elevator on the first floor. As they made their way to the back stairs, Mary talked about her life at Tudor Village.

MARY   I get so sad when I think about leaving this place.

MOLLY There are a lot of memories in these old walls, aren't there?

MARY   You know, when you and Jeff were little, I used to come down here late at night. You two were with your father, asleep upstairs. I liked to sit and read the newspaper while the clothes were in the wash.

MOLLY I bet that was the only quiet time you had for yourself all day.

MARY   Molly, something's wrong with the light switch. I think it's broken.

MOLLY Mom, I'm frightened. It's so dark. We can get the wash tomorrow.

MARY   Don't be silly. I know these stairs by heart. I'll just go down to get the clothes. You wait here.

MOLLY Mom, please. I'm worried. Let's go back.

MARY   Oh, it'll only take me a minute. Aaaah!

MOLLY Mom? Mom! Help. Somebody help us!

Questions

1 Could Molly blame the tenants if they decided to sell? Ask why not.
2 Where did Mary and Molly go after the meeting had ended?
3 What did Mary remember about the wash?
4 What did Mary use to do when Molly and Jeff were very young?
5 Was Molly worried? Ask what about.
6 What happened to Mary?

Past Perfect and Reported Speech with Tense Changes

They *say* they	*are* ready to vote.	They *said* they	*were* ready to vote.
	won't vote.		*wouldn't* vote.
	are planning to vote.		*were* planning to vote.
	were certain.		*had been* certain.
	have made a decision.		*had made* a decision.
	decided to sell.		*had decided* to sell.

When the main verb is in the **past** (*said, told, etc.*), we regularly shift the **past** and **present perfect** verbs in the rest of the sentence to the **past perfect tense** (*had* + V-*ed, en*).

 A Tell about the story. What did these people regret they *had done*?

1 MOLLY "I wasn't able to stop Mom from going down the stairs."
→ Molly regretted that she *hadn't been able* to stop her mother from going down the stairs.

2 WADE "I left Susan alone with Kemp."

3 SUSAN "I went to the restaurant with Kemp and my father."

4 JEFF "I wasn't able to get Susan to help the tenants."

5 PAULO "I didn't persuade Molly to marry me."

6 MOLLY "I didn't go down to the basement and get the clothes myself."

7 CARLOS "I haven't been able to catch the men who caused the accidents."

8 SUSAN "I trusted Kemp."

9 CARLOS "I didn't hire a security guard to watch the building."

10 JEFF "I haven't been able to forget about Susan."

11 MARY "I wasn't careful about the stairs."

B Since Susan won't speak to him on the telephone, Jeff decided to send her a note:

• Rewrite Jeff's note to Susan. Practice reported speech:

Jeff told Susan that he _____ to call her last week, but nobody answered. He asked if she _____ his messages. He wrote that he _____ by her house yesterday, but she _____ there. Jeff told Susan that _____ so much. He asked if _____ on Sunday.

> SUSAN,
> I TRIED TO CALL YOU ALL LAST WEEK, BUT NOBODY ANSWERED. DID YOU GET MY MESSAGES? I STOPPED BY YOUR HOUSE YESTERDAY, BUT YOU WERENT THERE. I'VE MISSED YOU SO MUCH. CAN WE GET TOGETHER ON SUNDAY?
> LOVE,
> JEFF

C Change these sentences to reported speech. Be careful of the tense and pronoun changes.

1 Did Wade make a reservation for eight o'clock at a very expensive restaurant? Wade told Susan . . .
→ Wade told Susan that he had made a reservation for eight o'clock at a very expensive restaurant.

2 Can Jeff get Susan to help the tenants? Jeff thought . . .
→ Jeff thought that he could get Susan to help the tenants.

3 Will Molly change her mind about marrying Paulo? Paulo hoped . . .

4 Does Carlos agree to sell his apartment? Mary didn't think . . .

5 Has Susan made up her mind not to see Jeff again? Jeff was afraid . . .

6 Is Kemp responsible for the accidents at Tudor Village? Molly believed . . .

7 Will the police ever catch Butch? Carlos wasn't sure . . .

8 Are the tenants going to accept Wade's offer? Wade expected . . .

9 Have the tenants decided to wait until Sunday for a final vote? Jeff was glad . . .

10 Is Mary going to recover from the fall? Molly hoped . . .

V-ed and V-ing Adjectives

| The dark room frightened Molly. | Molly is *frightened* by the dark room. The dark room is *frightening* to Molly. |

| Jeff is in a bad mood. | He's *depressed* about Susan. The Tudor Village situation is *depressing*. |

We use **v-ed adjectives** to tell about *people*. We use **v-ing adjectives** to tell about *things* or *situations*.

A Complete the sentences about the story with *V-ed* and *V-ing* adjectives.

1 The accidents at Tudor Village *terrified* the tenants. The accidents were _____ to the tenants. The tenants were _____ by the accidents.

2 Kemp's bad behavior *shocked* Susan. Susan was _____ by Kemp's bad behavior. Kemp's bad behavior was _____ to Susan.

3 Paulo's proposal of marriage *surprised* Molly. Molly was _____ by Paulo's proposal. Paulo's proposal was _____ to Molly.

4 Susan's refusal to drink champagne *annoyed* Kemp. Susan's refusal was _____ to Kemp. Kemp was _____ by Susan's refusal.

5 The tenants' decision to sell their apartments *disappointed* Mary. Mary was _____ by the tenants' decision. The tenants' decision was _____ to Mary.

6 Jeff's depression over Susan *distressed* Molly. Jeff's depression was _____ to Molly. Molly was _____ by Jeff's depression.

B After the meeting, Jeff felt very depressed. He and Carlos went to Paulo's apartment. They were in the mood for a cold beer.

I'm feeling . . .		I'm in the mood to . . .
positive	*negative*	go out and celebrate
happy	sad	have a cigarette and relax
terrific	depressed	watch TV
confident	anxious	see a movie
energetic	tired	play a set of tennis
I feel like . . .		**I'm in the mood for . . .**
celebrating	crying	a cold beer
laughing	screaming	a night on the town
relaxing	being alone	pizza

1 How do you usually feel after a long day at school or work? How are you feeling right now?

2 When you're in a good mood, what do you feel like doing?

3 When you're depressed, what aren't you in a mood to do?

● Ask each other about your feelings.

S1 You look like you're in a _____ mood.
S2 Yes, I'm feeling _____. In fact, I'm in the mood for a _____.
or Actually, I'm not feeling very _____ today. In fact, I'm not in any mood to _____. I feel like _____.

C Paulo and Molly are having an argument.

PAULO Do you really think football is boring?
MOLLY Yes, I do. I'm bored by all those rules. I can't imagine anything more boring than a bunch of grown men in those silly clothes chasing a leather ball around a field.

● Use the cues to make questions to ask each other.

1 confusing: English

S1 Do you think English is *confusing*?
S2 Yes, I do. I'm *confused* by all those tenses.
or No, I don't. I'm not *confused* by English. It's easy if you practice the language every day.

2 boring: golf
3 fascinating: politics
4 annoying: babies
5 entertaining: TV
6 irritating: rock music
7 frightening: horror movies

107

ONE   *Considering alternatives*

After the meeting with the tenants, Jeff discussed the situation with Carlos and Paulo. They are trying to decide what to do next.
Listen to the tape, then complete the conversation as you listen to the tape a second time.

CARLOS   We should decide whether to wait for the police to catch those men, or to try to find them ourselves.

JEFF   Do we have _____? The way I see it, either we can _____ or we can _____.

PAULO   What do you mean by that?

JEFF   It's obvious that the police _____. We should tell Wade that _____ Tudor Village.

PAULO   I get it. Then those men _____ to frighten us again.

CARLOS   And _____ to catch them!

JEFF   Right. And they won't _____

this time. We'll prove to the police that Wade Enterprises is _____ at Tudor Village.

PAULO   Let's do it. I prefer to try something _____ sit back and do nothing.

Role Play: Practice similar conversations to discuss:

Molly's choices: to stay with her family and job / to marry Paulo.

Susan's choices: to trust her father / to believe Jeff and Molly.

Kemp's choices: to force the tenants to leave / to wait until they sell.

Use expressions such as:
I have to decide whether to _____ or to _____.
Either I can _____ or else I can _____.
You prefer to _____ rather than _____.

TWO   *Showing disapproval with tact*

At breakfast the next morning, Preston Wade asked Susan about the celebration dinner:

WADE   You didn't enjoy yourself last night, did you?

SUSAN   Well, it wasn't the most exciting evening we've ever had, was it?

We often use tag questions to express mild disapproval in an indirect way. For example, we can use "not interesting" in place of the direct expression "boring."

Indirect / Tactful	Direct / Tactless
It wasn't a very interesting movie, was it? You weren't very interested in the movie, were you? It wasn't the most interesting movie we've ever seen, was it?	What a boring movie! I've never seen such a boring movie in my life! I can't believe how boring that movie was!

Practice short conversations about these situations. Some vocabulary cues are given.

1 Your best friend asks you:
  A new acquaintance asks you: | "Have you ever seen such a crazy movie?"
  cues *exciting; disappointing*

2 Your teacher asks you:
  Your brother asks you: | "Did you enjoy that book I gave you?"
  cues *interesting; boring*

3 Your husband / wife asks you:
  Your boss asks you: | "How did you like the President's speech last night?"
  cues *exciting; disappointing*

Making a decision

You and your friend are trying to decide which vacation to take, perhaps to a big city, to the seashore, or to the mountains. Consider the alternatives your friend proposes; then discuss your preferences.

● Act out the conversation between you and your friend. Follow the conversation guide below. Some vocabulary cues are given, but you may choose words of your own.

🔊 Listen to the sample conversations on the tape.

cues:	You	Your Friend	cues:
Have you thought about / decided about . . . —where we're going to go? —which place we're . . . ? —our vacation?	Ask for a decision.		
		Present alternatives.	Well, either we can go to _____, or to _____. We have to decide whether to _____ or to _____. We have three choices: _____ or _____ or even _____.
Where would you rather go? Which (place) do you prefer? What's your preference?	Ask for preferences.		
		Tell about your dislikes.	I know I don't want to go to _____. I can't stand / hate _____. I'm not crazy about _____. Let's not go to _____.
Me, too. / I agree completely. How about _____? / Let's go to _____. I really enjoy _____. / I love _____.	Agree. Tell what you like.		
		Offer a suggestion.	Instead of _____, why don't we go to _____? Rather than _____, let's _____.
Good idea. / Sounds fine. If we go to _____, we can _____.	Agree. Give reasons for the choice.		
		Agree. Offer your own reasons.	Absolutely, / You're right. Yes, and it's . . . —more enjoyable / interesting at _____. —cheaper / more fun to _____.
I can't wait to _____. What a great trip / vacation!	Express approval about your choice. End the conversation.		It's going to be . . . wonderful / exciting / great fun to _____.
I think so, too. I'm sure we will. We'll have a terrific time. I know what you mean.			I'm sure we're going to . . . have a great time / enjoy ourselves at _____. You bet! / Right. / Sounds great to me!

Butch must have loosened the boards. Carlos wishes Butch were in jail, but he isn't.

Scene One

🔊 It was a long night for Molly and Jeff and their friends as they waited outside the operating room at City Hospital. The doctors had examined Mary briefly in the emergency room before they rushed her into surgery. The x-rays had shown a broken hip and several fractured ribs. Mary was an old woman with a bad heart. The doctors weren't sure that she could survive the operation.

Without telling Jeff, Molly left the waiting room and took the elevator to the lobby of the hospital. She found a telephone booth and dialed Susan's number. When Susan heard what had happened to Mary, she burst into tears. Susan had been unwilling to face the truth. But now she realized that the broken stairs had been no accident. Susan was coming right over to the hospital to be with Jeff and Molly.

Mary was still in surgery when Molly returned. Jeff and Paulo had just brought back some coffee and Carlos had lit another cigarette. All eyes were on the operating room door.

JEFF   I wish the operation were over. It's been three hours since they took Mom into surgery.

PAULO   Why did this have to happen to Mary?

CARLOS   We should have sold the apartments. Then this wouldn't have happened.

MOLLY   I should have been more careful. I knew something was wrong when the light switch was broken. I shouldn't have let her go down those stairs.

JEFF   We've got to stop blaming ourselves.

PAULO   Jeff's right. Your mother is a stubborn woman. You couldn't have told her what to do.

MOLLY   Oh, Paulo. Someone must have done something to the stairs. There was nothing wrong with them before.

PAULO   Molly, we're going to get Wade Enterprises for this. I've talked with the other tenants. They're angry. You know how much they care about your mother. Nobody is going to think about selling until we get those men in jail.

CARLOS   Look, the doctors are coming out of the operating room!

JEFF   Molly, they're smiling! It must have gone well.

MOLLY   She made it, Jeff. Mom's going to be all right! I just know it. Thank God!

Questions

1 Where did the doctors take Mary after they had examined her?

2 Did the doctors expect the operation to be difficult for Mary? Ask why.

3 How did Susan hear about Mary's accident? Ask how Susan felt.

4 Could Molly have prevented Mary's accident? Ask what Paulo thinks.

5 What must have happened to cause Mary's fall?

6 Is Mary going to get better? Ask how Jeff knows.

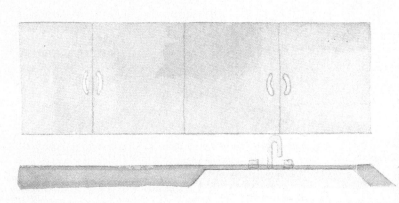

Susan, what are you doing here?

Scene Two

🔊 By the time Mary was out of the recovery room, Susan had arrived at the hospital. She rushed to Mary's room. Jeff and the others were standing around the bed. She was shocked when she saw all the tubes coming out of Mary's body. Mary must have had a terrible time, Susan thought. Mary could have died and it would have been her fault! She could have helped, but didn't.

Susan saw the grief on Jeff's face. Was Jeff ready to forgive her? She had treated him so badly. Susan wouldn't blame him if he never spoke to her again. Just then, Jeff looked up.

JEFF Susan! What are you doing here?

SUSAN Molly called me. I wanted to be with you.

JEFF Well, she shouldn't have. Your father's company is responsible for Mom's accident, Susan. Or don't you believe us?

SUSAN Of course I do. I know that now and I should have helped you when you asked me to. I'm to blame for this.

JEFF No, you aren't. You couldn't have done anything to prevent Mom's accident.

SUSAN I wish I were sure of that. Mary is here now because I didn't help you.

MOLLY Mother had a rough time, but she's going to make it. Susan, we're not going to let Wade Enterprises get away with this.

JEFF We'll get even with Kemp.

SUSAN This time I'm going to help. I can watch Kemp and find out where he's going and what he's planning.

JEFF Susan, Kemp's a dangerous man. Stay away from him.

SUSAN My father will know what to do about Kemp. Don't you see? He has to be told about this.

JEFF Your father trusts Kemp. Don't bother asking for his help. He won't believe that Kemp is behind the accidents.

SUSAN Of course he will. I'm his daughter. He has to listen to me.

Questions

1 Where was Mary when Susan arrived? Ask where Mary had been.
2 What was shocking to Susan?
3 Did Susan blame herself for Mary's accident?
4 Did Susan think she could have helped the tenants? Ask how.
5 Did Jeff want Susan to spy on Kemp? Ask why not.
6 Did Susan expect her father to help the tenants? Ask what Jeff expected.

Must Have, Could Have, Should Have—*Past Modals*

Jeff concludes that someone *must have loosened* the boards.

Molly feels responsible because she *shouldn't have let* her mother go down the stairs.

Susan believes that she *could have helped* Jeff, but she didn't.

We use **must have** (assumption), **could have** (possibility) and **should have** (obligation) when speaking in the *present*, but referring to a *past* situation. The **past tense** of **must/have to** (necessity) is **had to**; **must have** does not refer to necessity.

A Read each situation about the story. Then choose from the two options to complete the statements with *must have* and *could have*.

1 Molly refused to marry Paulo.
   Paulo *must have* . . .
   Molly *could have* . . .
   a been disappointed.
   b accepted his proposal.

2 The doctors rushed Mary into surgery.
   Mary *must have* . . .
   Mary *could have* . . .
   a died without the operation.
   b had a serious fall.

3 Molly called Susan from a phone booth in the hospital lobby.
   Molly *must have* . . .
   Susan *could have* . . .
   a refused to listen to her.
   b told her about Mary's accident.

4 The light switch at the top of the stairs was broken.
   Butch *must have* . . .
   Mary *could have* . . .
   a gotten the laundry another time.
   b cut the wires.

5 When Susan found out about Mary's accident, she rushed to the hospital.
   Jeff *must have* . . .
   Molly *could have* . . .
   a told him she had called Susan.
   b been surprised to see Susan.

B Give your opinion about the story. What *should have* or *shouldn't have* these people done? Give reasons for your opinion.

1 Molly feels responsible for her mother's accident.
→ Molly thinks she should have been more careful. She shouldn't have allowed her mother to get the laundry.

2 Susan blamed herself for Mary's accident.

3 Wade left Susan alone with Kemp.

4 Kemp stole thousands of dollars from Wade Enterprises.

5 Molly called Susan without Jeff's permission.

C This is today's *City Herald*. Describe the accident and the conditions which caused it to happen.

• Tell about someone you know who has had a serious accident:

What *must have caused* the accident? Who *could have prevented* the accident?

• Was anyone to blame for the accident?

What *should* or *shouldn't* this person *have done*?

Present Wishing

Carlos wishes (that)	Mary *didn't need* an operation (but she does). Mary *weren't* so ill (but she is). Mary *could leave* the hospital soon (but she can't).

We use **wish** statements to express a condition that is not true. The **past tense** (*didn't need, weren't*, etc.) is used with *wishing* about *present* situations.

A Tell about the story. What are these people thinking about?

1 The Ryans won't sell their apartment. Wade wishes . . .
→ Wade wishes that the Ryans would sell their apartment.

2 Susan can't forget about Jeff. Kemp wishes . . .
3 Wade's wife is dead. Wade wishes . . .
4 Molly won't marry Paulo. Paulo wishes . . .
5 Mary has a bad heart. The doctors wish . . .
6 Spike is afraid of Kemp. Spike wishes . . .
7 Kemp won't leave Susan alone. Susan wishes . . .
8 Susan blames herself for Mary's accident. Jeff wishes . . .

● Do you wish you could change your *present* situation?

1 I wish I were living . . .
2 I wish I owned . . .
3 I wish I knew how to . . .
4 I wish I could travel to . . .
5 I wish I had the time to . . .
6 I wish my (father) would . . .
7 I wish the leader of my country would . . .
8 I wish I were . . .

B Compare these statements with *wish* and *hope.* Then complete the sentences about the story.

> Molly *wishes* that Mary *didn't need* the operation. (impossibility)
> Molly *hopes* that the operation *will be* a success. (some possibility)

1 The doctors wish that Mary ___(not have)___ a heart condition. They hope that she ___(survive)___ the operation.
2 Wade wishes that the tenants ___(be)___ ready to sell their apartments. He hopes that they ___(move)___ out of Tudor Village soon.
3 Paulo wishes that Molly ___(not smoke)___ so much. He hopes that she ___(want)___ to give up smoking someday.

4 Kemp wishes that Susan ___(like)___ him more. He hopes that she ___(forget)___ about Jeff.
5 Molly wishes that Butch ___(be)___ in jail. She hopes that the police ___(catch)___ him soon.

C While Jeff was waiting outside the operating room, he thought about his life. He wasn't very pleased with himself. He made a list of all his negative characteristics. Then he made a list of "resolutions"—all the things he needed to do to change his life:

NEGATIVE CHARACTERISTICS
IRRESPONSIBLE
LAZY
STUBBORN
INCONSIDERATE
BITTER AND ANGRY
UNTRUSTING
IMPATIENT

RESOLUTIONS
GET A JOB
DO HOUSEHOLD CHORES
LISTEN TO MOLLY'S ADVICE
FORGET ABOUT THE PAST
MAKE MORE FRIENDS
KEEP TEMPER UNDER CONTROL

● Tell:
what Jeff regrets about his past actions.
what Jeff wishes to change about himself.
what Jeff hopes to do from now on.
→ Jeff should have gotten a job. He wishes that he weren't so irresponsible. He hopes that he will get a job soon.

● What don't you like about yourself?
What do *you wish* you could change about yourself?
What do *you hope* you will be like/do in the future?

ONE   Reassuring others

Susan was shocked when she saw Mary in the hospital bed. It was frightening to see all the machines and tubes coming out of the old lady's body. Susan went over to talk to Mary.

Listen to the tape, then complete the conversation as you listen to the tape a second time.

SUSAN   Mary. It's me, Susan. I came to see you as soon as I heard about the accident.

MARY   Oh, Susan. Is that you? I feel _____. I _____ a mess!

SUSAN   Nonsense, Mary. You _____. You're just a little tired _____. That's all.

MARY   I'm so afraid of hospitals, Susan. My husband died _____ 15 years ago. I just wish _____ right now.

SUSAN   Don't worry, Mary. You'll be up and around in no time. You just need _____ for a few days.

Later, Susan is talking to Jeff.

SUSAN   Oh, Jeff. Mary _____! It's amazing that she survived that operation.

JEFF   I know. She was lucky. The doctor said she _____ on the operating table.

Role Play: Practice short conversations about each situation, then explain why you chose or didn't choose to tell "little white lies."

1 Professor Cooper, the chairman of Paulo's department, invited Molly and Paulo for dinner. Molly didn't enjoy herself, and neither did Paulo. As she's leaving the house, Molly says to Professor Cooper and his wife. . . .
Later, Molly and Paulo are discussing the Coopers' dinner party. Molly says to Paulo . . .

2 Molly is showing her new dress to her boss, Ben Greene. Ben hates it. Ben says to Molly . . .
Molly is showing the same dress to Jeff. Jeff hates it and he says to Molly . . .

Do you ever tell "little white lies" to make people feel better?

Truth / Direct	Little White Lies / Tactful
What an ugly shirt!	It's an interesting design (fabric, color).
Look at that terrible haircut!	It's very stylish (fashionable, modern).
Wasn't that a boring party!	We had a lovely (very nice) time.
Those were the dullest people I've ever met!	It's always fun (enjoyable, interesting) to meet new people.

TWO   Blaming yourself

Jeff is thinking about his life since he went to fight in Vietnam. He's thinking about what he could have done: "After I had gotten out of the army, I should have gone back to law school. I wish I were a lawyer now. I could have been, but I'm not. I've wasted a lot of time."

- Do you blame yourself for what you *could have done* or *should have done* in a particular situation? Tell about a decision you made or something that happened to a friend of yours.
- What do your classmates think you or your friend could have done? should have done?

Mercy-killing and the Law

Three years ago, Sylvia Mason, 65, found out that she had cancer. Sylvia's doctors tried x-ray treatment, chemotherapy, and many experimental drugs, but there was nothing that they could do to save Sylvia's life. Sylvia knew that she had only a few months to live.

Sylvia went into City Hospital under the care of Dr. Richards. Dr. Richards knew that Sylvia couldn't live more than three or four months. He saw that she was in terrible pain. He knew that if he gave Sylvia an extra dose of morphine, she would die sooner.

One day, when Sylvia was in one of her calm periods, she asked Dr. Richards to help her. She told him that she didn't want to suffer from the pain any longer. Would he give her enough morphine to kill her? Dr. Richards considered Sylvia's request. He knew that mercy-killing was against the law. But he made his decision: he gave Sylvia the extra dose of morphine which ended her life.

By chance, Sylvia's husband walked into the hospital room just as Dr. Richards finished. It was too late to prevent Sylvia's death. Sylvia's husband knew about his wife's desire to end her life, but he was against her decision. Sylvia's husband reported Dr. Richards to the police.

Dr. Richards is on trial for murder, which carries a punishment of death. Dr. Richards admits he killed Sylvia Mason but he believes that he did the right thing. *Should* the jury decide to put Dr. Richards in jail, or to let Dr. Richards go free?

Thinkabout

		True	False
1	Sylvia could have lived for three more years but she decided to end her life.	___	___
2	Sylvia's husband would have given his wife the morphine but he didn't have the opportunity.	___	___
3	Dr. Richards could have obeyed the law against mercy-killing, but he didn't.	___	___
4	Sylvia's husband could have prevented his wife's death, but he didn't.	___	___

Talkabout

You are the jury who must decide the Dr. Richards mercy-killing case.
1 Could Sylvia have taken her own life?
2 Would you have made Sylvia's decision?
3 Would you have reported Dr. Richards to the police?
4 Should Dr. Richards have granted Sylvia's request to end her life?
5 Should Dr. Richards be given the death penalty *or* be put in jail *or* set free?

Writeabout Expository: Presenting an argument

Write a composition about the doctor's action in the mercy-killing situation. In your *first* paragraph, describe the doctor's point of view and give his decision. In your *second* paragraph, agree or disagree with the doctor's decision. Give at least three reasons to support your point of view. In your concluding sentence, decide to support or not to support a law which allows mercy-killing.

Dr. Richards was faced with a difficult situation. An old woman was in great pain and she was dying _____

Finally, the doctor decided to _____.

The doctor should(n't) have _____. In the first place, _____. Then we have to consider that _____. Also, _____.

I would support a law which permits / prohibits mercy-killing because a man like Dr. Richards should(n't) be punished.

←Start with:
Describe the situation.
Tell what the doctor did.

←Support your point of view:
Reason #1
Reason #2
Reason #3

←End with:
State your opinion.

20

Nothing Susan said made sense to Wade. Susan noticed her father looking at her untidy appearance.

Scene One

🔊 By the time Susan got back from the hospital, her father had just finished breakfast. When Wade first saw Susan, he was puzzled. His daughter looked a mess: her clothes were wrinkled, her hair wasn't combed, and her eyes were red and puffy. Wade concluded that Susan must have been out all night. It was a shock for him to see his daughter in this condition. He had trusted Susan, and he hadn't expected his daughter to betray that trust.

SUSAN Daddy, I'm so glad you're still home. I've got to talk to you.

WADE You've been out with that Jeff Ryan, haven't you?

SUSAN Yes, I just left him. Something terrible has happened.

WADE What did that hippie do to you? Susan, tell me!

SUSAN No, no. You don't understand. It wasn't like that. I was at the hospital.

WADE The hospital? Are you all right? Did he try to hurt you?

SUSAN Daddy, listen. It's not what you think. I'm fine. I think I love Jeff. But that's not what I want to tell you.

WADE Love? What do you know about love? You're just a child! When I get home tonight, we're going to sit down and talk about this.

SUSAN Daddy, please listen! I have to talk to you *now*.

WADE There's nothing more to say. I absolutely forbid you to see Jeff Ryan again. It's late. I have to leave for the office now, but you'd better be here when I get home.

Questions

1 Had Wade left for the office by the time Susan returned to the house? Ask where he was.

2 Was Wade pleased when he saw Susan's appearance? Ask how he felt.

3 Had Susan been out all night? Ask who she was with.

4 Did Susan tell her father where she had been all night?

5 Did Wade think that Susan was old enough to be in love?

6 Did Susan tell her father about Mary Ryan? Ask why not.

Scene Two

I want to get rid of Tudor Village completely.

📼 It took a while before Susan realized what had happened. Her father hadn't even given her a chance to explain. She had promised Jeff that her father would help them, but now it was all a terrible misunderstanding.

Susan was suddenly very tired so she went upstairs to lie down for a while. When she woke up, it was late afternoon. She took a shower, got dressed, and took a cab to her father's office. This time Susan was going to make him listen.

But her father wasn't there and the receptionist had left too. Susan could hear a voice coming from her father's office. When she recognized it, she hesitated. Without a sound, she picked up the phone on the receptionist's desk.

BUTCH What's the rush, Kemp? I thought those tenants were going to sell. Why don't you just pay them the money?

KEMP Thanks to you two, those tenants are still there. They won't even vote on the sale until that old lady is out of the hospital.

BUTCH Look, Kemp. We did just what you told us. We thought you wanted someone to get hurt.

KEMP Okay, okay. But I'm sick of waiting around. I want to get rid of Tudor Village completely.

BUTCH Wait a minute . . .

KEMP I mean *completely*. As soon as it gets dark, we're going over to Tudor Village. I want you and Spike to get some gasoline.

BUTCH Hey, Kemp. I don't know about this. You're going to burn down the place, aren't you? That's murder, Kemp.

KEMP Nah. Just listen. We'll go up the fire escape to the roof. If we set fire to the roof, the tenants will have time to get out but there'll be so much damage to the building that they'll have to sell.

BUTCH That's what I like about you, Kemp—your concern for other people.

KEMP That's right, Butch. I've got a big heart.

BUTCH Yeah, it's about as big as Spike's brain.

Questions

1 Did Susan try to find her father? Ask when.
2 Did Susan hear Kemp talking? Ask where.
3 How did she hear Kemp's conversation with Butch?
4 Did Kemp want to wait for the tenants to sell? Ask what his plan is.
5 Who's going to get the gasoline? Ask why.
6 Does Kemp really care about the tenants' safety?

Notice + *Noun/Pronoun* + *V-ing—Verbs of Perception*

Susan	noticed heard discovered	Kemp him	sitting at her father's desk. talking to Butch on the telephone. planning to burn down Tudor Village.

We regularly use the **noun/pronoun** + V-ing pattern after these special verbs to show that an action is observed while it is in progress: *catch, discover, feel, find, hear, notice, observe, see,* and *watch.*

A Complete these sentences about the story. Tell what each person learned or didn't learn by direct experience.

1 Was Kemp or Wade talking to Butch? Susan heard . . .
2 Were the doctors examining Mary or Susan? Molly observed . . .
3 Was Wade or Susan hiding behind the door? Kemp didn't notice . . .
4 Was Jeff or Carlos holding Susan's hand? Molly saw . . .

5 Was Susan leaving or coming home at 8 A.M.? Wade discovered . . .
6 Were Butch and Spike loosening the stairs in the basement or in the lobby? Carlos didn't catch . . .

B Molly is in Ben Greene's office. They are discussing a story that Molly is working on. It's about a bank robbery that occurred that morning. The police have arrested one of the men and charged him with the crime. Ben is going over the facts of the case with Molly.

• Complete the conversation with the correct form of the verbs:

BEN   How many men were involved in the hold up?
MOLLY The guard _____ three men _____ the bank together. (enter/observe)
BEN   _____ the guard _____ them _____ for the money? (ask/hear)
MOLLY No, only the bank teller did. She was scared, so she did what they asked. After she gave them the money, she pressed the alarm button.
BEN   Who _____ them _____ the bank? (see/leave)
MOLLY The guard did. The men were walking out the front entrance when the alarm went off. He _____ a man _____ a sack of money and two others _____ guns. (carry/point/notice)
BEN   Did the guard go after the men?
MOLLY Yes, and he fired a few shots at them. One of the bullets hit the

man with the money. The guard _____ him _____ on the sidewalk. (find/lie)
BEN   What about the other two?
MOLLY The guard _____ them _____ into a green pick-up truck. (get/watch) He _____ them _____ down Broadway. The police are looking for the truck now. In fact, the man took down the license number of the truck. (turn/see)
BEN   Good. Write all of this up, Molly. We've got to make the 2 o'clock deadline for the evening edition.

C Read these situations. Tell about a personal experience.

1 Has anyone ever tried to rob you? Did you notice a stranger standing next to you? Did you feel the person touching your coat? Did you catch the thief taking your wallet?

2 Have you ever seen an accident? Did you hear the cars crashing? Did you watch the police questioning the drivers? Did you see the ambulance taking someone to the hospital?

Nobody, Nothing—*Negative Quantifiers*

There isn't
anybody at home.
anything to eat.
anywhere to go.

There's
nobody at home.
nothing to eat.
nowhere to go.

The **pronoun quantifiers** *neither, none, nobody, no one* and *nothing* substitute for noun phrases and are regularly followed by singular verbs.

Molly and Jeff are at the hospital. *Neither* is at home.
All of the tenants are angry. *None* of them wants to sell.

A Tell about the story. Complete the sentences with the correct negative quantifier.

1 The tenants are angry about Mary's accident. *Nobody/nothing* is going to think about selling until Kemp is put in jail.

2 Wade won't let Susan explain. There's *none/nothing* to talk about. Wade won't permit Susan to see Jeff again.

3 When the tenants started their meeting, there was *nothing/nowhere* wrong with the stairs.

4 All of the tenants were at the meeting. *No one/neither* saw Butch and Spike entering the basement door.

5 *None/neither* of the tenants knew that someone was in the basement.

6 Mary has a mind of her own. *Nobody/none* could have stopped her from going down those steps.

7 There was *nothing/nobody* that Molly and Jeff could do but hope for Mary's recovery.

8 Molly was running out of cigarettes and there was *nothing/nowhere* to buy any in the hospital.

9 Susan and Jeff looked into each others' eyes. *None/neither* spoke for a long time.

10 Molly had to go to the lobby to call Susan because there was *nobody/nowhere* to find a telephone near the operating room.

B When Jeff worked abroad, he lived in a little town in the middle of nowhere. It was so dull there that he left after a few weeks. Jeff was so bored that he complained all the time:

There was *nowhere to go* at night. There wasn't even a bar or a movie theater.

There was *nothing to eat* that I liked. You couldn't even get fresh fruit.

There was *nobody to talk to*. I couldn't speak the language and nobody spoke English.

There was *nothing to do*. If you wanted to read, you couldn't buy even a newspaper.

● Change the underlined words to the negative form:

> Nov. 19
> HI!
> YOU WOULDN'T BELIEVE THIS
> PLACE. THERE ISN'T <u>ANYTHING</u>
> TO DO AND <u>NOT ONE PERSON</u> TO
> TALK TO. I'M GOING CRAZY.
> <u>NOT ONE</u> OF THE OTHER MEN
> SPEAKS ENGLISH. MY BOSS
> SPEAKS A LITTLE FRENCH, BUT
> WE REALLY HAVEN'T <u>ANYTHING</u>
> TO SAY TO EACH OTHER. THIS
> IS A PRETTY DULL TOWN. <u>NO</u>
> <u>PLACE</u> I'VE EVER BEEN IS AS
> BAD AS THIS. MAYBE IT'S TIME
> I CAME HOME.
> LOVE,
> JEFF
>
> MARY + MOLLY RYAN
> TUDOR VILLAGE
> 495 RIVERSIDE DRIVE
> NY, NY, 10025
> USA
>
> PER VIA AEREA
> · PAR AVION ·

● What's the dullest place you have ever been to? Tell why you were so bored there.

Was there:
anywhere to go?
anything to do?
anything to eat?
anybody to talk to?

ONE   Making observations

The doctors have just examined Mary. Molly watched them taking her pulse and checking the incision. She saw one of the doctors reading Mary's chart. Molly heard the doctors talking, but she didn't understand what they were saying. Later, Molly asked Mary's doctor about her progress:

Listen to the tape, then complete the conversation as you listen to the tape a second time.

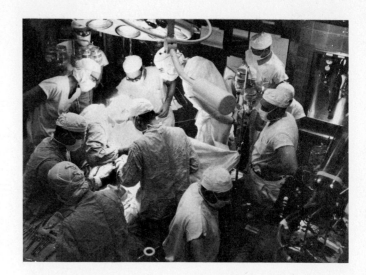

MOLLY   How is she doing, doctor?

DOCTOR   Better than _____, Miss Ryan.

MOLLY   I saw you _____ her pulse. How is her blood pressure?

DOCTOR   It's _____, but we have it under control. She's responding well to the medication _____.

MOLLY   I noticed _____ the incision. Is there anything wrong?

DOCTOR   Absolutely _____. It's healing perfectly. We _____ to take the stitches out in a few days.

MOLLY   How long _____ in the hospital?

DOCTOR   Your mother had a pretty bad fall. In my judgment, she _____ at least four weeks. She needs a lot of rest right now.

MOLLY   Doctor, you don't know my mother. No _____ can make that woman sit still for four weeks! You'll see.

Role Play: Jeff wasn't at the hospital when Molly talked to the doctor. Practice a short conversation between Molly and Jeff.

Jeff wants to know:
what the doctors found in their examination.
what the doctor said about Mary's progress.
when Mary is expected to leave the hospital.

Start with:
JEFF   What did you see the doctors doing?

TWO   Offering suggestions

Jeff is worried about Molly. Lately she has been spending most of her time at the hospital or at home alone. Jeff is trying to get Molly to go out and enjoy herself.

JEFF   What are you doing tonight after visiting hours?

MOLLY   I'm going home to do some work.

JEFF   Why don't you go to a movie instead? There's a terrific French movie at the *Strand*. If I were you, I would definitely see it.

MOLLY   It sounds like fun, but I really have to work tonight.

Ask each other about your plans for tonight. S2 gives his / her present plans; S1 offers a suggestion.

S1 What are you doing tonight?

S2 I'm _____ tonight.

S1 Why don't you _____ instead? If I were you, I would _____.

Expressing anxiety

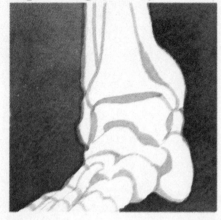 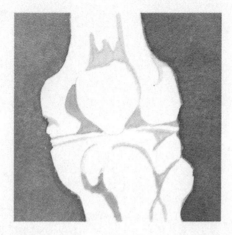 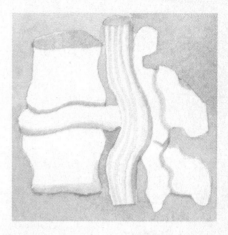

You are in the doctor's office. Perhaps you have a broken ankle, a bad knee, or a slipped disc in your back. Your doctor has just finished examining you and you are discussing the treatment.

🔊 **Listen to the sample conversations on the tape. Act out a similar conversation between you and your doctor.**

cues:	You	Your Doctor	cues:
How bad is my (ankle)? What did the tests / x-rays / examination show? Do you know what's wrong with my (ankle)?	Ask what the problem is.		
		State the problem.	It looks like a broken / fractured bone (a slipped disc). It's your ankle; it's (broken).
What seems to be the matter / the problem with my _____? What do you mean there's a (broken bone) in my _____?	Ask for more information.		
		Explain the problem.	The x-rays (tests / examination) shows . . . —a break in your _____. —a weakness in your _____.
That sounds bad / serious! Will I need . . . —an operation? —to go into the hospital? —more tests?	Express surprise / concern.		
		Explain the treatment.	You'll need surgery / an operation to fix your _____. I'm going to put you in the hospital today / next . . .
Is it dangerous / difficult / expensive? How (dangerous) is the surgery / operation?	Express anxiety / great concern.		I recommend surgery as soon as possible / right away.
		Reassure the patient.	This operation is very successful / routine. We've had great results with . . .
How long will the (operation) last? How long will I be in the hospital / out of work? How long does it take to get over a (broken ankle)?	Ask about your stay in the hospital.		There's nothing to worry about / to get concerned over.
		Give details.	The (operation) takes about ___ hours. Most people need about _____ weeks to recover / get over a (broken ankle). You'll be home / walking again in _____ days / _____ weeks.
Okay. / I guess I have no choice. I hope everything will be all right. I know the operation will be successful / work out okay.	End the conversation.		If I were you, I wouldn't worry. I'm sure everything will be fine.

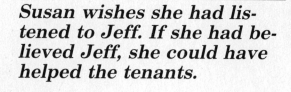

Susan wishes she had listened to Jeff. If she had believed Jeff, she could have helped the tenants.

Scene One

🔊 Susan hid behind the door so Kemp didn't see her when he left the office. Susan was scared. Her first thought was to call Jeff. The tenants had to be warned. She dialed the Ryans' number and waited, but no one answered. Frantically, she looked up Carlos's number in the telephone directory. The phone kept ringing and ringing. Susan was about to hang up when Carlos answered.

CARLOS Hello?

SUSAN Carlos, you've got to do something! Kemp is planning to set fire to Tudor Village. I heard him talking to someone about it.

CARLOS Calm down, Susan. Tell me what you know. Slowly.

SUSAN I can't remember all the details, but I do remember that they're going to get some gasoline. It's terrible!

CARLOS Susan, where's Kemp now?

SUSAN He left here a few minutes ago. I don't know. He must be on his way to Tudor Village.

CARLOS Susan, I want you to go home and stay there, where it's safe. I'll phone Jeff and Paulo at the hospital. We'll get the police.

SUSAN Isn't there anything I can do? I feel so helpless.

CARLOS No, Susan. It's going to be dangerous.

SUSAN Carlos, please. Oh, if I had only listened to Jeff, then I could have helped before. I have to do something now.

CARLOS There's nothing you can do, Susan. Believe me.

SUSAN I could have stopped all this long ago. I wish I hadn't been so stupid.

CARLOS Stop blaming yourself, Susan. We'll catch them, and this time, we'll have enough evidence to put Kemp in jail.

Questions

1 If Kemp had looked behind the door, who would he have found?
2 What will happen if Susan doesn't stop Kemp?
3 Did Susan know Carlos's number by heart? Ask how she got it.
4 Did Susan remember everything Kemp had said? Ask what she forgot.
5 Where did Carlos tell Susan to go? Ask what Carlos is going to do.
6 Does Susan wish she could have stopped Kemp? Ask why she didn't.

Scene Two

🔊 Susan knew that she ought to go home, but she couldn't. She felt that she was partly responsible and she wished that she had believed Jeff at the beginning. If she had helped him then, she probably could have found some evidence to connect Kemp with the trouble at Tudor Village.

Susan tried hard to remember what Kemp had said. The fire escape—that was it! Kemp was going to set *the roof* on fire. But the tenants would probably look for Kemp in the basement! Susan had to warn them that he would be on the roof.

She couldn't wait for her father to return to the office so she left him a note telling him about Kemp's plan. It took Susan quite a while to find a taxi. When one finally came, she jumped in and gave the driver the address of Tudor Village.

When Susan arrived, there weren't any lights in the windows of the Ryan or Rivera apartments. She walked around the side of the building, looking for Carlos.

BUTCH Grab her!

SUSAN Stop it. Let me go!

KEMP Don't hurt her. Susan, what are you doing here?

SUSAN I know what you're up to, Kemp.

KEMP What do you mean? We're here to . . . uh . . . look at the building. Your father wants us to . . . uh . . . look it over for him.

SUSAN You're lying! Then what do you need those cans of gasoline for?

BUTCH She knows, Kemp. We can't let her go. She'll warn the tenants.

KEMP He's right, Susan. I'm sorry, but you're coming with us. Spike, tie her hands behind her back.

BUTCH Give me your handkerchief, Kemp. We've got to keep her quiet.

SUSAN Take your hands off me! Help! Help!

SPIKE But, boss, what are we going to do with the girl?

KEMP Butch, give me a hand with this fire escape.

Questions

1 Did Susan follow Carlos's advice? Ask where Susan went.
2 What could have happened if Susan had helped Jeff at the beginning?
3 What did Susan leave for her father? Ask why.
4 Was Kemp surprised to see Susan? Ask what he said.
5 Did Susan know that Kemp was lying? Ask why.
6 Where is Kemp going? Ask about Susan.

Past Unreal Conditional with If

	Present Condition	Result
Type 1	If Mary gets through the operation,	she'll need time to recover.
Type 2	If you were Kemp,	would you set the roof on fire?

	Past condition	Result
Type 3	If Molly had gone down the stairs,	she would have been hurt.

The *third* **conditional** is used when the condition is *not possible* and *unreal* and the result refers to a *past* situation. We regularly use the **past perfect** in the *if-* clause and a **past modal** in the *result* clause.

A These events *actually happened* in the story. Guess what *could have happened* instead.

1 Both Molly and Mary went down to the basement to get the clothes in the washing machine. It was Mary who fell.
If Molly had gone down the stairs, . . .

2 Molly and Jeff rushed Mary to the hospital. Mary is alive today because they got her there as fast as they did.
If Jeff and Molly hadn't gotten Mary to the hospital so fast, . . .

3 The police weren't able to find Butch and put him in jail. Butch loosened the boards on the basement stairs.
If the police had caught Butch a week ago, . . .

4 Carlos told Susan to go home where it was safe, but she decided to go to Tudor Village instead.
If Susan hadn't gone to Tudor Village to look for Jeff, . . .

● **Give your opinion.**

1 If you had gone down to the basement at midnight and had noticed the broken light switch, would *you* have gone to get the clothes?

2 If you had been out all night, would *you* have called your father so that he wouldn't worry about you?

3 If you had remembered the plan to set fire to the roof, would *you* have gone to Tudor Village or would *you* have called the police?

4 If you had seen Kemp and the others with the cans of gasoline, would *you* have told Kemp that you knew about his plan?

B Complete these statements about the story with the correct conditional form.

1 If Wade (listen) to Susan, he probably would have agreed to help the tenants.

2 Would you want to set fire to Tudor Village if you (be) Kemp?

3 If Carlos (hurry), he'll find Jeff before he leaves the hospital.

4 Could Molly have stopped her mother from going down the stairs if she (try)?

5 If Kemp (not have) gambling debts, he could wait for the tenants to sell their apartments.

6 Will the tenants have time to get out of the building if Kemp (set) fire to the roof?

7 If Susan (not hear) Kemp's voice, she would have walked into the office where Kemp was on the telephone with Butch.

8 If Mary (have) a stronger heart, she would have a better chance for recovery.

9 Would Susan have had to go to Tudor Village if she (remember) all the details about Kemp's plan?

10 Will Kemp kill Susan if she (try) to escape?

C Wade has a dream. He wants to build Wade Plaza so the people of New York can remember him as a great man. What important contributions to history have these people made?

1. Columbus
2. Gandhi
3. Queen Victoria
4. Einstein
5. Beethoven

● **Ask each other:**

S1 If you had been Columbus, what would you have done?

S2 If I had been Columbus, I would have discovered a new land.

S3 If you had been Columbus, would you have sailed west?

S4 If Columbus hadn't sailed west, he wouldn't have discovered a new land.

● **Tell about famous people in *your country's* history.**

Present Wishing about the Past

Molly wishes (that)	the police *could have caught* Butch (but they didn't). Butch *hadn't been able* to loosen the boards (but he did). Mary *hadn't fallen* down the stairs (but she did).

With wishing about *past* situations, we regularly use the **past perfect** or **past modal** forms in the *wish*-clause.

A Tell about the story. What do these people wish they *had done,* but *didn't?*

1 Molly didn't accept Paulo's proposal of marriage. Paulo wishes that Molly...
If Molly had accepted, would she have felt guilty about leaving her family?

2 Kemp got drunk at the restaurant. Susan wishes that Kemp...
If Kemp hadn't drunk so much, would he have behaved so badly?

3 Mary went to the basement to get the wash. Molly wishes that Mary...
If Mary hadn't fallen then, would someone else have fallen the next day anyway?

4 Wade didn't give Susan a chance to explain. Susan wishes that her father...
If Wade had listened to her, would he have believed that Kemp was responsible for Mary's accident?

● What do you wish you *could do now* that you can't? What do you wish you *had done before?*

I wish I *could drive* a car.
I wish I *had learned* how to drive a car when I was younger.

cues *type; cook; speak (languages); dance; play (sports); fix cars; operate (a computer).*

B Molly is usually happy about her life, but sometimes she wishes she had been born in another time.

If she had been born in 1820, she wouldn't have to choose between marriage and a career. She would have been content to get married at 16, raise six children, and care for her husband and family. It's not easy to be a modern woman and have choices!

Do you wish you had been born in another time?
If you had been born then, what would your life have been like?

C Jeff knew that Molly was having a difficult time. Mary was in the hospital and Molly wasn't seeing Paulo as often as she used to. Jeff decided to take Molly to a rock concert to cheer her up. They didn't enjoy the concert because:

1 The theater was crowded.
2 The seats were in the last row of the balcony.
3 The musicians were late.
4 The teenagers in front of them were very noisy.
5 The music was too loud.

After the performance, Jeff said: I was disappointed that the theater was so crowded.
Molly agreed: I wish that the theater hadn't been so crowded.

● What else did Molly and Jeff complain about?

cues *disappointed; upset; annoyed; angry; irritated.*

ONE Asserting one's will

Jeff has decided to talk to Molly about Paulo. It's clear to Jeff that Molly should have accepted Paulo's proposal. Jeff is trying to convince Molly to change her mind. At first, Molly doesn't want to listen to him.
Listen to the tape, then complete the conversation as you listen a second time.

JEFF Paulo told me that he had asked you to marry him.

MOLLY Yes, and _____.

JEFF Could you _____? You love him and he loves you. What's _____?

MOLLY You make it sound so simple. There are _____ besides love.

JEFF Like _____?

MOLLY Like my job? And _____. Look. I don't want to discuss it.

JEFF Will you at least _____ about it?

MOLLY No. I've _____. I'm not going to marry Paulo.

JEFF Molly, I wish _____ to me. You're making _____. Paulo is a terrific guy. And you deserve some happiness too.

MOLLY How can I be happy when _____ about Mom? Who _____ of her if I go to Brazil?

JEFF I'll be here. I'm going to _____ and maybe _____ law school. Don't use Mom as an excuse.

MOLLY Paulo said _____. He said I was afraid.

JEFF He's _____, Molly. I felt _____ about Susan. But I know now that _____. I need her love.

MOLLY Jeff, I've hurt Paulo a lot. I don't think he even loves me anymore. It's _____, I know it.

Role Play: Wade was shocked when he realized that his daughter had been out all night. He didn't give Susan a chance to explain. If *you* had been Susan, what could you have said?

Practice a short conversation between Susan and her father.

Start with:
There's nothing more to say.

WADE There's nothing more to say.
I don't want to discuss it.
I've made up my mind.
I refuse to listen to you.

SUSAN Will you listen to me!
You're making a mistake.
I wish you'd give me a chance to explain!
Will you at least talk to me about it?

TWO Showing Regret

Jeff and Paulo are talking about Brazil. Paulo was surprised to find out that Jeff had never been to Rio de Janeiro, the most popular city in Brazil.

PAULO You went to Rio, didn't you?

JEFF No, I'm afraid I didn't get there. I spent all of my time in São Paulo and in the Northeast.

PAULO If you had gone to Rio, you could have seen Sugarloaf Mountain.

JEFF I know. I wish I had seen it. It's supposed to be a spectacular sight.

Ask each other about places you've been to.
If you had gone to _____, you could have seen _____.

I wish I had gone to _____. Then I could have seen _____.

Aunt Clara's Mailbox
Keeping a Promise

Dear Aunt Clara,

I am a fourteen-year-old boy and I have a problem. It all started last April when I told my father that I wanted to go to a computer camp for two weeks this summer. If I go, I can work with my own computer terminal every day and learn how to write programs myself. I've been studying about computers in school and I plan to become a programmer. My teachers suggested going to the camp and even arranged to get me a scholarship. I needed only $100 to pay for the train ticket.

I talked to my father about the money. He's always broke so he couldn't help me. However, he promised to let me go to the camp if I could save up the money myself. For the next two months, I mowed lawns, cleaned garages, and did all sorts of odd jobs for people in the neighborhood. I have the $100 now but if I hadn't done all that work, I wouldn't have saved it.

Last night my father asked me to give *him* the money. He told me that he needed it to fix his car. I don't know what to do. I know Dad needs his car to get to work, but I really want to go to the camp. If I hadn't worked so hard, the money wouldn't matter so much now.

I love my father and I'd like to help him, but he promised me that I could go to camp if I saved the money myself. I feel terrible. What should I do? Should I give up going to the camp or should I refuse to give my father the money to fix his car?

Yours truly,
Roger

Thinkabout

1 Roger learned about the computer camp from his
   a neighbors.
   b father.
   c teachers.

2 Roger saved $100 in order to pay for the cost of
   a computer camp.
   b a new car.
   c transportation.

3 The $100 belongs to
   a Roger.
   b Roger's father.
   c the scholarship fund.

4 Roger's father intends to
   a break his promise.
   b keep his promise.
   c borrow $100 from Roger.

Talkabout

Decide whether Roger should or shouldn't refuse to give his father the money. Consider these issues:
1 Why did Roger expect his father to keep his promise?
2 Why did Roger feel terrible when his father broke the promise? In general, why should promises be kept?
3 Is it important to keep a promise to a family member or to a close friend? Is it less important to keep a promise to a person who isn't a relative or close friend?
4 Is the child-parent relationship built on authority and / or trust? How would you describe Roger's relationship with his father?

Writeabout Expository: Using an experience to illustrate an idea

Write a composition about the importance of keeping a promise. In your *first* paragraph, show this importance with an example from personal experience. In your *second* paragraph, tell how you felt when the promise was broken and how this affected your relationship with the other person.

People shouldn't make promises they don't intend to keep. For instance, when I was (_____ years old / in _____ school) . . .

When (name) broke his / her promise, I felt _____. If I _____, then he / she would have . . .

Since that time, I haven't been able to . . .

←Start with:
Tell about the promise:
   Who made it?
   What was the situation?
   Why wasn't the promise kept?

←Give details:
Tell about your feelings.
Describe your options.

←End with:
Tell how your relationship with the other person was affected.

22

Kemp had Susan tied to the railing. Unless Jeff stops him, Kemp will kill Susan.

Scene One

 All the phone lines were busy, so Carlos raced to the hospital in his old pick-up truck. He arrived just as Jeff, Molly, and Paulo were leaving. Quickly, Carlos told them about Kemp's plan to have Tudor Village destroyed. Jeff was relieved that Carlos had told Susan to go home where it was safe.

Paulo and Molly got into the truck and Jeff had Carlos jump on the back of his motorcycle. It was rush hour so the streets were crowded with commuters. Right away, Paulo got the truck stuck in the early evening traffic, but Jeff was able to steer the motorcycle easily between the cars. It didn't take Jeff and Carlos long to reach Tudor Village.

Jeff pulled up in back of the building. He got there just in time to see some men climbing up the fire escape. There was no doubt in Jeff's mind about who they were. He had recognized Kemp right away. When Jeff looked more closely at the other three, he was horrified.

JEFF Carlos, look! They've got Susan!

CARLOS That can't be Susan. I told her to go home.

JEFF I know it's Susan. She must have come here to find me.

CARLOS They've got her tied up. What are we going to do now?

JEFF Carlos, call the police. When Paulo comes, you two go up the fire escape on the other side of the building. Oh, God! Poor Susan!

CARLOS You're not going up after them? Are you crazy? There are three of them. Wait for the police.

JEFF It'll be too late by then. I'm going after them. They might kill Susan if I don't stop them.

Questions

1 Who did Carlos see leaving the hospital?
2 Did Jeff and Carlos reach Tudor Village before Paulo and Molly? Ask why.
3 Who did Jeff see climbing the fire escape?
4 Did Kemp have Susan tied up? Ask who did it.
5 What did Jeff ask Carlos to do?
6 Did Jeff follow Kemp up the fire escape? Ask why.

Scene Two

📼 When they got to the top, Butch shoved Susan against the railing at the edge of the roof near the water tank. Kemp had Butch tie Susan's hands to the railing. Then Butch and Spike started to pour the gasoline around the water tank.

Susan was having difficulty breathing with the handkerchief tied around her mouth. The smell of gasoline was making her dizzy. Unless she did something soon, she would pass out. Although her hands were tied, Susan was able to bend over and reach the knob of the railing. Susan rubbed her face back and forth against the knob. The handkerchief was slipping off.

Just then, Jeff reached the top of the fire escape. Butch and Spike were behind the water tank, so they didn't see Jeff climbing onto the roof. Jeff saw Susan struggling to free herself. Kemp was standing in the middle of the roof with his back to Jeff. A box of matches was in his hand. Suddenly, Jeff rushed across the roof and knocked Kemp over. At that moment, Susan freed herself from the handkerchief. She saw the matches flying out of Kemp's hand. Jeff was holding Kemp down against the side railing.

SUSAN   Jeff, Jeff! Watch out! There's gasoline all around the water tank.

KEMP   Butch! Spike! Help me!

JEFF   Leave those matches alone, Kemp.

BUTCH   Spike, get over there and help Kemp.

JEFF   It's no use, Kemp. Give up. The police'll be here in a minute.

KEMP   You aren't going to stop me, Ryan. Get the matches, Spike!

SUSAN   Jeff, help me, please!

BUTCH   Ryan, look over here. I've got your girl. Let Kemp go, or I'll throw her off the roof.

JEFF   Susan? Susan!

SUSAN   Don't listen to him, Jeff. It's a trick!

BUTCH   It's no trick, Ryan. Get away from Kemp, or you won't see your girl alive again.

KEMP   He's right, Ryan. We've got you both now.

Questions

1 Did Kemp have Susan tied to the railing? Ask who did it.
2 What did the men do with the gasoline?
3 Did Susan manage to remove the handkerchief? Ask how.
4 Did Butch and Spike see Jeff climbing onto the roof? Ask why not.
5 What must have happened to Kemp's box of matches?
6 How did Butch help Kemp?

Get Something Done—*Passive Causative*

Active causative

Get Have	somebody	to do do	something	Jeff wants Carlos to get help, so he got Carlos to call the police.

Passive causative

Get Have	something	*done*	Kemp wants to keep Susan quiet, so he had Susan's mouth covered.

We use the **active causative** when a person causes another person to do something. We use the **passive causative** when a person causes something to happen to another person or thing. Use the past participle with have or get to form the **passive causative.**

A What are the results of these actions in the story?

1 Action Kemp had Butch cover Susan's mouth.
Result Kemp had Susan's mouth _____.

2 Action Kemp had Spike tie Susan up.
Result Kemp had Susan _____.

3 Action Kemp had Butch lower the fire escape to the ground.
Result Kemp had the fire escape _____.

4 Action Kemp had Butch and Spike pour the gasoline on the roof.
Result Kemp had the gasoline _____.

• Decide whether to do these things yourself or to have them done by someone else.

1 You bought a suit but it doesn't fit you well. The sleeves are too long and the pants are too wide. Who's going to shorten the sleeves? take in the pants?

2 Your car needs an oil change and a new filter. Who's going to change the oil? install the filter?

3 You wrote a 20-page report. Your instructor/boss wants a typed report. Who's going to type the report?

B Before Paulo met Molly at the hospital that evening, he stopped by the florist's. He picked out a dozen yellow roses and *had them sent* to Mary at the hospital.

• Have you ever had flowers sent to a friend, or do you usually bring them yourself?

• Do you have your groceries delivered, or do you usually carry them home yourself?

• Do you have your hair cut, or do you usually cut it yourself?

cues *shine shoes; do laundry; press shirts; clean house; wash car.*

C These are the orders the doctor left with the nurse in charge of Mary's care:

• Tell what the doctor *had* the nurse *do*:
→ The doctor *had* the nurse *take* Mary's blood pressure.

• Tell what *was done* to Mary:
→ Mary *had* her blood pressure *taken.*

• Was there a time when *you* or someone you know:
had an x-ray taken?
had blood taken?
had a bone set after a fall?

• Tell when and where it happened, who did it, and how it was done.

Doctor's Orders
1. take blood pressure
2. take temperature
3. change dressing on incision
4. take blood for laboratory tests
5. x-ray both hips
6. change diet from liquid to solid foods
7. decrease medication for pain

I had	an x-ray of my ____taken blood from my ____taken a bone in my ____set	when I ____in ____.

First, the doctor _____. Next, he/she _____. Then, _____. After that, _____. Finally, _____.

Negative Condition with Unless

If Unless	Jeff	doesn't stop stops	Kemp,	Kemp will kill Susan.
If Unless	Susan	doesn't do anything, does something,	she will pass out.

We use *unless* to express a **negative condition**. *Unless* means the same as *if . . . not*.

A Give your opinion about what will happen in the story.

1 Mary has just had major surgery. What will happen if she doesn't get plenty of rest?
Unless Mary gets plenty of rest, . . .
2 Kemp has to get the tenants out of Tudor Village. What will happen to Kemp's job if he doesn't?
Unless Kemp gets the tenants out of Tudor Village, . . .
3 The tenants have to stop Kemp. What will happen if they don't?
Unless the tenants stop Kemp, . . .
4 Susan can't breathe very well. What will happen if she can't get the handkerchief off?
Unless Susan gets the handkerchief off, . . .
5 Butch is threatening to throw Susan off the roof. What will happen if Jeff doesn't release Kemp?
Unless Jeff releases Kemp, . . .

● What would happen to you in these situations?

1 Unless I get a driver's license, I won't be allowed to . . .
2 Unless I have a passport, I can't . . .
3 Unless I have a good job, I can't . . .

B This afternoon, Molly and Jeff made arrangements to meet at the hospital. Neither of them is sure of the exact time. Complete the telephone conversation between Molly and Jeff with *unless* or *if . . . not*:

MOLLY I'll be at the hospital entrance about 6 o'clock _____ I get caught in traffic.
JEFF Well, _____ you're _____ in the lobby by 6, I'll just meet you in Mom's room.
MOLLY I'll try to call you _____ I can _____ leave the office by 5:30.
JEFF All right. _____ I hear from you, I'll expect to meet you at the hospital at 6.

● Do you have plans for tonight? tomorrow night? next weekend? Is there anything that might make you change your plans?

S1 Do you have plans for (tonight)?
S2 Unless I _____, I plan to _____.

cues *work; transportation; money; babysitter.*

ONE   Getting repairs done

Last week, Jeff had his motorcycle repaired. Jeff explained the problems to the mechanic. Then he asked him for an estimate of the cost of the repairs.
Listen to the tape; then complete the conversation as you listen a second time.

JEFF   There seems to be something wrong with the transmission. I have trouble with second gear.

MECHANIC   Let me _____. You're _____. The gears are worn out. You _____ the transmission _____.

JEFF   Are you _____? That's an expensive job.

MECHANIC   Well, it's an old cycle, but it's in _____. With a new transmission, it'll be _____.

JEFF   How _____ going to cost me?

MECHANIC   Well, most _____ is labor. We need to have the engine taken apart first. You should _____ the carburetor _____ at the same time and maybe _____ the fuel pump _____. Altogether, I'd say about _____.

carriage return
ribbon
keys
space bar

JEFF   That much? Well, I guess I don't have _____.

MECHANIC   We'll start on it right away. It should be ready by early next week.

Role Play: Last month, Molly had her typewriter repaired. Practice a similar conversation between Molly and the typewriter repairman.

Start with:
There seems to be something wrong with _____.

Gordon's Typewriter Repairs
2700 Broadway
NEW YORK, NY

repair carriage return
clean keys
replace ribbon
adjust space bar

Total $40

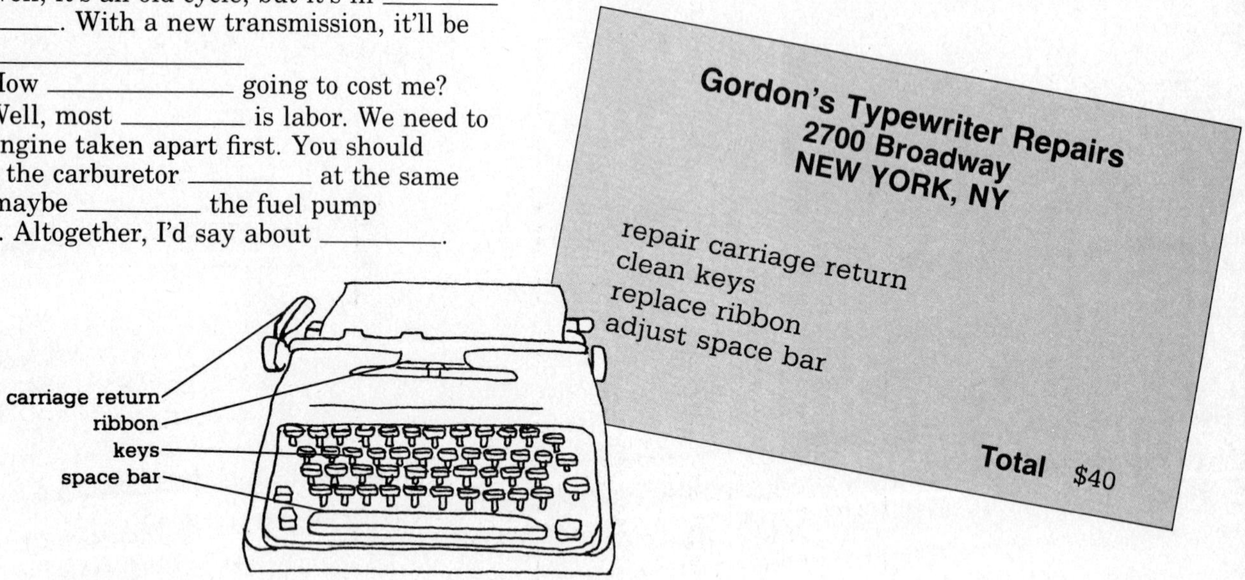

TWO   Showing doubt and certainty

Jeff saw some men climbing up the fire escape. There was no doubt in Jeff's mind about who they were. He had recognized Kemp right away.

Discuss what has happened in the story up to now. *How certain are you* that . . .
• Kemp will carry out his plan to set fire to Tudor Village.

• Paulo and Molly will get back together.
• Wade will forget about his dream to build Wade Plaza.
• The police will rescue Jeff and Susan.

Talk about events or issues in the news.

Doubt	Certainty
There is some doubt that . . .	There is no doubt that . . .
I'm not sure that . . .	I'm sure that . . .
I doubt that . . .	I don't doubt that . . .

Handling an emergency

You're suddenly involved in an emergency situation. Perhaps (1) you're on a ship and someone falls overboard; (2) you're at home and the curtains near the stove catch fire; or (3) you're on your way to work and a child gets hit by a truck. Take charge of the situation. Give others directions on what to do in the emergency.

🔊 **Listen to the sample conversations on the tape.**

- Act out the situation between you and another person at the scene. Follow the conversation guide below.

cues:	You	The Other Person	cues:
Help! / Fire! / Man overboard! Watch out for (the fire). Be careful of (the fire).	Call the alarm.		
		Show surprise / panic.	What? / Where is it / he? Oh, no! / What happened? It's horrible / terrible!
Calm down. / Relax. Slow down. / Move away. Let me through. Do what I say!	Show confidence and control.		
		Offer help.	What can I / we do? I / we want to help. Is there anything I / we can do? What do you need? Need any help / assistance?
Find (give) me . . . —the lifeboat / the fire extinguisher / a first-aid kit. Look (call) for / get . . . the captain (a doctor, the fire department / the police).	Suggest something.		
		Volunteer.	Here's the _____. I'll get the _____. Let me call the _____. I / we can find the _____.
It looks like we've got . . . the man aboard / the fire controlled, the child pulled out from under the truck.	Evaluate the situation.		
		Express relief.	I'm relieved that . . . Thank goodness that . . . the fire's out / the man's safe the child's alive.
I appreciate / I'm grateful for your help / assistance. You were wonderful / terrific. It was nothing. I was happy to help. We were lucky to be here.	Show appreciation. End the conversation.		Thanks to you. / You acted quickly. You're the one who . . . put out the fire / saved the man's (child's) life.

Paulo meant to stop Spike. But the match fell on the gasoline, setting the roof on fire.

Scene One

Jeff was on top of Kemp, holding him down against the railing along the side. He saw Butch pushing Susan against the back corner of the railing. Unless Jeff released Kemp, Butch would push Susan off the roof.

Just then, Jeff spotted Carlos and Paulo coming up the back fire escape. Slowly, Carlos crept behind Butch. At the same time, Paulo moved toward the middle of the roof where Spike was lighting a match. Paulo jumped on Spike, trying to knock the match out of his hand, but he was too late. Suddenly, the gasoline was on fire. The roof around the water tank burst into flames.

Carlos quickly shoved Butch aside and pushed Susan away from the flames. Butch picked Spike up and the two of them headed for the other fire escape at the front of the building. By now, the roof near the water tank was completely on fire.

In all the confusion, Kemp managed to break away from Jeff, making his way around the burning areas of the roof toward the front fire escape. Jeff went after him, avoiding the flames. Kemp got as far as the front railing before Jeff was able to grab his leg and pull him down. Kemp fought back, pushing Jeff against the fire escape. The two men struggled on the edge of the roof.

CARLOS Paulo, I'll untie Susan. Go into the building and pull the fire alarm.
PAULO Where are the fire extinguishers?
CARLOS Behind the door to the roof. Hurry!
SUSAN We've got to help Jeff. Look, Carlos. Behind the flames! He's going after Kemp!
CARLOS Jeff, Jeff, come back!
SUSAN I've got to help Jeff! Let me go, Carlos.
CARLOS Susan, come back here! Susan! Jeff!
PAULO Where's Susan?
CARLOS I couldn't stop her. She ran after Jeff.
PAULO I can't see either of them. The fire's spreading and there's too much smoke. Susan! Jeff! Can you hear me?
CARLOS We can't put out this fire, Paulo. It's hopeless.
PAULO We've got to try, or Susan and Jeff won't have a chance!

Questions

1 What would Butch do to Susan if Jeff didn't let Kemp go?
2 Did Jeff see someone coming up the back fire escape? Ask who he saw.
3 Who started the fire? Ask how it happened.
4 Did Kemp get away from Jeff? Ask where he went.
5 Where did Paulo go? Ask about Susan.
6 Can Carlos and Paulo put out the fire?

Scene Two

🔊 Preston Wade picked up the note Susan had left on his desk. The broken stairs, Mary's operation, and Kemp's plan to burn down Tudor Village—it was all there. By the time he finished reading, Wade's hands were shaking. His anger at Kemp changed to horror as he realized the danger Susan might be in. He called the house, only to discover that Susan wasn't there. Suspecting the worst, Wade rushed out of the office.

When Wade arrived at Tudor Village, he saw police cars and fire trucks everywhere. There was total confusion, as the firemen tried to control the flames coming from the roof. The police were leading two men with handcuffs into a car. Wade remembered seeing the one with the scar in Kemp's office the week before. He didn't recognize the other.

Wade went over to a group of tenants to look for Susan. Molly was there. He followed her gaze to the roof. There were two men on the edge; they seemed to be fighting. Immediately, Wade recognized Kemp and Jeff. The fire was spreading dangerously close to them. At any moment, either of them could fall to his death.

MOLLY You! What are you doing here? Haven't you already done enough?
WADE You're Miss Ryan, aren't you? I'm sorry about your mother. I truly am.
MOLLY Do you know who's on that roof? Jeff. And Paulo and Carlos. They could die up there and it's your fault!
WADE Believe me. I didn't know Kemp was behind this. I swear I didn't.
MOLLY Look! There's someone else up there! It looks like a woman. No, it couldn't be . . .
WADE What? My God, it's Susan! My daughter's on the roof!
MOLLY She's trying to help Jeff. Oh, no! Kemp is pushing Jeff over the railing!
WADE I can't see them. There's too much smoke!
MOLLY Someone is falling!
WADE Who is it?
MOLLY I don't know! I can't tell who it is.

Questions

1 What did Wade find on his desk? Ask who left it.
2 How did Wade react when he read about Kemp's plan?
3 Who were the two men wearing handcuffs?
4 Was Molly pleased to see Wade standing next to her? Ask why not.
5 Did Molly and Wade recognize the woman on the roof? Ask who she is.
6 Who could have fallen from the roof?

135

Participial Clauses

Jeff	was on top of Kemp. trapped Kemp against the railing.	Jeff was on top of Kemp, *trapping* him against the railing.
Susan	bent over. reached the knob on the post.	Susan bent over, *reaching* the knob on the post.

When *both* actions take place *at the same time,* we use the *present* form of the **participle** (*V-ing*) to join the sentences.

A Combine these sentences by changing the italicized verb to a present participle:

1 Jeff rushed to Tudor Village. He *steered* the motorcycle between the cars.
→ Jeff rushed to Tudor Village, steering the motorcycle between the cars.

2 Jeff climbed up the fire escape. He *followed* Kemp to the roof.
3 Butch got rough with Susan. He *shoved* her against the railing.
4 Susan rubbed the handkerchief against the knob. She *managed* to slip it off.
5 Carlos grabbed Susan. He *pushed* Butch aside.
6 Paulo went into the building. He *searched* for the fire extinguishers.
7 Jeff grabbed Kemp. He *pulled* him down.
8 The two men struggled on the edge of the roof. They *fought* for their lives.
9 Wade watched the burning roof. He *feared* for his daughter's life.
10 Susan cried out to Jeff. She *hoped* to warn him.
11 Jeff caught Kemp's leg. He *pulled* Kemp off the fire escape.
12 The police arrested Butch and Spike. They *took* them away in handcuffs.

B Paulo bought a tape recorder at an appliance store on Broadway. When he tried to use it, it didn't work because the switch was broken.

● Complete the sentences to tell what *you think* happened:

Paulo wrote a letter to the store manager, complaining about . . .
The store manager replied, offering to . . .
Paulo returned to the store, bringing . . .
Paulo left, thanking . . .

● Have you ever returned something you bought because it was defective? Tell about *your* experience.

C When they first met, Susan told Jeff about her life at the London School for Girls, which was not a pleasant experience.

Four years ago, I went to London, *expecting* that I wouldn't miss my father. I thought I would make new friends at School, but I didn't. After the first year I wanted to leave, *thinking* I could return to New York. But my father wanted me to stay in London, *promising* that he would visit me more often. I stayed there, *hoping* that my father would keep his promise, but he didn't. This year I came to New York, *wanting* to live here in Manhattan to be with Dad.

● Tell about a disappointing experience, for example:

a vacation you had looked forward to, but was actually very unpleasant.
a movie or play someone had recommended, but was really very boring.
a restaurant which had received excellent reviews, but was in fact terrible.

I went to _____, expecting that . . .
I wanted to _____, thinking that . . .
I stayed/waited until _____, hoping that . . .
I left _____, promising myself that I would never . . .

Verbs + Gerunds or Infinitives

Wade denied	responsibility for the Tudor Village accidents.
	gerund
	causing the accidents at Tudor Village.

Molly refused	Paulo's proposal of marriage.
	infinitive
	to marry Paulo.

The **gerund** (V-ing) form can substitute for a noun in the direct object position after *particular* verbs. The **infinitive** (to+V) form can also substitute for a noun after *particular* verbs.

A Complete these sentences with the gerund or infinitive.

Verbs followed by *V-ing*:

appreciate	imagine
avoid	keep
consider	mind
deny	miss
enjoy	postpone
finish	suggest

Verbs followed by *to-V*:

agree	mean
arrange	promise
decide	refuse
determine	seem
hope	

1 Molly refused (marry) Paulo. She couldn't imagine (leave) her family and (give) up her career.
2 The tenants postponed (vote) on the sale of Tudor Village. They agreed (wait).
3 Susan considered (wait) for her father, but she decided (leave) him a note.
4 Paulo arranged (meet) Molly. He didn't mind (wait) at the hospital.
5 Mary hopes (leave) the hospital soon. She misses (see) her family.
6 Wade seems (trust) Kemp completely. If Wade asks him, Kemp will deny (take) money from the company accounts.
7 Mary appreciates (see) her family during visiting hours. She enjoys (hear) all the gossip about Tudor Village.
8 The police keep (look) for Butch. They are determined (find) him.
9 Jeff promised (help) Paulo paint the kitchen. He suggested (buy) the paint after they visit Mary.
10 Susan never finished (tell) her father about Mary's accident. Because Wade was so angry, he avoided (listen) to her story.

B After Molly had applied for the job as a reporter at the *City Herald*, she had an interview with Ben Greene, the editor. Molly gave Ben a hard time, but he liked her straightforward manner. These are some of the questions Ben asked her. How do you think Molly responded?

B What made you *decide* to be a reporter, Miss Ryan?
M Ever since I was a little girl, I was *determined* . . .
B You *appear* to be a very intelligent woman. Have you *considered* going into another profession like law or medicine?
M I can't *imagine* . . .
B I've *finished* reading your résumé and your stories are quite good. What do you *like* writing about?
M Thank you. As a matter of fact, I really *enjoy* . . .
B I wonder whether you'd *mind* telling me a little about your personal life. Are you married?
M My personal life is private. Those are the kinds of questions I *refuse* . . .

B Miss Ryan, you *seem* to have the kind of experience and personality we're looking for. When can you *start* working?
M It's *Ms.* Ryan, please. I can *arrange* . . .

● **What questions would you ask . . .**

a woman who wants to join the army?
a man who wants to be mayor of your city?
a person who wants to teach in this school?

Use expressions, such as:
What made you decide . . . ?
Have you considered . . . ?
What do you plan . . . ?
What do you enjoy . . . ?
Would you mind . . . ?
Can you imagine . . . ?
When can you arrange . . . ?

23 EXPRESSION

ONE Offering sympathy

When Ben Greene heard about Mary's accident, he called Molly right away to express his sympathy.
Listen to the tape, then complete the conversation as you listen a second time.

BEN   I was so sorry to hear about your mother, Molly.
MOLLY Thank you, Ben. It's _____ to call.
BEN   How _____?
MOLLY Much better. The operation went well. The doctors say _____.
BEN   I'm glad to hear that. Is there _____ to help?
MOLLY Right now she just needs a lot of rest. Ben, I _____ a favor. Would it be all right if I _____ off from work?
BEN   Take _____ you need.
MOLLY Thanks. I appreciate it.

Role Play: Maria Rivera is shocked to hear about Mary's accident. Maria calls Molly at the hospital.

MARIA asks how Mary is feeling
      offers to help

MOLLY tells about Mary's condition
      asks Maria if she would feed Morris, Mary's cat

Practice a similar telephone conversation between Maria and Molly.

TWO Reporting past events

Ben Greene is at the *City Herald*. He's listening to the *Eleven O'clock News* on television:

"A three-alarm fire destroyed the top three floors of one of the city's oldest buildings this evening, killing one person and injuring another.
  The fire, at Tudor Village on Manhattan's West Side, began on the roof around 9:15, spreading quickly to the top three floors. Firemen rescued several tenants from the twelfth floor, rushing them to City Hospital . . ."

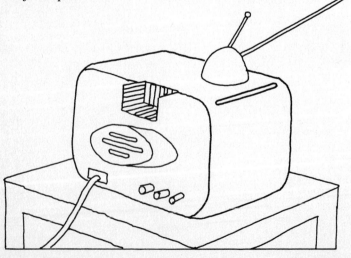

Tell what Ben Greene heard on the News.
Ben heard that an alarm *had gone off* at one of the city's oldest landmark buildings.

Tell what *you* heard on the news last night. What did *you* read in today's newspaper?

cues   *world affairs; local news; editorials; sports; advertisements.*

138

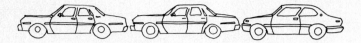

A Nation on Wheels

Although the price of gasoline continues to climb, the automobile remains at the center of American life. In 1980, 82% of trips of 100 miles or more were made by people in cars, while travel by airplanes, trains, and buses accounted for less than 18%. Americans are accustomed to using their cars and they are not likely to change their driving habits. However, America's dependence on the automobile has had serious results, including air pollution and traffic congestion.

In Los Angeles, the air is so dirty one day out of every three or four that people with lung and heart problems risk their lives. Each year, air pollution results in $1.5 to $2 billion of damage to human health, vegetation, and buildings in Los Angeles alone.

Mayors of big cities and commuters continue to complain about the problem of traffic in urban areas. New York probably has the worst traffic jams in the country. Over 555,000 vehicles enter midtown Manhattan daily. The city has tried increasing parking fees and tolls to discourage auto commuting, but regular drivers seem willing to pay the extra cost of their riding habits.

For Americans, the automobile is not a luxury. It is a necessity to get to work, to take vacations and to have the kind of privacy not available in a bus or train. By comparison, dirty air and traffic problems seem a small price to pay. The simple fact remains: motorists are just not interested in giving up their cars.

Thinkabout

	True	False
1 Americans used to take their cars on trips, but now depend on buses and trains for transportation.	____	____
2 People with lung and heart problems should move to Los Angeles.	____	____
3 Public officials in New York City have encouraged people to take their cars to work every day.	____	____
4 Americans' concern for privacy is greater than their worry about dirty air and traffic congestion.	____	____

Talkabout

As members of the city council, you must discuss and vote on the proposal to build a new highway along the river. The Alco Steel Company, which employs one-fourth of the city's workers and pays high taxes, wants the new highway built. If it isn't built, Alco might move to another city with a better transportation system. However, the people who live in the expensive homes along the river object to the proposal because the highway will destroy Riverside Park and add to the city's pollution problems. There is no other place to build the highway.

Discuss the points of view of:
the people who live along the river
the Alco Steel Company
the workers in the steel mill
the city council who must do what is best for the majority of the citizens

Vote on the proposal to build a new highway along the river. Give a reason for voting YES or NO.

Writeabout Expository: Developing an idea with cause and effect

Write a composition of two paragraphs to show how the automobile has changed the way of life of people in *your* country. Discuss two areas of change: (1) in family life, and (2) in social customs.
The first sentence of each paragraph should describe *the causes*. The sentences which follow should give examples to describe *the effects*.

The appearance of the automobile has caused important changes in the life of the family in (country).

Perhaps most changes caused by automobile habits have occurred in our social customs. In the *first* place . . .
Second . . .

For (people in your country), the automobile is . . .

←Start with:
Emphasize family life.
Effects on: fathers, mothers, children.

←Continue:
Emphasize social customs, travel, housing patterns.

←End with:
Give your opinion.

Wade was terrified of losing Susan. She was with the others on the burning roof.

Scene One

🔊 Molly ran toward the police as they examined the broken body. She was terrified that it was Jeff who had fallen from the roof. But from the blue suit and dark hair of the dead man, she realized that it was Kemp. Molly's worries weren't over. The others were still somewhere in the burning building.

Wade went over to talk to the Fire Chief who was trying to get a rescue team up the fire escape to the roof. Wade learned that some other firemen were inside the building on the twelfth floor, just below the roof. In the stairway, they had found two men overcome by smoke.

Molly wept as the firemen brought Paulo and Carlos out of the burning building. They were unconscious, but alive. Molly touched Paulo's bruised cheek, then she put her hand on his. How could her life have any meaning without him?

There was still no word on Susan and Jeff. It was possible that they had managed to reach the fire escape at the back of the building. The firemen were up there now but the Fire Chief estimated that the roof would collapse in a matter of minutes. Wade tried to comfort Molly.

WADE Is this man your husband?

MOLLY No. We've talked about getting married, but . . .

WADE I'll do anything I can to help you.

MOLLY Why should you? After all you've done to break up Susan and Jeff? You haven't helped anyone.

WADE I was a selfish old man. I wanted Susan to love only me. I thought that if she fell in love, I would lose her again.

MOLLY We may have lost both of them right now. Look at the roof—it's collapsing. Oh, I can't bear to watch!

WADE Wait, Molly, I see them! Over there, with those firemen coming out of the side entrance. Susan and Jeff are alive!

MOLLY Jeff, Susan! We're over here . . .

JEFF We're okay, Molly. We made it!

SUSAN Daddy, it was horrible! I was so frightened!

WADE Susan, Susan. You're safe now. Thank God, you're safe. I promise I'll make it up to you. Jeff, I was wrong, so terribly wrong. Believe me. I'll make it up to *both* of you.

Questions

1 Who fell from the roof? Ask how Molly knows.
2 Where were Paulo and Carlos? Ask how they were rescued.
3 Is Molly planning on marrying Paulo?
4 Could Jeff and Susan still escape from the burning building? Ask how.
5 Did Molly get angry at Wade? Ask why.
6 Does Wade feel sorry about treating Jeff so badly? Ask what Wade hopes to do.

Scene Two

It took all night, but the fire was finally put out. There was a lot of damage; the top three floors were completely destroyed by the collapsed roof. Wade put all the homeless tenants in a hotel, but he insisted on having the Ryans move into his house until Tudor Village was repaired.

The tenants agreed to let Wade pay for their losses and rebuild Tudor Village instead of taking legal action against Wade Enterprises. Wade asked Paulo to redesign Wade Plaza. It would be a smaller project now, but somehow that didn't matter.

Wade was counting on having Jeff and Susan take over the business someday. But Jeff was reluctant to accept Wade's offer of a job at Wade Enterprises; he insisted on finishing law school before he made that decision. Susan was thinking about going back to school too.

Mary came home from the hospital today. Tonight they are having a special dinner to celebrate her recovery.

MARY   It's wonderful to be with my family again.
WADE   I'm delighted that you're here, Mary.
SUSAN   Mary, did I tell you? I'm going back to college soon. But in New York, not in England.
MARY   Does that mean that you and Jeff aren't getting married?
JEFF   We've just decided to wait a while, that's all. I'm planning on getting my law degree first.
SUSAN   We need to be on our own for now.
WADE   I guess I'll lose you both for awhile.
MOLLY   Now we all know one thing—sometimes you almost have to lose someone to know your true feelings.
PAULO   Give them time, Preston. Just hope Jeff isn't as stubborn as his sister.
WADE   Okay, okay. The business can wait until you finish school. But there is one thing I want to do for you both now, if you let me.
JEFF   What's that?
WADE   Do you mind accepting—let's say—a little present?
SUSAN   Oh, Daddy. What is it? C'mon, tell us!
WADE   Frankly, I was thinking of a new car. Somehow I'll never get used to a daughter of mine riding a motorcycle.
SUSAN   Oh, Daddy!
JEFF   Preston . . .

Questions

1 Was there much damage from the fire? Ask where.
2 What happened to the tenants who lost their homes in the fire?
3 What will happen to Tudor Village? Ask about Wade Plaza.
4 Did Wade have plans for Susan and Jeff? Ask what they were.
5 What decisions have Jeff and Susan made?
6 Is Wade thinking of giving Susan and Jeff a present? Ask what it is.

Pronouns that Function as Nouns

The police handcuffed the two men, but they suspected that *another* was responsible for the fire. ("one more")

Wade recognized the one with the scar, but he didn't recognize *the other one*. ("the remaining one")

Kemp had fallen to his death, but *the others* were still on the roof. ("the remaining is more than one")

Pronoun substitutes, such as *another*, *the other(s)*, and *the other one*, refer only to *count* nouns.

A Susan's dinner party for Mary is a success. Everyone is having coffee and dessert now.

● Complete the conversation with: *the other one, the one, another.*

SUSAN Would you like some more tea, Mary?

MARY I've already had two cups, but I'd love _____, thank you.

SUSAN What about you, Daddy? Are you having any more coffee or tea?

WADE None for me, thanks. I'll try one of your cakes, though. I'll have _____ with the strawberries and vanilla frosting. It looks delicious.

SUSAN Are you ready for dessert, Jeff?

JEFF I'm always ready for dessert! Let me have a piece of _____. I love chocolate.

● Respond to these situations with:

No, thank you./None for me, thanks.
or
Yes, thank you. I'll have _____.

1 Would you like some more coffee?
2 Which pie will you have? How about the apple?
3 Do you like red or rosé wine? Paulo's drinking *Mateus*.
4 I have two flavors of ice cream. Would you like the strawberry?

B Complete this short passage about the story with the correct form of the verb:

> plural
>
> *All* of them *hope* the firemen can put out the fire.
>
> plural
>
> *Both* of them *were* standing on the edge of the roof.
>
> singular
>
> *Either* of them *is* capable of overcoming the other.
>
> singular
>
> *Neither* of them *has* much of a chance to survive the fire.

Susan has prepared a special dinner to celebrate Mary's return from the hospital. Right now, all of them ___(sit)___ around the dining room table. Jeff and Susan have an announcement. Both of them ___(go)___ back to school. It seems that neither of them ___(be)___ interested in getting married right now. Mary and Wade are disappointed; either of them ___(be)___ willing to give the children a big wedding. They'll just have to wait until Jeff and Susan get their degrees.

● Are you ready to get married? Ask each other these questions. Put a check in one of the boxes to record your responses.

	yes	no
1 Are you bored with being single?		
2 Do you look forward to quiet evenings at home?		
3 Are you interested in dating other people?		
4 Do you dream about having children?		
5 Are you afraid of taking responsibility for others?		

● Compare your responses with a classmate.

Both of us _____.
Only one of us _____.
Neither of us _____.

Gerund Expressions

Paulo and Molly	have talked about	marriage. getting married.
	are planning on	a small wedding. having a small wedding.
Jeff	is interested in	a career in law. pursuing a career in law.

Certain verb and adjective expressions are completed by a prepositional phrase. **Gerund** (*V-ing*) clauses are regularly substituted for nouns which follow the preposition.

 A Complete these sentences with the preposition and gerund.

Verb expressions followed by gerunds:

confess to	look forward to
count on	plan on
depend on	talk about
dream about	think about
insist on	

Adjective expressions followed by gerunds:

accustomed to	interested in
afraid of	proud of
capable of	quick at
excited about	worried about
happy about	

1 Preston Wade has been dreaming (build) Wade Plaza all his life. He's a man accustomed (get) what he wants.
2 Butch confessed (set) the Tudor Village fire. He's not looking forward (spend) ten years in jail.
3 Molly is happy (get) married. She's planning (have) a small wedding.
4 Wade insists (have) Jeff work for him, but Jeff isn't interested (get) a job.
5 Wade was afraid (lose) Susan, but now he's proud (have) Jeff as a son-in-law.
6 Jeff is quick (do) figures. He's capable (examine) the Wade Enterprises accounts.
7 Susan is thinking (go) back to school. She's depending (get) her father's help.
8 Molly is excited (live) in Brazil, but she's worried (leave) her family.
9 Mary is talking (give) Jeff and Susan a big wedding. She's counting (invite) all her friends.

B Molly and Mary have different points of view. Molly is complaining about her mother to Paulo.

Molly says, "My mother will never get used to my smoking. She doesn't believe that a lady should smoke, especially in public. She also doesn't approve of my wearing make-up, but I think she's just old-fashioned."

● Tell about some of the things *you* do that your parents object to.

cues *smoking; drinking; dating; living away from home; wearing certain clothes; choosing a particular career; listening to popular music; having certain interests, etc.*

| My parents | will never get used to my _____.
don't approve of my _____. |

| They | believe
feel | that _____, but I | argue
think | that _____. |

● Are there some things about the United States or American customs that . . .

you don't approve of?
you'll never get used to?
you are interested in?
you confess to liking?

cues *the traffic; the noise; the pollution; the crime; the food; the music; the clothes; sports; entertainment.*

ONE   Giving advice and counsel

Molly and Paulo have decided to get married right away. Paulo has to stay in New York until the end of the year. Paulo is worried about going back to Brazil. Perhaps Molly won't like living there. Paulo is asking Jeff's advice.

Listen to the tape, then complete the conversation as you listen a second time.

PAULO I'm not so sure about going back to Brazil next year. Molly has her career and family here.

JEFF Why don't you _____ in New York? I'm sure Susan's father would be happy _____ for his construction company.

PAULO He's already _____. It's an excellent opportunity.

JEFF You could go back to your job in São Paulo.

PAULO I know that. But somehow I can't imagine Molly _____. She's accustomed _____ a career. Frankly, I don't think she's _____ about staying home all day.

JEFF She doesn't have to. She's _____ learning the language and finding a job if she _____ with playing housewife. If I were you, I would discuss this with Molly.

PAULO You're right. It's a big decision. I had better get used to sharing the responsibility.

JEFF Take my advice. Talk to Molly. It's too important a decision to make by yourself.

Role Play: Molly knows that Paulo is thinking about staying in New York. She's not sure if Paulo will be happy living away from his family and friends.

Molly is asking Susan's advice. Practice a short conversation between Molly and Susan.

Start with:
MOLLY I'm not sure about staying in New York. Paulo has his job and family in Brazil.

Useful expressions:
Why don't you. . . ?
You could. . . .
If I were you, I would. . . .
Take my advice.

TWO   Stating strong opinions

Can you imagine yourself living . . .
    on an island in the Pacific Ocean?
    in an old castle in Austria?
    on a cowboy ranch in Wyoming?
    in a solar house in Maine?

Ask each other:
How do you feel about
Have you ever thought about | (living) _____?
Can you imagine yourself |

Pro
I love the idea of living . . .
I enjoy (swimming, riding, etc.) . . .
I wouldn't mind living . . .

Con
I can't stand the thought of living . . .
I can't imagine myself (swimming) every day.
I'd never get used to living . . .

Making an important decision

You have to tell your father (mother, brother, sister) about an important decision you have made. Perhaps you have decided to move to a city far away, to change job or career, or to go to law (medical, business) school. The other person will be disappointed about your plans, but you are sure you have made the right decision.

Listen to the sample conversations on the tape.

- Act out the scene between you and the other person. Follow the conversation guide below. Some cues are given, but you may choose words of your own.

cues:	You	The Other Person	cues:
I'm planning on . . . I've been thinking about . . . —moving to _____ / quitting my job / going to _____ school. I want to tell you / let you know that I'm (moving) . . .	Tell about your decision.		
		Express surprise.	Moving to _____? / Quitting your job? / Going to _____ school? Does that mean you're leaving _____? / quitting _____? What do you mean you're (moving)?
Yes, I've been thinking about (moving) for a long time / since . . . I've always wanted to (live in _____) because . . .	Give reasons for your decision.		
		Oppose the decision.	You shouldn't. . . . You're too (old / young) to . . . If I were you, I wouldn't . . . Why don't you think about it some more before you (move) to . . .
It's important to me that I move to _____ / find a new job / have a career in _____. I've dreamed about (moving) for _____ years / since _____.	State your decision again with emphasis.		
		Express disapproval.	I'm not sure about it. It doesn't make sense to (move) . . . I don't think it's a good idea to (move) . . .
I appreciate what you've done for me, but . . . I'm grateful for your advice, but . . . I need to be on my own / to try a new (place, career, job).	Show appreciation and determination.		
		Give or deny approval.	You (don't) seem to know what you want. I (don't) think / I'm (not) sure . . . you should _____.
I knew you would(n't) understand / see it my way.	End the conversation.		Why don't you think about it some more? Let's (not) talk about this again. I hope you know what you're doing.

Unit 1

OPERATOR Trans American information and reservations. May I help you?
KEMP I'm calling about flight 487.
OPERATOR From London to New York?
KEMP Yes, that's the one. What's the arrival time?
OPERATOR 10:25 A.M.
KEMP Is the flight on schedule?
OPERATOR Yes, it's arriving on time. Gate 3.
KEMP Thanks.
OPERATOR Thank you for calling Trans American. Have a nice day.

Unit 2

KEMP Take me to Kennedy International Airport.
DRIVER Do you want me to take the 59th Street Bridge or the Midtown Tunnel?
KEMP Go south. Take the Tunnel. Get on Route 495. That's the Long Island Expressway.
DRIVER Does the Expressway go to Kennedy?
KEMP No, you have to get on the Van Wyck Parkway. That's Route 678 South.
DRIVER Is that going to take us to Kennedy?
KEMP Yes, it goes directly to the airport.

Unit 3

MOLLY This room is a mess!
JEFF What's wrong with it? It looks fine to me.
MOLLY Are you kidding? Jeff, aren't you going to pick up those magazines?
JEFF Oh, Sis. I can't. I'm too busy.
MOLLY What do you mean "you can't"?
JEFF I'm too tired to get up. Leave me alone.
MOLLY Well, I'm tired of your excuses. You're old enough to take some responsibility for this house. Get up and help me.
JEFF When Mom was here, I didn't have to do the housework.
MOLLY I'm not your mother. Now pick up those magazines.

Unit 4

MOLLY Did you see today's paper?
JEFF No, I haven't looked at it yet.
MOLLY Look on page 32, under "sales" The Sanderson Hospital Supply Company is looking for a New York area sales representative.
JEFF What do you have to do?
MOLLY The sales rep has to visit hospitals and show company products.
JEFF What's the salary?
MOLLY The starting salary is $10,000, but you get 10% commission on all sales. There are lots of benefits, too, like free medical insurance and tuition.
JEFF I'm not sure I have the qualifications. I've never done sales work.

MOLLY They don't require any experience. They want someone with a college degree and a friendly personality.
JEFF No, thanks. I'm not interested. I'm not very good at meeting new people.

Unit 5

PAULO What about this coffee maker? It's called *Mrs. Coffee*.
MOLLY I haven't heard of that brand. How many cups does it make?
PAULO From 4 to 12 cups. You can make as many cups as you want.
MOLLY How does it work?
PAULO Well, first you set the dial, then you add the coffee.
MOLLY Where do you put the water?
PAULO The opening is on the top.
MOLLY How much is it? I bet it's expensive.
PAULO $32.50, but it has a special feature. You can select the kind of coffee, from very weak to very strong.

Unit 6

PAULO Are there any good restaurants around here?
MOLLY Actually, there are several good ones.
PAULO Which one is your favorite?
MOLLY Gino's. It's an Italian restaurant. They serve excellent lasagne and spaghetti and the food is reasonably priced.
PAULO Is it close by?
MOLLY Not very far. It's on the corner of 93rd and Broadway.
PAULO How about joining me for dinner? We could go to Gino's tonight.
MOLLY Well, I'm writing a story and I really should finish it tonight.
PAULO C'mon. You've been working too hard lately. Take a break.
MOLLY Oh, all right. But you should call and make a reservation. They're usually crowded on weekends.
PAULO Let's make it for 8 o'clock.
MOLLY That sounds fine. Come by for me at 7:30.

Unit 7

CLERK May I help you?
PAULO Yes, I'd like to buy a bottle of wine.
CLERK What kind would you like? We have an excellent selection of red and white wines.
PAULO Actually, I think I'd like to have a rosé wine. Do you have any wines from Portugal?
CLERK How about a bottle of *Mateus*? It's one of our popular wines.
PAULO Fine. I'll take it.
CLERK That'll be $4.39 plus tax.
PAULO Here's a twenty.
CLERK Your change, sir. And your wine.
PAULO Thanks.

CLERK Thank you. Have a pleasant evening and come again.

Unit 8

MARY Paulo, would you like another piece of roast beef?
PAULO Yes, please. This salad is delicious, Mary. How do you make your dressing?
MARY With fresh lemon and olive oil. I added some oregano and other spices.
PAULO This bread is wonderful. It's so fresh and light. Is it homemade?
MARY Yes, Molly and I baked it this afternoon. It's my grandmother's recipe for Irish white bread.
PAULO Molly, could you pass me the bread, please? I think I'll have another slice.
MOLLY Here it is. Would you like more potatoes, Paulo?
PAULO No, thank you. I've had enough. After all, I have to leave some room for dessert.
MARY That's right. Molly made us a beautiful chocolate cake.
PAULO This is an excellent dinner, Mary. My compliments to the chef and her lovely assistant.

Unit 9

SUSAN There's an article here about the Wade Plaza Project. Have you seen it?
WADE No, I haven't. What does it say?
SUSAN It says that the construction is going to start next month. Here, look at it.
WADE What do you think of the article, Susan?
SUSAN It's terrific! I really enjoyed the part about the new restaurants and shops. In fact, I liked all of the story.
WADE Let me see it. Well, generally, I agree with you. But the section which shows the plans looks rather boring.
SUSAN Oh, I don't agree. I thought that it was wonderful, especially the artist's drawing.
WADE Do you really think so? Well, you're probably right. I guess I have to agree with you. It is an excellent article.

Unit 10

SUSAN I'll never forget the time when I was at that school. It was awful. The teachers made us get up at 7 o'clock in the morning, even on Saturday and Sunday. We had to be in class by 8.
JEFF You think that's bad? When I was in the army, they had us get up at 5 A.M.! Then they made us line up for inspection. The sergeant walked up and down and checked our uniforms. Sometimes he made us shine our shoes again before we could eat breakfast.
SUSAN They made us wear uniforms at school, too. We had to wear old-fashioned gray wool skirts and ugly white blouses. When we were in class, we had

to wear our navy blue sweaters. They made us keep them on even in hot weather.

JEFF At least you were in a classroom all day! I spent all my time in the mud. The sergeant had us march 10 miles a day in the heat. We had to carry 40 pounds of equipment on our backs. It's a part of my life that I want to forget.

Unit 11

MOLLY Dinner's ready. We're waiting for you, Jeff.

JEFF Start without me. I'm busy.

MOLLY Haven't you fixed that sink yet?

JEFF Not yet. I just need a few more minutes.

MOLLY It could be too difficult for you. Why don't you get Carlos to help you?

JEFF Because I'm determined to fix it myself. That's why.

MOLLY You always want to do everything yourself. I've never met anyone so stubborn.

JEFF Stop talking, Molly, and hand me that wrench.

MOLLY The one on the table?

JEFF Right. That's the one.

MOLLY Here it is.

JEFF Thanks. There, I've got it. The sink should be okay now.

MOLLY Well, it's about time! You've been working on it all afternoon.

JEFF *I* might be stubborn, Molly, but at least *I'm* patient!

Unit 12

MOLLY Can you believe this place? First they made us wait for a half-hour, then they brought us to that horrible table.

PAULO Well, we were given this wonderful table next to the window. Why don't you just relax and enjoy the view?

MOLLY Relax! How can I relax when I'm so hungry? Where's our food? Our order was taken hours ago!

PAULO C'mon, Molly. It hasn't been that long. Besides, the waiter is bringing our food now.

MOLLY Paulo, I can't eat this roast beef. It's well done. And these potatoes! They were cooked in oil! I wanted a baked potato.

PAULO Waiter. We specifically ordered rare meat and baked potatoes. We'd like to have the food we ordered.

WAITER I'm sorry for the mistake, sir. I'll take this back to the kitchen and get your order.

MOLLY Terrific. Now we'll have to wait another half-hour!

PAULO Molly, have some more wine. Here, let me fill up your glass.

MOLLY Oh, all right. But pass me the bread. I'm starved.

Unit 13

GREENE City Desk. Greene speaking.

KEMP Greene, this is Wade Enterprises. I'm calling for Preston Wade.

GREENE I hope Mr. Wade liked our story on The Plaza. Molly Ryan did a fine job on that article.

KEMP That's exactly the person I'm calling about. I want you to fire her. Immediately.

GREENE Now, hold on. Molly's one of our top reporters. Who are you?

KEMP Kemp's the name. Mr. Wade's personal assistant. Let me make myself clear. Miss Ryan and her brother are responsible for a tenant protest here at Wade Enterprises. Mr. Wade does not want to employ political people. Do you understand?

GREENE Sorry, Kemp. Molly's personal life is her business. My concern is what goes on at this newspaper.

KEMP Listen carefully, Greene. If you don't fire her, you'll have to answer to Preston Wade.

GREENE Don't you dare threaten me, Kemp! I run this paper, not Wade Enterprises.

KEMP Get rid of her, Greene, or I'll see that you lose your job, too.

GREENE You try that, Kemp, and we'll see who leaves—you or me. Get lost!

Unit 14

JEFF What do you suppose Wade is up to?

CARLOS What do you mean? You heard what he said. He offered us a lot of money to sell. And he's going to give us new apartments at Wade Plaza.

JEFF Molly, do you suppose Mom will want to sell our apartment?

MOLLY I don't think so. She cares a lot about Tudor Village. Do you realize how long she's lived there? Almost fifty years. No, I don't think she'll sell.

CARLOS What about the money? Doesn't Mary care about what she can do with the money? She could buy new furniture, or take trips.

MOLLY Mom really doesn't need the money. She has everything she needs. The money isn't important to her.

JEFF I suppose you're right. I'm sure Mom won't vote to accept Wade's offer.

Unit 15

PAULO What about going to the football game at Giants Stadium?

MOLLY Football? Are you kidding? I hate football. How about the opera? There's a performance of *Aida* at Lincoln Center.

PAULO No, thanks. You know I don't really enjoy the opera.

MOLLY All right. Then why don't we go to a concert? Ella Fitzgerald is at Carnegie Hall. And Elton John is giving a free concert in Central Park.

PAULO Won't the park be crowded and noisy? Well, what do you prefer?

MOLLY Well, I'd rather go to Carnegie

Hall. It's a lot more comfortable and less noisy there.

PAULO Fine. I'd really like to see Ella Fitzgerald. Besides I'm not too crazy about rock music.

MOLLY Okay. I'll pick up the tickets after work tomorrow. It's my treat.

PAULO Molly, I can't let you pay for the tickets.

MOLLY Oh, yes you can. You'll pay me back when you help me wallpaper my bedroom!

Unit 16

JEFF Susan is the kindest and most wonderful person I've ever met. She's the best thing that's ever happened to me.

PAULO It's certainly true that Susan is a very special person.

JEFF She's the most important part of my life, and now I've lost her.

PAULO I can see that, Jeff, but you can't say that you've lost her forever. She'll come back to you.

JEFF I don't know about that. She's pretty angry with me. Susan's father is more important to her than I am. Do you really think she'll change her mind?

PAULO I'm sure of it. I know that Susan is very confused right now, but she cares about you very much. Give her some time to think about everything. Don't worry. She'll see what's really best for her.

JEFF I hope you're right.

Unit 17

WADE I propose that we cut the welfare budget in half. There's a lot of waste there. These people on welfare could get jobs.

MAYOR That's not true, Mr. Wade. Most of the people on welfare are too old or too disabled to work. Besides, there aren't any jobs.

WADE The City has to create jobs for people. Why don't we increase the budget for building projects? New construction means new jobs.

MAYOR The City can't afford to increase the budget whatsoever. We have to cut the budget, not add to it.

WADE What about education? Do we really need those special programs for preschoolers and the gifted?

MAYOR If I were you, Mr. Wade, I would think about the future of this City. We need to train the best people for leadership positions.

WADE I'm not so sure about that. We didn't need those special programs when I went to school. Let's hear what the other Council members have to say.

Unit 18

CARLOS We should decide whether to wait for the police to catch those men, or to try to find them ourselves.

JEFF   Do we have any choice? The way I see it, either we can do nothing, or we can take some action of our own.

PAULO   What do you mean by that?

JEFF   It's obvious that the police can't help us. We should tell Wade that the tenants aren't going to sell Tudor Village.

PAULO   I get it. Then those men will have to come back to frighten us again.

CARLOS And we'll be waiting to catch them!

JEFF   Right. And they won't get away from us this time. We'll prove to the police that Wade Enterprises is behind the accidents at Tudor Village.

PAULO   Let's do it. I prefer to try something rather than sit back and do nothing.

Unit 19

SUSAN   Mary. It's me, Susan. I came to see you as soon as I heard about the accident.

MARY   Oh, Susan. Is that you? I feel so terrible. I must look a mess!

SUSAN   Nonsense, Mary. You look fine. You're just a little tired after the operation. That's all.

MARY   I'm so afraid of hospitals, Susan. My husband died in this same hospital 15 years ago. I just wish I were home right now.

SUSAN   Don't worry, Mary. You'll be up and around in no time. You just need to rest here for a few days.

Later, Susan is talking to Jeff:

SUSAN   Oh, Jeff! Mary looks terrible! It's amazing that she survived that operation.

JEFF   I know. She was lucky. The doctor said she could have died on the operating table.

Unit 20

MOLLY   How is she doing, doctor?

DOCTOR Better than we expected, Miss Ryan.

MOLLY   I saw you checking her pulse. How is her blood pressure?

DOCTOR It's high, but we have it under control. She's responding very well to the medication we're giving her.

MOLLY   I noticed the surgeon examining the incision. Is there anything wrong?

DOCTOR Absolutely nothing. It's healing perfectly. We'll be ready to take the stitches out in a few days.

MOLLY   How long will she have to stay in the hospital?

DOCTOR Your mother had a pretty bad fall. In my judgment, she should be in the hospital at least four weeks. She needs a lot of rest right now.

MOLLY   Doctor, you don't know my mother. No one can make that woman sit still for four weeks! You'll see.

Unit 21

JEFF   Paulo told me that he had asked you to marry him.

MOLLY   Yes, and I refused.

JEFF   Could you tell me why? You love him and he loves you. What's the problem?

MOLLY   You make it sound so simple. There are other things to consider besides love.

JEFF   Like what?

MOLLY   Like my job. And this family. Look. I don't want to discuss it.

JEFF   Will you at least talk to me about it?

MOLLY   No. I've made up my mind. I'm not going to marry Paulo.

JEFF   Molly, I wish you'd listen to me! You're making a big mistake. Paulo is a terrific guy. And you deserve some happiness too.

MOLLY   How can I be happy when I'm worried about Mom? Who'll take care of her if I go to Brazil?

JEFF   I'll be here. I'm going to get a job and maybe go back to law school. Don't use Mom as an excuse.

MOLLY   Paulo said the same thing. He said I was afraid.

JEFF   He's right, Molly. I felt the same way about Susan. But I know now that I need her. I need her love.

MOLLY   Jeff, I've hurt Paulo a lot. I don't think he even loves me anymore. It's too late, I know it.

Unit 22

JEFF   There seems to be something wrong with the transmission. I have trouble with second gear.

MECHANIC Let me try it. You're right. The gears are worn out. You have to get the transmission replaced.

JEFF   Are you kidding? That's an expensive job.

MECHANIC Well, it's an old cycle, but it's in pretty good condition. With a new transmission, it'll be as good as new.

JEFF   How much is this going to cost me?

MECHANIC Well, most of the cost is labor. We need to have the engine taken apart first. You should get the carburetor cleaned at the same time and maybe have the fuel pump replaced. Altogether, I'd say about $350.

JEFF   That much? Well, I guess I don't have much of a choice.

MECHANIC We'll start on it right away. It should be ready by early next week.

Unit 23

BEN   I was so sorry to hear about your mother, Molly.

MOLLY   Thank you, Ben. It's nice of you to call.

BEN   How is she doing?

MOLLY   Much better. The operation went well. The doctors say she'll be all right.

BEN   I'm glad to hear that. Is there anything I can do to help?

MOLLY   Right now she just needs a lot of rest. Ben, I'd like to ask a favor. Would it be all right if I took a few days off from work?

BEN   Take all the time you need.

MOLLY   Thanks. I appreciate it.

Unit 24

PAULO   I'm not sure about going back to Brazil next year. Molly has her career and family here.

JEFF   Why don't you consider working in New York? I'm sure Susan's father would be happy having you work for his construction company.

PAULO   He's already offered me a job. It's an excellent opportunity.

JEFF   You could go back to your job in São Paulo.

PAULO   I know that. But somehow I can't imagine Molly living in Brazil. She's accustomed to having a career. Frankly, I don't think she's too excited about staying home all day.

JEFF   She doesn't have to. She's capable of learning the language and finding a job if she gets bored with playing housewife. If I were you, I would discuss this with Molly.

PAULO   You're right. It is a big decision. I had better get used to sharing the responsibility.

JEFF   Take my advice. Talk to Molly. It's too important a decision to make by yourself.

Unit 2

Conversation 1

A Hello, Carol. How are you?
B Good, Jack. And you?
A Fine, thanks. Carol, do you have any plans for tonight?
B Well, I'm going to see a movie.
A Oh. What movie are you going to see?
B It's a French movie. My French teacher wants us to see it. She's going to ask us about it in class tomorrow. Do you want to come with me?
A Sure. Let's go.
B Okay. The movie starts at 8. Can you meet me at 7:30 in front of the library?
A Fine. See you at 7:30 then.
B See you soon, Jack.
A Goodbye, Carol.
B Bye.

Conversation 2

A Hey, Bob. Hi. *How are you doing?*
B John! Hey, *terrific*. And you?
A *Pretty good,* thanks. Hey, *are you* busy tonight?
B Well, I'm *going to* the game.
A What game?
B The *Jets*! They're *playing* Boston. Say, I have an extra ticket. *Can you* come?
A Great. I really like football.
B *I can give you* a ride. Meet me at 6 o'clock on the corner of *86th Street and* Broadway.
A *See you* at 6 then.
B Fine.
A Bye, Bob. *See you* later.
B Bye, John.

Unit 4

Conversation 1

A Greg Larson! Is that you?
B Dick! What a surprise!
A How long has it been?
B Five years, at least. I haven't seen you since college.
A What have you done since graduation? Are you still with that Wall Street company?
B No, I haven't worked for them for four years. I'm in law school now. At Columbia. And you?
A Still in business with my father. We've opened up two new stores in Manhattan. What happened to Betty? Did you two finally get married?
B Three years ago. She's doing fine. We haven't started a family yet. I want to finish school first. Say, let's get together soon. Here's my phone number.
A How about tomorrow? Let's have a drink.
B That sounds terrific. Can I call you tomorrow? I want to check my class schedule.
A Good. Here's my business card. My office phone number is on it.
B Bye, Dick.
A Take care, Greg.

Conversation 2

A Why, it's Sally! Sally Rogers, *isn't it?*
B Edith? Edith Carlson? *Is that* really you?
A *It's been* over 40 years, Sally, hasn't it?
B For ages! Since *we were* in high school.
A *Are you still living* in Brooklyn Heights? On Elm Street?
B Yes, *I'm still* there. With my parents. *I have a job* at the bank. *You know,* the one on Atlantic Avenue. What about you? *I heard you got* married and moved to Manhattan.
A I'm divorced now. My son and daughter are away at college. But I've *kept the apartment* on the East Side. *How's your* family? *Where's your* brother Ed now?
B He's still *living in* Boston. Ed's *doing* well. He's in real estate. *How about* lunch soon? I come *to the* city *every* Wednesday.
A Well, *how about* next Wednesday? *Let's meet* at the Russian Tea Room. Is noon okay?
B Sounds fine. Wonderful.
A *See you* next Wednesday. At noon. And *give my love* to your parents.
B Fine. *See you* next week. *Goodbye,* Sally.
A Bye, Edith.

Unit 6

Conversation 1

A May I speak to Linda, please.
B Is that you, Bill? This is Linda. Where are you?
A Hi, Linda. I'm on Broadway, near Café Paris. Would you like to go for a cup of coffee?
B Now? Oh, I can't. My mother is visiting. We're just leaving to go to Bloomingdale's. Mother wants to do some shopping.
A Really? That's a shame. It's such a beautiful day to sit outside. Could we get together on Sunday? There's a concert in Central Park.
B Wonderful. I can make it then. My mother is leaving on Saturday.
A Good. Could you call me on Sunday, about noon?
B Fine. Bye, Bill.
A Talk to you later, Linda. Bye.

Conversation 2

A *This is* Carol Wilson. Is Betty there?
B Carol, *this is* Betty. What a surprise! *How have you been?*
A Hi, Betty. Oh, *I'm pretty good,* thanks. *I've been traveling* a lot lately. I *just got back* from a business trip to London. Say, *how about* a game of tennis tomorrow? I need the exercise.
B Tomorrow? No, I'm sorry. My boss *is coming in.* I have meetings all day at *the office.*
A *That's too* bad. *How about* Saturday, then?
B Sounds fine. *In the morning,* okay? I

have a lunch date at 1. Call me at *the office* on Friday.
A Okay.
B Talk *to you* then. Bye, Carol.
A *Goodbye,* Betty.

Unit 8

Conversation 1

A Do you see that kid? Over there, on the motorcycle.
B That's really strange. I can't believe it. He must be 10 years old!
A It's incredible!
B It's my guess that he's waiting for his father. He can't be riding the motorcycle by himself.
A He must be. He's putting the key in and starting the engine. Look, he's pulling out into the traffic.
B Well, I'll be! Isn't it against the law for children to drive?
A I'm certain it's not allowed.
B It's dangerous. That kid must be crazy.
A Maybe times have changed. Kids grow up pretty fast today.
B Not my kids. They'll never drive around on motorcycles. I won't permit it.

Conversation 2

A *Look at that old* lady! The *one on the* rollerskates.
B *What old* lady? Oh, *wow!*
A *Isn't that something? She's actually* on rollerskates!
B I bet she's from California. It's a real fad there. *Everyone* in Los Angeles *is buying* rollerskates. I read it *in the papers.*
A *You're probably* right. People from the West Coast are strange.
B *It's dangerous* in all this traffic. *Is she* permitted *to skate* in the street?
A I'm *sure it's* allowed. People ride bicycles. Why not skates?
B *Actually,* it looks like fun.
A Well, *you won't* see me on rollerskates.
B *I think I'll* try it myself sometime. Why walk when *you can* skate!

Unit 10

Conversation 1

A I went to a wonderful restaurant last night.
B Really? Which one is it?
A It's called *Hawaiian Village.* It's on the corner of Broadway and 57th Street.
B What's so special about it?
A It's a place where you can get wonderful seafood. They serve only fresh fish. And the prices are very reasonable. All you can eat for $7.95.
B Maybe I should try it.
A Why don't you have your boyfriend take you?
B That's a good idea. Bill loves seafood.
A It really is a terrific restaurant.
B Thanks for telling me about it.

Conversation 2

A *Boy, have I found* a great discotheque!

B Oh? *Where is* it?

A In Soho, on West Broadway. *It's called The Garage.* It just opened.

B *What's it* like?

A *It's a* place where *you can dance* all night. They close at 6 A.M. There're three floors with great dance music. And the *lights are* fantastic! The *prices at* the bar are high, but *it's worth* it.

B *Sounds like* fun. Pretty wild, huh?

A *It sure* is. Maybe *you can* get Carol *to go.* She likes *to dance,* doesn't she?

B Right. We *could go* next Saturday.

A I'm sure *Carol'll love* it. *You'll have a* great time.

B Maybe we'll *see you* there? Thanks *for the* tip.

Unit 12

Conversation 1

B May I help you?

A Yes. It's these pants. I've gained some weight and now they're too small for me. The seams came apart.

B Could you show me the place where it's ripped?

A Here, in the back. It happened when I bent down to tie my shoe.

B We'll take care of it. We can open the seam a bit to give you more room.

A Terrific. They're my favorite pants. I guess I need to go on a diet, huh? When will they be ready?

B How about next Thursday?

A Fine. What's the charge?

B Let me see. There's the sewing, and the pressing. That will come to $8.00.

A Good. I'll stop by Thursday morning.

B Very good. Your pants will be ready for you.

Conversation 2

B What *can I do for you,* Miss?

A Well, there seems to be *something wrong with the* radiator. It leaks all the time, even *when it's* filled with water.

B *Let me* take a look at it.

A There, under the car. *You can* see the water *that's coming* out.

B *It looks* like there's a hole in the radiator. It's damaged all right, but *we can* fix the hole *for you.*

A I'm glad to hear that. I thought I needed a new radiator.

B The car'll be ready *tomorrow* afternoon.

A *That's great.* Oh, how *much will it* cost?

B Well, it *should be about* $20 *for the* labor.

A I'll *come and pick* up the car after work. *About* 6. Okay?

B Sure. It'll be ready then.

Unit 14

Conversation 1

A My car! Do you realize that you've just gone through a red light?

B Young man, young man! Look at what you've done to my car. There's a big scratch on the fender.

A It was your fault, lady. Didn't you see that red light?

B My fault? That's not true, young man. I'm afraid you're mistaken.

A You didn't see the red light, did you?

B I know I'm getting old and my eyes aren't as good as they used to be, but ... I'm an excellent driver, young man. Why, I've been driving for over 50 years!

A Ma'm, we should let the insurance companies handle this.

B I know my registration should be here in my handbag, but I can't seem to find it. Anyway, my insurance company is Metropolitan. Their office is on Main Road. Why, I don't even know what your name is?

A Reynolds. Bob Reynolds. Here's my registration. Look, I'll stop by your insurance company and report the accident, Mrs. . . . ?

B . . . Edna Wilkins. Yes, please do that for me. I'm so upset, right now. I just want to go home and lie down.

A Let me handle it. I'll call you tonight, Mrs. Wilkins. Oh, I don't know what your telephone number is.

B It's WATSON 2-5381, Mr. Reynolds.

A If I need more information, I'll call from the insurance company. Everything will be all right.

B I hope so.

Conversation 2

A Hey, you hit my car! *Didn't you* see the sign?

B What sign? *Wait a minute.* Look at the damage to my truck! The whole back *end is* smashed!

A I *suppose* you didn't see that one-way sign? You caused the accident. My car, my brand new car!

B You're crazy! I *was just* backing up.

A *Didn't you* look *where you were* going?

B Me? You weren't looking! How *could you miss* this truck? You blind, or *something?*

A Look, I *don't want to* fight about this. *Let's just* exchange information. *Why don't you give me* your registration.

B Here *it is. Give me your* registration and *your* telephone number.

A *I don't know* where to call you. *Give me your* work number.

B It's 673-4847. *The Hi-Rise Bakery. Call me tomorrow,* after 10. I'll *get my* boss to talk to you.

A I'll *call you at* 10. If you're not there, I'm *going to go to the* police.

B Okay, *okay,* Lady.

Unit 16

Conversation 1

A Don't you think we should get a larger apartment?

B What do you mean? This apartment is fine. It's big enough for us.

A It's obvious that this apartment is too small. We don't even have a dining room. I'm tired of eating in this kitchen. We've lived here since we were married. It's time we moved.

B I'd rather stay here. I like this old place. Besides, we don't need all that extra room.

A Yes, we do. We need a larger apartment with an extra bedroom. Then it'll be more comfortable for my mother when she visits.

B Your mother? Wait a minute. No. No, we just can't afford it.

A That's not true! Of course we can afford a more expensive apartment. You got a raise last month and my salary certainly helps. What am I working for, if I can't have a better apartment?

B Well, if it means that much to you, I guess we can look at a few apartments.

A Thanks, honey. You know we really need the extra room.

B Okay, okay. You're probably right. Your mother's not coming to visit us again, is she?

Conversation 2

A Dad, *why don't we get* a new TV?

B *What's wrong* with ours?

A *Come on. Can't you* see the *picture is* too small? And it's black and white. We *need a* bigger screen. Besides, I'd rather *watch the* programs in color.

B You *know I'm* not crazy about television. You watch too much TV as it is.

A But a color TV *is a* lot better. The *picture is* clearer and it's more fun. Why *can't we get a* new TV?

B Because we don't need one, *that's why.* You should spend more time on your homework, not at the TV.

A Ah, Dad. That doesn't make sense. I always do my homework. I'm *getting A's in* school, aren't I?

B Well, *let me* think about it.

A I still think we *should get* a color TV.

B We'll see.

Unit 18

Conversation 1

A Have you decided about our vacation?

B We have some choices: a week in Paris, Greece, or Switzerland. Here're the brochures. I got them from the travel agent. Take a look.

A Wow! They all look great. What's your preference?

B Well, let's not go to Paris. I'd like to get away from city life for a while.

A Me, too. How about a nice quiet place. I need the rest.

B Rather than the beach, let's do something different. I've always wanted to do some mountain climbing.

A If we go to Switzerland, we can take one of those camping and climbing tours. They even have special groups for beginners.

150

B I haven't been camping since I was a kid! It certainly will be more interesting than lying around a beach all day.

A Let's go to the mountains, then. Call and make the reservations. It's going to be a great trip.

B It will be wonderful to get out of the city and breathe some clean, fresh air for a change.

A I know what you mean.

B We're really going to enjoy ourselves on this trip. Now, what will I wear?

Conversation 2

A *Have you* thought about where *we're going* this weekend?

B Well, either we *can go* to my brother Bob's place in the mountains *or to the* shore. Betty invited *us to her* parents' beachhouse on Fire Island.

A Where *would you* rather go?

B I know I *don't want to* spend another weekend with *Betty and her* parents. Her mother drives me crazy.

A Yeah, I know *what you* mean. But I really enjoy the beach. And the weather's *going to be* perfect this weekend.

B *Instead of* Betty's house, *why don't we* get a room at *one of those* little hotels along the beach?

A Good idea!

B Yeah, *it'll be* more expensive, but a *lot more* fun if we don't stay at Betty's house.

A Man, I *can't wait* to get *out on that* beach. It's been a tough week *at the office.*

B Yeah, *it's going to be* fun. Maybe we *can get* some *of the other guys to go,* too. Play a little volleyball on the beach? *Huh?* Think Jerry and Paul *might be* interested?

A I think so. *Give them* a call.

B Right. Sounds like a great weekend *to me.* Fire Island, here we come!

Unit 20

Conversation 1

A Do you know what's wrong with my knee?

B It's the knee cap.

A What seems to be the matter with it?

B Well, the tests show that there's a broken bone. You had a bad fall.

A That sounds serious.

B It is. You'll need surgery on it. If you don't have it done, I'm afraid you'll have trouble walking for the rest of your life.

A How dangerous is the operation?

B There's really nothing to worry about. This operation is very successful.

A How long does it take to get over it? I mean, I start classes again next month. I want to graduate in June.

B Well, you could be walking again in a few weeks. You'll have to use a cane, but I don't think you'll miss your classes.

A That's good to know. I just hope everything will be all right.

B If I were you, I wouldn't worry about it.

Conversation 2

A *What did the* x-rays show?

B *It looks* like a slipped disc.

A A slipped disc? *What does that* mean?

B Well, take a look at the x-ray. There's definitely a weakness here, *in the lower* back.

A Will I need an operation?

B Not yet. *I'm going to put you* in the hospital for a while. We'll try bed rest and traction.

A Will it hurt?

B No, *it's a little* uncomfortable, *that's all.* But we've had great results without surgery.

A How long'll I be in the hospital?

B You'll be home again in 10 days to two weeks.

A Okay, I guess I have no choice.

B I'm sure *everything will be* fine.

Unit 22

Conversation 1

A Help! Man overboard!

B What? What happened? Oh, this is terrible.

A Calm down! Do what I say.

B What can I do?

A Help me get this lifeboat into the water. Here's the line. Now pull.

B You get in. I think I can lower the boat. *(pause)*

A I've got him. He's okay.

B Thank goodness, he's safe. If you bring the boat over to the side, I'll pull him in.

A I'm grateful for your help.

B You're the one who saved his life.

A Lucky for him we were both here.

Conversation 2

A Watch out! The *curtain's on* fire!

B Oh, no!

A Move away from the stove.

B What can I do?

A Find the fire extinguisher in the hall. *It's behind* the door.

B I'll get it, Mom. *(pause)*

A Give it *to me* and move away. That's it. *It* looks like we've got the fire out.

B Whew! *I was* really scared, Mom.

A You were terrific, honey. I'm proud of you.

B Thanks to you, Mom. Hey, maybe we should eat out tonight. Huh?

Unit 24

Conversation 1

A Mr. Reynolds, I'd like to tell you something. Please don't get upset, but I've decided to leave my position here.

B Quit your job? But I thought you liked working here?

A Well, the salary's good, but I don't want to work in business for the rest of my life. You know I've always wanted to be a lawyer.

B A lawyer? But you'll have to go back to school, for at least three years. Why don't you think about it some more before you quit this job?

A I've always dreamed about being a lawyer. I have to try now before it's too late.

B It doesn't make sense to leave your job now. You have an excellent future ahead of you with this company.

A I'm grateful for your advice, Mr. Reynolds, but I've made up my mind. I'm going back to school.

B Well, you seem to know what you want. I'm sorry you'll be leaving us.

A Thank you, Mr. Reynolds. I knew you'd understand.

B Good luck.

Conversation 2

A Dad, *I've been thinking about moving* to the city and *getting* my own apartment.

B What do you mean you're getting your own apartment?

A Well, *I've been thinking about having* my own place for quite a while now.

B You're too young to be on your own. You belong at home with your mother and me.

A *Don't you* understand? I'm 24 years old. It's important *to me* that I have a life of my own. I can't be your little girl forever.

B Honey, I *just don't think it's a* good idea for you to live alone. The city is dangerous. Your mother and I'd worry *about you* all the time.

A *I appreciate* all you and mom've done for me, but all my friends live in the city. My job's there and I *want to* take some classes at night at the university. There's *nothing for* me here in this town.

B I'm still not sure you should move into the city.

A I knew you wouldn't see it my way.

B *Let's not* talk about this again.

Infinitive	Past Tense	Past Participle	Infinitive	Past Tense	Past Participle
be	was/were	been	lie	lay	lain
beat	beat	beaten	light	lit	lit
become	became	become	lose	lost	lost
begin	began	begun	make	made	made
bend	bent	bent	mean	meant	meant
bet	bet	bet	meet	met	met
bite	bit	bitten	pay	paid	paid
blow	blew	blown	put	put	put
break	broke	broken	quit	quit	quit
bring	brought	brought	read	read	read
build	built	built	ride	rode	ridden
buy	bought	bought	ring	rang	rung
catch	caught	caught	rise	rose	risen
choose	chose	chosen	run	ran	run
come	came	come	say	said	said
cost	cost	cost	see	saw	seen
cut	cut	cut	sell	sold	sold
dig	dug	dug	send	sent	sent
do	did	done	set	set	set
draw	drew	drawn	shake	shook	shaken
drink	drove	driven	shine	shone	shone
drive	drove	driven	shoot	shot	shot
eat	ate	eaten	shut	shut	shut
fall	fell	fallen	sing	sang	sung
feed	fed	fed	sink	sank	sunk
feel	felt	felt	sit	sat	sat
fight	fought	fought	sleep	slept	slept
find	found	found	slide	slid	slid
fit	fit	fit	speak	spoke	spoken
fly	flew	flown	spend	spent	spent
forget	forgot	forgotten	stand	stood	stood
freeze	froze	frozen	steal	stole	stolen
get	got	gotten (got)	stick	stuck	stuck
give	gave	given	strike	struck	struck
go	went	gone	swear	swore	sworn
hang	hung	hung	sweep	swept	swept
have	had	had	swim	swam	swum
hear	heard	heard	take	took	taken
hide	hid	hidden	teach	taught	taught
hit	hit	hit	tear	tore	torn
hold	held	held	tell	told	told
hurt	hurt	hurt	think	thought	thought
keep	kept	kept	throw	threw	thrown
know	knew	known	understand	understood	understood
lay	laid	laid	wake	woke	woken
lead	led	led	wear	wore	worn
leave	left	left	win	won	won
lend	lent	lent	wind	wound	wound
let	let	let	write	wrote	written